sydney ARCHITECTURE

First published in 1997 by
The Watermark Press
Sydney, Australia

This publication is supported by the
Australia Foundation for Culture
and the Humanities Ltd.

Project Director: Graham Jahn
Assistant: Ann-Elise Hampton

Advisory Group: Professor Jennifer Taylor, Professor GP Webber,
Jennifer Hill, Trevor Howells, Maisy Stapleton, Dr John Phillips, Roy Lumby,
Philip Thalis, Jackie Cooper

Editor: Simon Blackall
Managing Editor: Siobhan O'Connor

For Jack and Eva

Redrawn Plans: Kim Bazeley   Maps: Cartodraft and IKON Graphic Design
Contributing Writers: Peter Bridges, Maisy Stapleton,
Trevor Howells, Jennifer Hill

National Library of Australia
Cataloguing-in-Publication data

Jahn, Graham.
    Sydney architecture.

    Includes index.
    ISBN 0 949284 32 7.

    1. Architecture — New South Wales — Sydney — Guidebooks.
    2. Historic buildings — New South Wales — Sydney — Guidebooks.
    3. Buildings — New South Wales — Sydney — Guidebooks.
    4. Sydney (N.S.W.) — Buildings, structures, etc. — Guidebooks. I. Title.

720.99441

Design and Production:
IKON Graphic Design
Printed in Australia by Southwood Press

sydney ARCHITECTURE

GRAHAM JAHN

The Watermark Press

Sydney Exhibition Centre, Darling Harbour

CONTENTS

INTRODUCTION

The city's name derives from Sydney Cove, which was named after the British Home Secretary, Lord Sydney, in 1788. In two centuries, it has grown from a piecemeal provincial Georgian township into a visually dramatic city within the constraints of four physical barriers: Sydney Cove to the north, Darling Harbour to the west, the Royal Botanic Gardens and Hyde Park to the east and Central Railway to the south.

Effective town planning only came with the arrival of Governor Lachlan Macquarie in 1810. In addition to establishing a monetary system and promoting agriculture, Macquarie recruited the talents of convict architect Francis Greenway to help formalise his grand design. A legacy of his buildings fringe the city – Hyde Park Barracks, St James' Church and the former Government House Stables.

By the 1850s, Georgian architectural refinement was on the wane and by the 1870s the financial effects of the gold discoveries, expanding wool and wheat trade and adoption of British trends gave rise to a decorative commercial 'Victorian' architecture of the self-made man. This prosperous era featured confident businessmen and merchants who often designed and built their own premises — tracts of the city west of York Street and south of Bathurst Street are testimony to these naive yet self-assured projects.

Following the thriving Centennial years, a second generation of architects, more attuned to contemporary styles from Europe and the United States of America in particular, practised Edwardian, American Romanesque and Beaux-Arts persuasions until World War I. Architectural styles centred on particular types of buildings; warehouses used neo-Romanesque arcading, while a Beaux-Arts treatment gave status to office buildings. Independently, between the wars, cinemas and related entertainment forms lavishly displayed Hollywood and Art Deco influences. As always, clear-cut divisions between these so-called styles is difficult.

Art Deco and then functionalism, in various forms, were indicative of Sydney's avant-garde architecture of the 1930s. World War II was a watershed; new technologies and building practices superseded the sandstone and terracotta building practices of the 19th and early 20th centuries. Road construction and government land sales have allowed the suburbs to spread, gradually filling out the natural confines of the Cumberland Basin. Today four transitional conditions characterise Sydney: a very compact vertical city centre of high-rise office and residential towers, medium-density 'new urban ring' of recycled suburbs, two-storey suburban sprawl, and intimate bushland sites for the 'isolated' single house. These conditions seem to attract their own architectures and, in Sydney, the single house has been the most fertile ground for a definable architectural approach.

HOW TO USE THIS BOOK

The sample page below is typical of those found in the listings throughout the book. Each period of architecture has its own chapter and is colour-coded for easy reference. Individual numbered entries contain standard information and symbols, as well as text outlining details about the building itself.

Colour-coded chapter tabs for quick and easy reference

Building name, which may be either present or former name, or both

Address or location, including opening hours

Condition, Visibility and Accessibility of the building or site

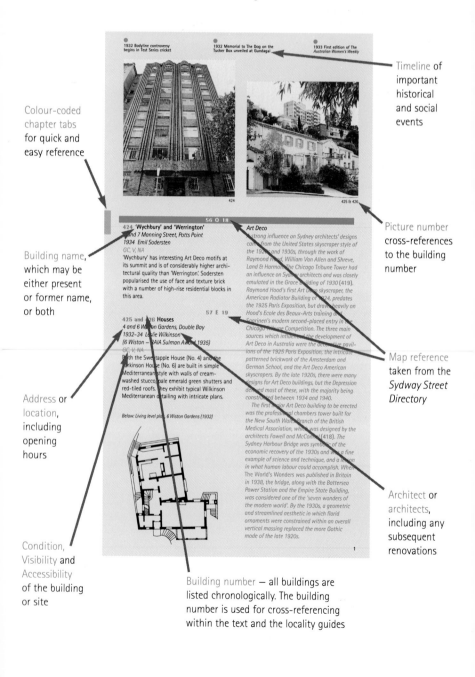

Timeline of important historical and social events

Picture number cross-references to the building number

Map reference taken from the *Sydway Street Directory*

Architect or architects, including any subsequent renovations

Building number — all buildings are listed chronologically. The building number is used for cross-referencing within the text and the locality guides

---

Text within sample page:

1932 Bodyline controversy begins in Test Series cricket

1932 Memorial to The Dog on the Tucker Box unveiled at Gundagai

1933 First edition of The Australian Women's Weekly

424

425 & 426

424 'Wychbury' and 'Werrington'
5 and 7 Manning Street, Potts Point
1934 Emil Sodersten
GC, V, NA
'Wychbury' has interesting Art Deco motifs at its summit and is of considerably higher architectural quality than 'Werrington'. Sodersten popularised the use of face and texture brick with a number of high-rise residential blocks in this area.

425 and 426 Houses
4 and 6 Wiston Gardens, Double Bay
1932–34 Leslie Wilkinson
(6 Wiston – RAIA Sulman Award 1935)
GC, V, NA
Both the Sweetapple House (No. 4) and the Wilkinson House (No. 6) are built in simple Mediterranean style with walls of cream-washed stucco, pale emerald green shutters and red-tiled roofs. They exhibit typical Wilkinson Mediterranean detailing with intricate plans.

Below: Living level plan, 6 Wiston Gardens (1932)

Art Deco
A strong influence on Sydney architects' designs came from the United States skyscraper style of the 1920s and 1930s, through the work of Raymond Hood, William Van Allen and Shreve, Land & Harmon. The Chicago Tribune Tower had an influence on Sydney architects and was closely emulated in the Grace Building of 1930 (419). Raymond Hood's first Art Deco skyscraper, the American Radiator Building of 1924, predates the 1925 Paris Exposition, but draws heavily on Hood's Ecole des Beaux-Arts training and Saarinen's modern second-placed entry in the Chicago Tribune Competition. The three main sources which influenced the development of Art Deco in Australia were the decorative pavilions of the 1925 Paris Exposition, the intricate patterned brickwork of the Amsterdam and German School, and the Art Deco American skyscrapers. By the late 1920s, there were many designs for Art Deco buildings, but the Depression delayed most of these, with the majority being constructed between 1934 and 1940.
The first major Art Deco building to be erected was the professional chambers tower built for the New South Wales Branch of the British Medical Association, which was designed by the architects Fowell and McConnel (418). The Sydney Harbour Bridge was symbolic of the economic recovery of the 1930s and was a fine example of science and technique, and a lesson in what human labour could accomplish. When The World's Wonders was published in Britain in 1938, the bridge, along with the Battersea Power Station and the Empire State Building, was considered one of the 'seven wonders of the modern world'. By the 1930s, a geometric and streamlined aesthetic in which florid ornaments were constrained within an overall vertical massing replaced the more Gothic mode of the late 1920s.

1

HOW TO USE THIS BOOK

Buildings are listed chronologically so that it is possible to trace the history of the city through the architecture. A timeline runs along the top of each page relating current events in Australia.

The listings are divided into five periods: 'Colonial' (1790–1860); 'Victorian' (1860–1895); 'Arts and Crafts' (1895–1920); 'Moderne' (1920–1940); and 'Contemporary' (1940–1996). The buildings are numbered so that the first digit relates to the section in which they are found. Each section is preceded by an introduction, written by guest authors, providing an overview of the period relating to the architecture in the pages following. Brief explanations of styles and movements are provided alongside the entries, approximately where a change of style has occurred.

Each entry in the listings is located by a *Sydway Street Directory* map reference and an indication of its condition, visibility from the street and accessibility.

Condition/Visibility/Accessibility

GC — Good Condition
AC — Average Condition
BC — Bad Condition
V — Visible
NV — Not Visible
A — Accessible
NA — Not Accessible

Abbreviations

CA — Colonial Architect
RE — Royal Engineer
E — Engineer
NSWGA — New South Wales Government Architect

Where possible, an indication of opening times is provided, although it is important that these be confirmed before visiting.

Tours of areas of concentrated architectural interest are provided at the end of the book. Entries are cross-referenced to the listings.

The Colonial City
1790–1860

1790–1860

The First Fleet had to bring everything its people needed to survive in a wilderness.

Their first shelters were tents or rough structures made from whatever they could find; but within thirty years Sydney had grown from a penal camp into a busy seaport. The newcomers had little information about the place they were coming to and expected to find the materials needed for building; however, they quickly discovered that the Sydney red gums were iron-hard, brittle and crooked, the cabbage palms were soft and pithy, and the only usable timber was the she-oak, which made very fine shingles. There was good building stone, but the urgency of the moment made its use beyond reach; workable clay was found within easy distance of Sydney Cove, but with no lime mortar, bricks had to be laid in clay or mud. This meant that high walls could not be built and walls had to be made extra thick for safety. When Captain John Hunter arrived as the new governor in 1794, he found all the brick buildings so fragile that he hastily put convicts to collecting sea shells and making lime to plaster them against the rain. With its whitewalled houses, Sydney took on the appearance of a small Mediterranean town.

Earnshaw Chronometer 520, made by Thomas Earnshaw (1749–1829) between 1790 and 1800. It was used by Matthew Flinders in his circum-navigation of Australia from 1801 to 1803.

Powerhouse Museum, Sydney

The first real building in Sydney was a house for the governor. The First Fleet had brought some window glass, 10,000 bricks and a little lime. Augmenting these supplies with local material, Governor Arthur Phillip built himself a modest two-storey Georgian house such as would have suited any English country gentleman. Its unique solidity and architectural quality set it apart from its primitive neighbours and made it stand out as a lone symbol of order and authority.

As building methods improved, the town's first houses began to follow English patterns of building without regard for the local climate. When, in 1793, Lieutenant-Governor Francis Grose built his own house with a veranda, the benefits of this feature were quickly appreciated and soon after a veranda was added to Government House. This quickly became a common element of Australian domestic architecture.

The government back in England had refused to sanction any public buildings except utilitarian structures for the penal establishment. However, as religion was recognised to be useful in the maintenance of order, Hunter was allowed to start building churches at Sydney and Parramatta. While architecturally crude,

St Philip's and St John's at Parramatta stood above their utilitarian neighbours.

Nevertheless, there were some buildings of architectural interest. In 1799, Captain William Kent built a mansion in the Palladian manner which was praised as the finest house in the town and, in 1800, Robert Campbell, a merchant from Calcutta, built himself an Indian bungalow with verandas 'finished in an elegant manner with colonnades & two fronts'. The leading emancipist merchants also built well for themselves. In about 1804, the trader and ship builder James Underwood built a Regency-style house overlooking the Tank Stream with two storeys of lime-washed brick set on a stone podium. The house was crowned by a balustraded flat roof with a 'captain's walk' from which he could survey his shipyard. Between 1800 and 1806, Dr John Harris built Ultimo, a two-storey Georgian country house set in landscaped grounds overlooking Cockle Bay (now Darling Harbour). He was followed by Simeon Lord who built a large four-storey townhouse and place of business facing what was later to become Macquarie Place.

In the decade from 1800, the population of the colony doubled. More than 6,000 people lived in Sydney, of whom less than a thousand were serving convicts. It was a town of emancipist merchants, shopkeepers, publicans and craftsmen who lived at their places of business.

As good tradesmen and better materials became more common, the crude huts of the first years of colonisation were gradually replaced by more substantial structures. However, the erection of public buildings still languished as both Hunter and his successor, Philip Gidley King, were constrained by labour shortages and the home govern-

Hyde Park Barracks replica hammocks.

Historic Houses Trust of NSW

ment's parsimony. They built little but gaols and windmills; work on the two churches dragged on sluggishly and storehouses fell into decay, a situation which worsened with the neglect of the rebel regime after the overthrow of Governor William Bligh.

Governor Lachlan Macquarie arrived in Sydney in January 1810 with instructions to restore order in the turbulent community, a challenge he willingly accepted as it offered him the chance to make his mark in a career which up till then had been disappointing. Unlike the home government, Macquarie saw the future of the colony as a free community and believed in the principles of the 'Enlightenment'; that is to say, that public works were instruments of civic reform and progress: roads, wharves and bridges promoted commerce and agriculture, public buildings and orderly town plans were signs of a prosperous society — all symbols of order to the respectable and of authority to the unruly.

Within weeks of arriving, Macquarie had restored civil order and prepared a list of essential buildings; convict gangs were making urgent repairs, soldiers were patching the streets and the Tank Stream was cleansed of filth. In May, he announced he would be building a new hospital. The **Rum Hospital**, as it came to be called, was to be the first grand building in Australia; far larger than needed, it was a stage set in the theatre of public power and a pointer to the colony's future importance. The eager Macquarie did not allow inadequate resources to stand in his way. However, this first attempt to translate his 'Enlightenment' vision into reality was marred by a lack of architectural expertise, and by the work of unskilled craftsmen. Yet this naive and badly built Georgian version of tropical architecture was, in its imposing scale and setting, an affirmation of Macquarie's Enlightenment policy.

In August, Macquarie proclaimed a plan for *'the Improvement and Ornament of the town'*: streets were to be re-formed and widened, householders were to build 'neat, regular and durable' fences, and nobody could erect a house without permission. His next steps were to demolish old buildings to form Macquarie Place, lay out a new Market Square, proclaim the common as Hyde Park, and rename the streets according to the status of the

Early Colonial costume, makers unknown, pelisse (left) probably made in England c. 1815; pelisse (centre) probably made in Australia c. 1815; gown (right) muslin with silk petticoat made in Sydney c. 1822.

Powerhouse Museum, Sydney

town he wanted to create. In addition, he formed a number of new streets to stop the straggling growth of the past. By the end of his first year, Macquarie had enlarged St Philip's church, completed the military barracks, and marked out sites for five new towns in the Hawkesbury district.

Macquarie's building zeal drew charges of extravagance from London, but these did little to restrain him and he continued to build according to his own generous views of the colony's needs. When new houses were needed for the Judge-Advocate and the Colonial Secretary, Governor Macquarie, with his request for an architect having been turned down, used a pattern book of 'elegant' house designs belonging to his wife, Elizabeth. Later, when an architect, Daniel Dering Matthew, arrived as a free settler, Macquarie commissioned him to design an edifice combining a Court House and Town Hall. The new building was to be paid for by public subscription and Macquarie contributed £50 from his own pocket. Alas, Macquarie's generosity was not emulated by the settlers and the project had to be abandoned.

Although Matthew turned out to be incompetent, when Lieutenant John Watts arrived in 1814, Macquarie found in him a more able helper. Watts had some architectural training and collaborated with the governor as a family friend. Beginning with a military hospital in Sydney, he moved on to Parramatta where he built a barracks and a hospital and, in close association with

Mrs Macquarie, rebuilt St John's Church and Hunter's old Government House. Watt's buildings were an improvement on anything yet seen in the colony.

The coming of the convict Francis Greenway finally gave Macquarie the professional instrument required for achieving his ambitions. Greenway was a gifted architect, obsessive in his search for recognition, and each man excited the mind of the other, sometimes to the point of fantasy. Macquarie granted Greenway a ticket-of-leave and gave him small tasks as the Inspector of Public Works before appointing him Acting Colonial Architect and Assistant Engineer in 1816. Greenway then offered to prepare a plan of Sydney with 'regular streets, upon the same principle that they are in London [with] the most elegant, convenient and substantial buildings for every public accommodation to last for some centuries'.

About this time, the shortage of labour which had been an obstacle to Macquarie's building program was removed as, with the end of the war with France, convicts flowed into the colony in large numbers. Macquarie was only too willing to keep this workforce busy, until the arrival in 1819 of Commissioner John Thomas Bigge put an end to his building plans.

The first of Greenway's buildings were the Macquarie Lighthouse at South Head and the Hyde Park Barracks in the town. Greenway's lighthouse did not imitate the plain structures common to the coasts of Britain; this was an architectural monument in the form of a sturdy Doric tower. Nor was the barracks merely a convict dormitory; it was a formal urban set piece.

Greenway's impact extended beyond his own buildings; he touched the work of others both in design and building methods. One such person was the supervisor of the government's bricklayers, Francis Lawless, who built the Sydney Benevolent Asylum, the convict barracks at Parramatta and St Peter's church at Campbelltown, all of which showed the Greenway influence.

From early in 1816 until the arrival of Commissioner Bigge, Macquarie pursued a brisk course; he personally marked out sites, laid foundation stones, inspected work in progress and officiated at opening ceremonies. In his final report written after he left the colony, Macquarie listed 87 projects in Sydney and Parramatta alone, including hospitals, orphanages, schools, barracks, churches, storehouses and granaries. However, late in 1819, Macquarie's building career was cut short by the arrival of Commissioner Bigge and the banning of projects which the governor and his architect had dreamed up together. Work was stopped on a court house with a 40-foot (12.2-metre) high Ionic portico and a metropolitan church set in a great square, as were their proposals for a landscaped Domain, a monumental

Government House and a miniature fort on Bennelong Point. Only the fort and the stables for the Government House were realised later.

The force driving Macquarie's compulsive building came from deep within his own nature and he was strongly supported by his wife, Elizabeth. At her suggestion, the towers of St John's Church were copied from a church in Kent, and her family house in Scotland was the model for the Female Orphanage at Rydalmere. She was involved in the design of the little water temple in Macquarie Place and her personal interest in the rising fashion of Neo-Gothic architecture can be seen in the little toll house on the road to Parramatta and the small fort on Bennelong Point. On a larger scale, her influence is evident in the design of Macquarie's intended great Government House. Nor were her interests limited to matters of taste, as is seen in the businesslike directions she gave Greenway for the number of rooms and horses to be accommodated in the Government House Stables.

One of a pair of chairs owned by Governor and Mrs Macquarie. Carved from rose mahogany, casuarina and Australian red cedar, in Gothic style, the chairs are upholstered in eastern grey wallaby fur. They are attributed to carver John Webster and cabinet maker William Temple.

Powerhouse Museum, Sydney

The public buildings of Macquarie and his architect were as much for their own satisfaction as for the pursuit of Enlightenment ideals. Within the colony, people held sharply divided views. Free settlers such as John Blaxland saw little virtue in fine public buildings in a pioneer settlement; they wanted convicts for their own use and resented them being employed on buildings 'not necessary for this generation'. The architect Henry Kitchen criticised Greenway's extravagance and prodigious expenditure on 'puerile and frivolous' works. On the other hand, the Sydney Gazette regularly reported on the 'vast improvements' and the 'daily increasing Beauty and Improvement' of the town, on the benefits gained from the new country roads and 'the excellent buildings presenting themselves on every side ... as a demonstration of the liberality which leads us forward'. The Sydney Gazette spoke for the Macquaries' loyal emancipist supporters and its approval was an antidote to the otherwise uncontested denunciations of Macquarie's projects by his detractors.

Macquarie's departure in 1822 marked the end of an era. Under Sir Thomas Brisbane, strict limits were placed on public building and the colony became once again a place of retribution rather than a land of opportunity. With the coming of free settlers in increasing numbers, old houses in Sydney gave way to larger two and three-storey structures built in continuous blocks and often expressly designed as shops, hotels or business premises. In 1837, the traditional colonial way of building was affected by new town regulations introduced to prevent the spread of fire. Timber buildings and shingle roofs were banned, window and door frames had to be recessed from the wall face and party walls carried up above the roof line.

Many people still lived in the town itself, but the more affluent tended to build their mansions on the outskirts, thus starting Sydney's later suburban pattern. Also, as more architects arrived, matters of style became of increasing interest. The simple Georgian Colonial buildings of earlier times gave way to Regency, and later, Neo-Gothic styles. During the 1830s, John Verge built Regency houses such as **Elizabeth Bay House**, **Tusculum** and **Rockwall** and **Camden Park** on the Macarthur estate. Sir Thomas Mitchell's **Carthona** on Darling Point was a Gothic trendsetter. In the town itself, conventions of style dictated that important institutions such as banks followed solid classical models while churches, except for the nonconformist preaching houses, were commonly in the Gothic style. An oddity was a synagogue built on a pseudo Egyptian model.

With the appointment of Mortimer Lewis as Colonial Architect in 1835, the government began to overcome the shortage of public buildings. Lewis's style was eclectic. His first assignment, the lunatic asylum at Gladesville, was a simple colonial building; in his 1837 **Courthouse at Darlinghurst**, he adopted the latest Neo-Grecian style. His other public buildings were a personal blend of Georgian and Regency, although at St John's Church, Camden, he produced a fine example in the early Gothic Revival fashion. His own townhouse, **Richmond Villa**, was essentially a colonial design, but its decorative bargeboards and veranda woodwork were early signs of the coming 'Carpenters Gothic'. Lewis was also responsible for building perhaps the most important public building of the time, the new **Government House**, which was designed in London by the eminent Gothicist Edward Blore.

The 1840s was a period of economic depression, but it was also a decade of change. In 1842, Sydney had its first Municipal Council and with it a gradual improvement in its streets and water and sewerage systems. Advances in manufacturing led to the common use of cast-iron veranda columns and decorative balustrades which, later in the century, were to become a distinguishing feature of Sydney architecture.

Snuff box presented to Captain TB Daniel of the Hercules 'for services rendered by him to the Colonists of New South Wales', attributed to Joseph Forrester, Hobart, 1835. Cast, embossed, chased and engraved silver with gilt interior. The scene on the lid depicts Port Jackson in the 1830s.

Powerhouse Museum, Sydney

By the mid-century, Sydney had become a town of some 50,000 people, but its pattern of growth had been organic and untouched by the hand of planners since the days of Macquarie. The quarter near Sydney Cove was still the centre of commerce with large commercial houses and banks. On the rise of Bridge Street, the government offices remained where Governor Phillip had first put them in 1788, the retail shops clustered near Macquarie's Markets, the lawyers congregated in Phillip Street near the law courts, and the doctors in Macquarie Street close to the hospital. This pattern was to remain a characteristic of Sydney until the latter part of the 20th century.

PETER BRIDGES

103

253 B 18   252 R 17   253 A 17

Early Parramatta Houses
101 Elizabeth Farm
70 Alice Street, 1793 John Macarthur
102 Experiment Farm Cottage
9 Ruse Street, 1798 John Harris
103 Hambledon Cottage
Hassall Street, 1822 John Macarthur
Open: Tue–Sun 10am–4.30pm
Closed: Mondays, Christmas and Good Friday
GC,V,A

Elizabeth Farm is said to be the oldest surviving building in Australia, but this claim is the subject of spirited debate because of ongoing rebuilding during the 19th century. In all probability designed by its owner, the prominent businessman John Macarthur, it was altered five times during its first seventy years. The modest four-room house has walls of soft brick, a roof of shingles cut from local swamp oaks and narrow eaves cropped close to the walls. This is the evolutionary prototype for Australian country farmhouses in New South Wales.

Built five years later than Elizabeth Farm, but having undergone far fewer physical changes since that time, Experiment Farm Cottage may be a more authentic example of early colonial architecture. It displays the emerging hallmarks of the colonial verandahed bungalow with its cedar-panelled front door flanked by glazed sidelights and with an elliptical fanlight above. Built on the first grant of land (No. 1) in New South Wales, made to James Ruse for a farm, the cottage remained in the Harris family, the original owners, from 1793 until 1923.

Hambledon Cottage *(above)*, built in 1822, is the third cottage in this trilogy. It was built by John Macarthur for his governess Penelope Lucas. It shows the low-pitched roof, wide veranda and elegant proportions later found in the single-storey homesteads in Sydney. It is conserved by Parramatta City Council.

Colonial Style

Between the landing of the first settlers in 1788 and Governor Macquarie's arrival in 1810, the most basic necessities for survival such as food, water and protection had first priority. With the first experimental attempts at farming, Parramatta (where the river water turns from salt to fresh) became a centre for free settlers. Buildings were modest and made from available materials. Few survive of any architectural importance, however, those that do have great historical significance for the nation. Colonial architecture did not draw on the high styles of London. It related to simpler county work using face or plastered brick and limited stone. Columns were usually circular timber, but were occasionally made of stone.

Plan of Hambledon Cottage (1822), designed under John Macarthur's direction for his governess Penelope Lucas.

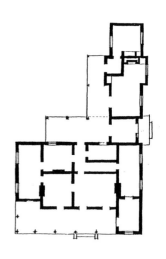

1795 First plough used
by John Macarthur

1797 Waterhouse and Kent import
13 Merino sheep from South Africa

1802 Matthew Flinders
circumnavigates Australia

104

105

252 L 14

104 Old Government House

Grounds near O'Connell Street, Parramatta
1799, 1815 Governor Hunter and John Watts
Open: Tue–Fri 10am–4pm; Sun 11am–4pm
Variable, check in advance.
GC, V, A

The matron of all surviving European public buildings in Australia, and possibly the only public building of which some part can be traced to the 1700s, Old Government House at Parramatta was for years forgotten and derelict.

Originally a simple two-storey brick house erected by Governor John Hunter in 1799, it underwent a major remodelling and extension in 1814–15 designed by Lieutenant John Watts (1786–1873). In perhaps one of his first tasks, the future Colonial Architect Francis Greenway (1777–1837) is credited with the supervision, if not the design, of the front porch.

More the residence of a part-time ruler than a formal public building, the lime-washed walls capture the closing moments of English penal militarism before the political realisation that this 'outpost' could be more than a dumping ground for British criminals. At one time a boarding house of The King's School, it is now open to the public.

Old Government House Grounds

A curious collection of early architecture and artifacts can be seen in the former grounds of Old Government House.

In 1823, Governor Brisbane erected a bath-house, now altered, which can be seen behind Old Government House. Brisbane also built an observatory, and Sir Charles Fitzroy laid out a racecourse in the park. A small obelisk near the main gateway to the park marks the spot where Lady Mary Fitzroy, the Governor's wife, was killed in 1847 when her runaway carriage capsized and she was thrown against a tree.

129 A 12

105 Presbyterian Church

Coromandel Road, Ebenezer
1809 attrib. Andrew Johnson
GC, V, A

In a European settlement of only twenty years, the erection of a solid hewn-stone building was a newsworthy event. Now the oldest existing religious structure in Australia, this tiny, modest church erected by Presbyterians cost its congregation of free settlers in excess of £400. Situated above the Nepean River flood plain, this multi-use building was originally divided in half with a schoolroom at one end and a place of worship at the other.

The 600-mm walls have four windows on each of the two long sides, while two central doors have been blocked up in favour of an entrance at one end. Remarkably, it has survived the pressures of urban development because, although Ebenezer was intended to be one of Governor Macquarie's five major townships, the predicted growth did not happen.

348 R 7

106 'Varroville'

St Andrew's Road, Minto
1814 architect unknown
Handmade sandstock brick homestead.

310 K 17

107 'Glenfield'

Leacocks Lane, Casula
1817 architect unknown
Almost original colonial farm homestead.

326 B 19

108 'Denbigh'

Private road, 8 km south of Bringelly
1817-37 architect unknown
Large homestead with wrap-around verandas and later two-storey addition.

109

26 L 18

109 The Mint Museum
Macquarie Street, Sydney
1811–14 architect unknown
Open: 10am–5pm daily
Closed: Christmas Day
GC, V, A

The Mint Museum and the NSW Parliament House are the two surviving 'bookend wings' of the very early triple wing General Hospital commenced in 1811, barely 20 years after first settlement. Refused both funding and permission by London, Governor Macquarie accepted a proposition by three businessmen to provide a hospital in exchange for three years' exclusive rights to the importation of rum. The architect is unknown, but the design is typical of barracks designed by military engineers for warmer climates. Unfortunately, the buildings were badly built by the entrepreneurs, using stone-faced rubble rather than solid stone and faulty roof framing design, which was later rectified by Francis Greenway. The entire centre wing, erected on poor foundations, was demolished in 1879. (As the result of an 1880 competition, a new building was erected in its place to accommodate the Sydney Hospital **(254)**). The two veranda-faced wings, originally surgeons' barracks, are what remain today.

A branch of the Royal Mint was located in the southern building from 1852–1927, immediately after the New South Wales gold rush, making it the first British currency mint established outside Britain. After 1927, when the Mint moved to Canberra, a variety of taxation and judicial offices were haphazardly housed inside. The building was repaired and conserved between 1975 and 1982, after which the Mint Museum was reopened as a branch of the Powerhouse Museum.

The Royal Mint established international metals expertise as seen in the Mint Museum collection.

26 L 17

110 NSW Parliament House
Macquarie Street, Sydney
1811–14 architect unknown
GC, V, A

Of the two wings which survive from the Rum Hospital **(see 109)**, the northern wing was requisitioned and converted to accommodate the first NSW Parliament House in 1829, it being the largest building available in Sydney at the time. The parliamentary chamber for Legislative Members was soon added (attached at the northern end), while the Legislative Council Chamber (attached at the southern end) was assembled in 1856. This second chamber is actually a prefabricated cast-iron building, initially shipped to Victoria from Glasgow, Scotland. Destined to be a church, it was diverted to Sydney during shipment where it was erected as one of the two parliamentary chambers. It is still the seat of government in NSW today.

190 L 17

111 Rouse Hill House
Windsor Road, Rouse Hill
1813–18 Richard Rouse
1875 John Horbury Hunt (stables)
Open: Check with Historic Houses Trust
GC, V, A

This is possibly the oldest undisturbed early colonial house in Australia, and was occupied by the same family for more than a century. Rouse Hill House, set on 12 hectares, is a two-storey building of thirteen rooms made of sandstone-faced, cavity rock wall construction. The encircling veranda of twin timber columns was probably added during the 1850s or earlier, and was recorded in an 1860 photograph. Such simple colonial Georgian architecture, relying on proportion, scale, symmetry and rhythmic spacing, was reminiscent of the English country houses of Richard Rouse's youth.

113

112

24 L 13

26 L 18

112 Cadman's Cottage

*110 George Street North, The Rocks
(below street level)
1815–16 (possibly) Francis Greenway
Open: Tue–Sun 10am–4.30pm
Closed: Mondays, Christmas and Good Friday
GC, V, A*

With this one exception, all the smaller non-descript buildings of the period of first settlement at Sydney Cove have vanished. This sandstone structure was built in 1815–16 as the 'Coxswain's Barracks' attached to Governor Macquarie's dockyard and stores on the shores of Sydney Cove. The present name comes from John Cadman, who took up residence there in 1827. The building has largely survived because of constant Government or institutional ownership, first as a barracks, then as Cadman's residence as superintendent of Government Craft (1826-45). From 1845-64, it was the Water Police Headquarters, and, from 1865-1970, the Sydney Sailors' Home Trust. Restoration began in 1972 and the building is now used as an information centre by the National Parks and Wildlife Service.

*Above: Elevation of Cadman's Cottage
Below: Plan of Hyde Park Barracks (after Morton Herman)*

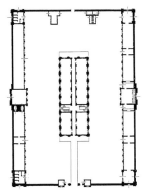

113 Hyde Park Barracks

*Macquarie Street (opposite
Queens Square), Sydney
1817–19 Francis Greenway
1990–92 Tonkin Zulaikha Harford (conversion
to museum) and Clive Lucas (restoration)
Open: 10am–5pm daily
Closed: Good Friday and Christmas Day
GC, V, A*

One of Sydney's earliest examples of refined architecture, Hyde Park Barracks was built to house transported convicts in a self-contained walled compound in a bid to solve night-time crime. It was miraculously saved from demolition after it had been left to decay for a century. The three-storey main building is the centrepiece of the walled compound, which included a cookhouse, bakery, cells and soldiers' quarters. Its primary purpose was to house the large working convict population, which, until this project, roamed the streets at night causing street crime.

Each floor has four large rooms divided by staircases, with rows of hammocks attached to wooden rails and upright posts fixed to the floor and roof. Seventy convicts were crammed into each large room and thirty-five into the smaller rooms, to bring the total to more than 800 inmates. In 1887, the interior was rebuilt to house the District Law Courts of NSW. Later, it became a project of the Historic Houses Trust, being carefully restored, conserved and converted into a museum in the early 1990s.

The modern interpretation of the museum, which demonstrates a sensitive approach, is well regarded in architectural circles. Modern materials such as glass and steel are used in ways which clearly distinguish the new work from the original fabric. In summer, during the Sydney Festival, the grounds are crowded with people who come to the night-time jazz concerts.

115

24 L 15	168 D 5

114 Sydney Conservatorium of Music

Conservatorium Road, Sydney
1817–21 Francis Greenway (Gov. Stables)
1912–15 Richard Seymour Wells (NSWGA)
GC, V, A

Of the surviving buildings from Sydney's first renowned architect, Francis Greenway, this is his and his master's greatest whimsy. The design for the Governor's stables is said to be based on Inveraray Castle (1745), which would have appealed to the Governor and Mrs Macquarie. Regarded as an excessive structure in its day, it only housed an exercise yard, stable rooms on three sides, and sleeping quarters for servants on the other. It was, however, conceived as a minor element in a much grander scheme for remodelling the landscape and building a new Gothic Government House. Such plans were severely criticised by the Crown as 'a state of magnificence far exceeding the wants or allowance of any Governor'.

In 1910, a sensational election promise by the McGowan government to abolish the role of the Governor came to nought, except that it did release the stables to become the Sydney Conservatorium of Music. In the conversion, Wells's austere central auditorium design was economical, but uninspired.

115 St Matthew's (Anglican) Church and Rectory

Greenway Crescent, Windsor
1817–23 Francis Greenway (CA)
GC, V, A

Governor Macquarie's visionary settlement plan to build five towns along the Hawkesbury River inspired the erection of this Anglican church at Windsor. After condemning an earlier building recently commenced by the architect Henry Kitchen, Francis Greenway managed to take over the project, demolish Kitchen's attempt and start again. The John Soane-influenced building is considered architecturally informed yet original (not copybook Georgian), skilful in proportion and detailing, well built and dignified. It is the least altered of all Greenway buildings and as such is a national treasure.

The Rectory

The elegance and simplicity of Greenway's architecture is clearly present in what many believe to be his best domestic design, a house for the Rector of St Matthew's Church. The fabric is in good condition and has undergone relatively minor changes.

23 G 14

116 Glover Cottages

124–126 Kent Street, Millers Point
1820–23 Thomas Glover (builder)
GC, V, A

The earliest pair of attached terrace houses in Australia are made of coursed random sandstone with dressed reveals and a simple hipped roof. Nicknamed 'The Ark' when left stranded by the lowering of Kent Street, they are now occupied by The Australian Institute of International Affairs.

Left: Plan and elevation of the Governor's Stables, 1820 attributed to Francis Greenway (Courtesy Mitchell Library)

● 1819 Governor Macquarie
suffers criticism and is forced
to return to London

● 1824 Wentworth and Wardell
publish *The Australian* newspaper

● 1826 Government campaign to
force Aborigines into Tasman
Peninsula area

117

25 H 20   **66 J 6**

117 The Judge's House (private offices)
531 Kent Street, Sydney
1821–22 William Harper, Assistant Surveyor
1978 Gordon Fuller (restoration)
1992 further renovations and underpinning
GC, V, NA

A survivor from the redevelopments of the
1960s and 1970s, this house is now the oldest
surviving free-standing dwelling in the central
business district of Sydney.

The building's name stems from its most
famous occupant, Judge Dowling, the second
Chief Justice of New South Wales (1828–1830),
and it was thereafter associated with judges and
magistrates for many years. It was later part of
the Sydney Night Refuge (Sydney City Mission)
until it was finally sold for demolition in 1970.
However, intense lobbying by The 1788–1820
Association and other heritage interest groups
succeeded in saving the building.

As a result of severe dry rot, only the timber
columns on either side of the doorway are
original. The fanlight over the front door is
unusually delicate and the concave stone
chamfered door framing is noteworthy.
Interestingly the house is now occupied by
businesses run by descendants of William
Harper, who designed the building.

Below: Ground floor plan (JAA)
The Judge's House by William Harper (1821–22)

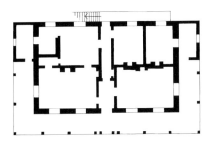

118 Cleveland House
51 Buckingham Street, Surry Hills
1824 architect unknown
GC, V, A

This is one of only seven surviving large private
houses built before 1830 to be found in the
greater Sydney area. Only two of these are in
the inner city. Although authorship is unknown,
possible Greenway signature details, including
the entry door and fanlight, are remarkably
similar to 'Hobartville' (1829) at Richmond.

There are no clearly documented city houses
surviving by Francis Greenway, Australia's first
distinguished architect (he appears to have only
designed three in any case), and records of his
private work from the time of his dismissal
(1822) to his death (1837) are scant.

24 J 12

119 'Clyde Bank'
Formerly 'Bligh House'
43 Lower Fort Street, The Rocks
1823–24 attrib. Francis Greenway
1962–63 Morton Herman (renovations)
1972 Fisher, Jackson and Hudson
GC, V, A

One of two surviving colonial Georgian townhouses in the inner city area **(see 118)**, 'Clyde
Bank' was built for Robert Crawford, Principal
Clerk to the Colonial Secretary, but was leased
for twenty years after completion. It was then
purchased by Robert Campbell in 1845, a
parliamentarian and the first provincial Scottish
Grand Master Freemason in Australia. Later a
boarding house and then offices of the RACGP,
it underwent two renovations. The walls are
rendered handmade sandstock bricks, with full-
height veranda doors of cedar and turned
timber Doric columns. 'Clyde Bank' is an important example of the scale and design of buildings
during this period of the first governors.

● 1830 First Australian novel,
Quintus Servinton, published

● 1831 The *Sydney Morning Herald*
newspaper first published

120

26 K 18 **66 R 4**

120 St James' (Anglican) Church

King Street and Queen's Square, Sydney
1820–22 Francis Greenway (CA)
1832 John Verge (porch additions)
1894 Varney Parkes (additions)
1978 Woodhouse and Danks (conservation)
GC, V, A

Governor Macquarie had wanted a courthouse and town hall soon after his arrival in 1810, but lacked both an architect and funds. However, within five years, the Macquarie–Greenway team had developed grand plans for a large 'European' quadrangle in the vicinity of Queens Square to be enclosed by civic buildings, including a new courthouse and school. During an early phase of construction, the scheme was criticised as being grandiose; a directive from the visiting Commissioner of Enquiry, John Thomas Bigge, ordered the conversion of the court plans into a church (now St James'), and the school into the less than successful Supreme Court.

The result was an urban church for Greenway after his two earlier pastoral churches, St Matthew's **(115)** and St Luke's. The tower and spire of St James' are finely proportioned and were meant to be viewed when approaching from King Street. The main body and tower are built of sandstock bricks set in lime mortar, and red rubbing bricks form all the arches. The interiors (1824) are not by Greenway. The porch by John Verge (1832) is also highly regarded.

Below: Ground floor plan (after Morton Herman),
St James' Church (1820–22)

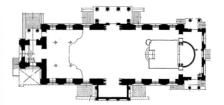

121 Juniper Hall (private offices)

248–250 Oxford Street, Paddington
1824 architect unknown
1892 (extension of two bays to the east)
GC, V, A

The oldest surviving house in Sydney's eastern suburbs was saved from destruction in 1984 only moments before bulldozers moved in to begin demolition. It was later restored by the National Trust.

For more than half a century, Juniper Hall had been subdivided into flats and hidden from view by a string of shops built on its front lawn. It was named after the juniper berry (used to flavour gin) by Sydney's first private distiller, Robert Cooper (1776–1857). He built the villa for his third wife to house his family of twenty-eight children from three marriages.

The Georgian Influence

By 1814, the first architects had arrived — the free settler Henry Kitchen; an army officer, John Watts and the Bristol-born convict, Francis Greenway. The rediscovery of Palladio in England through architectural pattern books in the early 1700s revived Italian architecture throughout the world. The Palladian, or Georgian as it was known in the British colonies, style incorporated classical columns, cornices, pilasters and fanlights into a carefully proportioned, often symmetrical, brick shell. While brick was favoured by proponents of the Georgian style, sandstone became the material of choice during the later Regency and Greek Revival styles. Church designs were influenced by Sir Christopher Wren's tower, spire and basilica designs, and houses reflect published estates. Greenway is credited with original thinking in the Georgian framework, having a fine eye for proportion and a mind for quality.

122

59 A 11

122 Vaucluse House

Wentworth Road, Vaucluse
1829 George Cookney (stables)
1839 architect unknown (front wing, veranda)
1847 architect unknown (remodelled)
Open: Tue–Sun 10am–4.30pm
Closed: Mondays, Christmas and Good Friday
GC, V, A

Vaucluse House, which is well preserved, is both historically and architecturally important. This castellated Tudor Gothic home was built by the explorer and statesman William Charles Wentworth (1780–1872), for his wife Sarah and family who resided there from 1827–1853.

It was built in three successive periods and has been owned by the public since 1910, making it the first house museum of its kind in Australia. Wentworth furnished the house with artifacts from around the world including Bohemia glass,

Below: Ground floor plan, Vaucluse House (1839–1910)

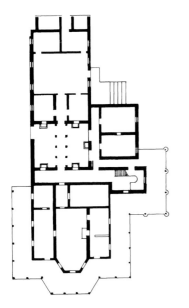

a dining room setting from the Doge's Palace in Venice, Meissen china and Italian floor tiles. The most influential statesman in the colony, Wentworth was author of the Australian Constitution and President of the Legislative Council of NSW in 1872. Vaucluse House remains a rare example of a 19th-century estate with kitchen wing, stables and outbuildings set in 27 acres of gardens.

26 K 18

123 NSW Supreme Court Building

Cnr King and Elizabeth Streets, Sydney
1819 Francis Greenway (design)
1822–28 (completed by others)
1859–62 Alexander Dawson (registry office)
1868 James Barnet (colonnade)
1895–96 Walter Liberty Vernon (Banco court)
1978 NSWGA and Philip Cox and Partners (renovations)
GC, V, A

Originally designed as a school, Commissioner Bigge decided, while it was already under construction, that it should become a court. The school was built later in Macquarie Street. Generally little evidence of Greenway remains except for the handsome geometrical staircase.

24 J 13

124 Argyle Stores

Cnr 14–20 Argyle Street, The Rocks
1826 on; 1826–35 attrib. Henry Cooper
GC, V, A

This grouping of early masonry and timber framed warehouse buildings set around a granite courtyard was the nucleus of revived commercial activity in the historic area of The Rocks. It has been restored twice and currently houses Australian speciality retailers. The nearby Argyle Cut was completed in the 1860s and bridged over during the 1920s.

126

26 K 18

125 Newington House

In the grounds of Silverwater Women's Prison
1829-32 architect unknown
1840 J Houson (veranda colonnade)
GC, NV, NA

This stately house was built of stuccoed brick on stone foundations. Of particular interest are the columns, each carved from single blocks of stone, which support a well-designed entablature and parapet. The house, which has a private chapel, is surrounded by formal gardens.

Regency Style

As wealthier free settlers, particularly merchants, began to settle in Sydney in the late 1820s and the 1830s, the architecture began to take on some style and even elegance. Regency style (named after the Prince Regent, later George IV) is only a shade more mannered than Georgian style (named after George III), which, in domestic architecture, exhibited an increasing tendency towards more detailed Italianate or Greek references in the interiors, while the exteriors displayed a lighter touch. Greater opportunities for architects to travel in Europe, together with a growing number of reference books, helped diversify domestic architecture. However, public and religious buildings remained trapped in the traditions of Greek and Gothic Revival.

56 Q 18

126 Tusculum Villa

(Royal Australian Institute of Architects)
3 Manning Street, Potts Point
1830-32 John Verge (original building)
1851 attrib. JF Hilly (two-storey colonnade)
1905 JB Clamp (internal alterations, stair)
1988 Neil Durbach and Harry Levine
GC, V, A

The first homes for the emerging well-to-do in Sydney were built on land grants on Woolloomooloo Hill (now called Potts Point) and were subject to a set of 'villa conditions'. A time and value restriction was imposed with the grant: houses were to be of a minimum value of £1,000, they had to face the city and they were to be approved by the then Governor, Sir Richard Bourke. Verge's design for Tusculum Villa, commissioned by the merchant Alexander Brodie Spark, was for two storeys with an open colonnade of Doric columns at ground level. The present building's appearance stems from an 'aggrandisement' in the early Victorian Italianate style for merchant William Long. He introduced the current two-storey Ionic colonnade to replace the single-storey Doric affair. It was saved from complete dereliction by the Royal Australian Institute of Architects who restored the villa and built a new wing to house offices and an auditorium.

Below: Ground floor plan, Tusculum Villa (1830–1905)

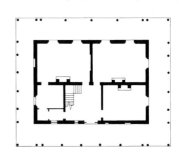

Below: Ground floor plan, Newington House (1829–1840)

127

56 R 18

65 C 2

127 Elizabeth Bay House

7 Onslow Avenue, Elizabeth Bay
1832–37 John Verge
1973–75 Clive Lucas and Partners (restoration)
Open: Tue–Sun 10am–4.30pm
Closed: Mondays, Christmas and Good Friday
GC, V, A

This is the finest house by John Verge (1782–1861), with probably the most sublime interior built in the colony in the first half of the 19th century. The entrance vestibule leads through to an oval domed saloon around which the geometrical (cantilevered) stair rises to an arcaded gallery. The window and door joinery are exceptionally well detailed. Designed for Alexander Macleay, a distinguished scientist and Colonial Secretary of New South Wales (1825–1837), Elizabeth Bay House was last used as a private residence in 1927. Thereafter it served various purposes until, in 1941, it was divided into fifteen apartments. In 1963, it was purchased by the State government and carefully restored with a complete redecoration of the interior, including furnishings and furniture. The gardens were also revived. In 1837, shortly after completion of Elizabeth Bay House, John Verge suddenly announced his retirement and moved to a land grant near Kempsey in northern New South Wales.

128 'Lyndhurst'

(Historic Houses Trust)
61 Darghan Street, Glebe
1833–36 John Verge
1979–84 Clive Lucas and Partners (restored as Headquarters of the Historic Houses Trust)
GC, V, A

Conceived as an impressive Regency villa for Dr James Bowman, son-in-law of John Macarthur and Inspector of Colonial Hospitals, its use as a residence was short-lived. The fashionable architect Verge, assisted by John Bibb (1810–62), was allowed free rein to position and design the building on 36 acres of land. He used a total of 29,000 bricks, rendered to look like stone, ironbark shingles on the roof and cedar joinery and furnishings imported from around the world. The villa was surrounded by ornamental gardens, an orchard and flowering shrubberies.

From 1847, 'Lyndhurst' was used by various institutions before being subdivided for the terrace houses which surround it today. Later uses included an ice cream factory, a printing works and a timber workshop. Its planned demolition in the 1970s became the centre of a public outcry and it was eventually saved and restored in part. It has since become the headquarters of the Historic Houses Trust.

Below: Ground floor plan, Elizabeth Bay House (1837)

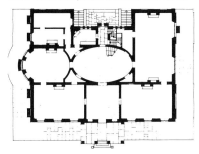

Below: Ground floor plan, 'Lyndhurst' (1837)

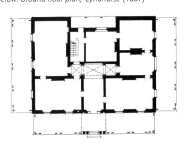

133

133

66 N 2

129 'Camden Park'
Old Hume Highway, Camden Park
1834 John Verge
1821 Henry Kitchen ('Home Farm')

66 N 4

130 Durham Hall
(Royal College of Pathologists of Australasia)
207 Albion Street, Surry Hills
1835 Architect unknown
1986 Brewster Murray (restoration)
GC, V, A
An early colonial villa built for George Hill, then
Mayor of Sydney. A representative building of
the era, it was made with handmade sandstock
bricks, which were rendered over in 1923.

24 J 12

131 Australian American Association
39–41 Lower Fort Street, Millers Point
1834–36 John Verge
GC, V, A
The only remaining example of small-scale
domestic work by this well-known architect.
Originally built on speculation, this elegant pair
of late Georgian townhouses has margined
pattern French windows with semicircular fanlights to the doors and windows at ground level.

57 E 17

132 'Lindesay'
1 Carthona Avenue, Darling Point
1834–36 attrib. Edward Hallen
1840s attrib. James Hume (south wing)
1914 Robertson & Marks (major additions)
GC, V, A
An early, square plan Gothic Revival villa with
attractive false gablework and a rather powerful
display of chimney architecture. Each year the
house is open for special events.

66 N 2

133 East Sydney TAFE
Formerly Darlinghurst Gaol
Cnr Forbes and Burton Streets, Darlinghurst
*1836–40 Mortimer William Lewis (CA) and
George Barney (RE)*
1885 James Barnet (CA)
GC, V, A
Darlinghurst Gaol was one of two purpose-
designed gaols built concurrently (the other
being Parramatta Gaol) by Mortimer Lewis
(1796–1879). These were needed to address the
appalling prison conditions of the 1820s. Lewis's
experimental design, arrived at as a result of the
tension between the architect, government and
the Royal Engineers, was a plan of six radial
wings centred on a circular chapel. The scheme
attempted to mediate and incorporate competing concepts about prisoner reformation and
amenities from Britain and America.

The design debate turned on the argument of
individual prisoner separation and the size and
accommodation of cells. The final built design
expressed a compromise, with prisoner
separation at night and common exercise during
the day. The open central galleries to the cell
buildings were introduced during construction.
The gaol was ready for occupation by the
middle of 1841 and public executions became a
popular entertainment in early Sydney.

•••

*The head gaoler is reported to have announced,
'We can hang seven together at a pinch, six
comfortably.' Progress!*

•••

*The last hanging at the gaol was in 1907. It was
closed in 1912, but, during World War I, was
used to detain 'enemy aliens'. After the war, it
was used as a technical college with an emphasis on the arts; today it houses an exhibition
gallery, painting studios and pottery kilns.*

134

23 H 13

264 F 2

134 Argyle Place
Millers Point
1830s–1850s
GC, V, A

This is the only urban space in Sydney which survives intact from the 1830s. Since the beginning of the century, Argyle Place buildings have been under the control of the Sydney Harbour Trust and its successor, the Maritime Services Board. Once used as a tram terminus, Millers Point has many fine houses and terraces from the Georgian and Victorian eras and retains its mid-19th century scale dominated by Holy Trinity Church. No. 50 Argyle Place is a classic 'five lighter', with iron lace, long cedar shutters and fanlight. The area was saved from wholesale high-rise redevelopment in the 1960s by the intervention of building unions.

24 J 13

135 Westpac Bank and Museum
Formerly Martyn & Combes
47 George Street, The Rocks
1841–42 John Bibb
GC, V, A

Originally a colonial store, this building shows architectural principles of Georgian England. It was first used as a plumbers store, and later housed a wholesale chemist. In 1987, Westpac established Australia's first banking museum, where real transactions can be made in a re-created Victorian setting.

23 H 13

136 Holy Trinity Anglican Church
Lower Fort and Argyle Streets, Millers Point
c. 1840 Henry Ginn
1878 Edmund Blacket (additions)
GC, V, A

Known as the 'Garrison Church', Ginn's original design was spired and picturesque.

137 'Fernhill'
Mulgoa Road, Mulgoa
1842 Mortimer Lewis
GC, NV, NA

Distinguished by its semicircular projecting bay and veranda, the original house was built by Edward Cox who brought twenty stonemasons out from Ireland. They arrived under Governor Bourke's 'bounty' system, which effectively subsidised passages for skilled immigrants chosen by individual colonists.

The entrance elevation has a classical severity and was possibly intended to be two storeys in height rather than one. The front door is set in an arched recess and the walls are divided into bays by plain, slightly projecting pilasters which frame tall French windows. The low 'hipped' roof has projecting eaves.

The interior has delicate Greek Revival details, embellished plasterwork and extensive polished cedar timberwork.

●●●

'Fernhill' is considered to be one of the most valuable properties in Sydney. It commands 730 hectares spread over seventeen lots.

Below: Ground floor plan, 'Fernhill' (1842)

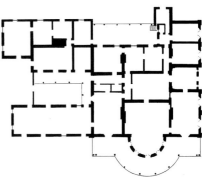

139

26 J 20

138 St Andrew's Cathedral

George and Bathurst Streets, Sydney
1837–42 James Hume
1847–74 Edmund Blacket
1886 Cyril Blacket (Chapter House)
1949 Leslie Wilkinson (George Street entrance)
GC, V, A

By 1812, this site had been chosen for a major
Anglican Cathedral by Governor Lachlan
Macquarie. Its position in what was then
considered to be the future commercial heart of
Sydney led Francis Greenway (1777–1837) to
envisage a noble square, 200 metres long by
100 metres wide, flanked by 50-metre wide
streets on either side.

He imagined a divinity school, a library and a
museum around a cloistered quadrangle with a
bishop's palace where the Town Hall now sits
beside Druitt Street. Opposite would be the city's
town and market hall (the present-day Queen
Victoria Building). From there 'streets ran broad
and straight, flanked with ornate mansions and
majestic terraces. Gardens flowered in ordered
spaces. Ionic columns gave a classic air to the
squares. Vistas had a proper ending in Gothic
toll-gates. Obelisks and fountains lent distinction
to small gardens.'

Unfortunately, Greenway never saw his vision.
Work on the cathedral was prevented by
Whitehall until 1837, when the English Gothic
design of James Hume was adopted. In 1847,
Edmund Blacket (1817–83) continued the work,
modifying Hume's design as he went along.

A cathedral in name, but a large English
parish church in scale, St Andrew's originally
had its main entrance to the west before the
interior layout was reversed to address George
Street. The square, with its trees and the
church's relationship to the Town Hall, are
compelling reminders of the lost visions of a
noble and stately city.

56 Q 18

139 'Rockwall'

Macleay Street, Potts Point
1830–37 John Verge
GC, V, A

'Rockwall' was commissioned by the surveyor
and engineer John Busby, who came to Sydney
for the purpose of establishing a permanent
fresh water supply (Busby's Bore is his legacy).
He immediately commissioned the society
architect John Verge (1782–1861) to build a
small house, described in 1837, when it was
finally completed, as 'a splendid Italian villa'.
It unfortunately changed hands between three
owners during construction (Busby overestimated
his fortunes). The striking Italianate verandas
were added by the last owner, Thomas Ryder,
during construction.

During the 1960s and 1970s, 'Rockwall' was
left to rot in a terrible state of disrepair, its site
overshadowed by the Chevron Hotel, which has
since been replaced by the Landmark Hotel.
After years of dereliction, the recently restored
villa now provides a useful comparison with the
few other surviving houses by this important
architect, from the grandly scaled Elizabeth Bay
House (127) to the simply planned villa of
Tusculum (126).

Below: Ground floor plan, 'Rockwall' (1837)

140

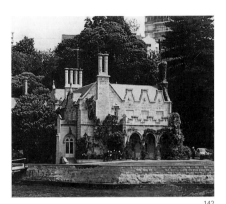

142

23 J 13

140 Lord Nelson Hotel
Kent and Argyle Streets, Millers Point
1834–43 architect unknown
GC, V, A
Possibly Sydney's oldest hotel, the Lord Nelson
is one of the few remaining pubs of the thirty-
seven original licensed premises in The Rocks
area. It would originally have had a columned
veranda to the edge of the footpath. Like its
neighbour, the Hero of Waterloo, it commemorates the British naval and military successes
in the early 1800s.

23 H 15

141 St Patrick's Church
20 Grosvenor Street, Sydney
1840–44 John Frederick Hilly
GC, V, A
Hilly, an Anglican architect, redrew the scheme
after a design brought from England by Father
Francis Murphy. The Early English Gothic style
was straightforward, decorative and influential
in the design of rural churches in the colony.
The sanctuary was extended c. 1928.

57 E 17

142 'Carthona'
5 Carthona Avenue, Darling Point
1841–44 architect unknown
GC, V, NA
A well-preserved early house of castellated
design copied from an English pattern book,
'Carthona' was built by the NSW Surveyor
General Sir Thomas Mitchell when he decided to
move away from Darlinghurst because it was
'too built up'. True to its name (*carthona* is
Spanish for 'meeting of the waters'), the
sandstone house is built on a levelled site on
the harbour edge, and is only visible from a
boat. Owned by a family of tea merchants, it is
one of Sydney's most valuable properties.

66 N 2

143 Darlinghurst Courthouse
Taylor Square, Sydney
1844 Mortimer Lewis (CA)
1884 and 1888 James Barnet (CA)
(flanking courts)
GC, V, A
Buildings designed by Mortimer Lewis during
this period are unmistakable, with their
pedimented Greek Revival temple facades,
fluted Doric columns and matching bookend
wings. Lewis designed countless courthouses
and police stations during his period as Colonial
Architect (1835–49), enabling the police and the
judiciary to assert their presence. The original
courthouse is only the small centrepiece of the
present elevation to Oxford Street. It was
designed with five columns, but built with six
and faced a dirt road across which was an open
field. On entering, the grand jury room is to the
right and clerk's office to the left. Note that the
fluting on the columns stops 2 metres from the
ground to prevent chipping by the public.

*Below: Measured drawing by Morton Herman before
matching additions were added by James Barnet.*

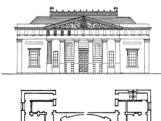

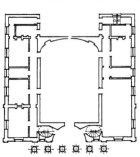

Government House Plan 144
Courtesy Historic Houses Trust

145

24 M 14

144 Government House
Royal Botanic Gardens, Sydney
1837–45 Edward Blore and Mortimer Lewis (CA)
Open: Fri–Sun 10am–3pm, Thu: groups
GC, V, A

To build a grand and worthy Government House was the dream of every notable Sydney architect, including Francis Greenway. However, when it was finally commissioned, the design came from the established English architect Edward Blore (1789–1879), as Governor Bourke felt that no colonial architect had sufficient experience to plan such a building.

Blore, working in the romantic Gothic style, produced a mock castle which matched the crenellations of the existing Greenway stables. The new building immediately became the talk of the town and helped establish the romantic Regency style in residential architecture which became popular in the colony over the next twenty years.

The large reception area is a richly decorated two-storey hall with a musicians gallery. Government House reputedly introduced the first modern water closet to Australia. The *porte-cochère* was added in 1873, and the two front rooms extended about 1900. Although there had been earlier proposals (c. 1900) to move the vestigial Governor into more modest premises, it was not until 1996 that this finally occurred under the premiership of Robert Carr.

Below: Blore's design for Alupka (1837–40), Crimea

24 J 14

145 Susannah Place
58–64 Gloucester Street, The Rocks
1844 architect unknown
1993 Robert Moore with Noni Boyd from Sydney Cove Authority (restoration and conservation)
Open: Sat and Sun:10am–5pm
Closed: Good Friday and Christmas Day
GC, V, A

This terrace of four houses with simple interiors, external brick toilets and open laundries is one of the few survivors of the clearances of the 19th century and the redevelopments of the Sydney Cove Redevelopment Authority.

It provides a rare insight into some of the earliest washing and sanitary amenities.

Below: Ground floor plan, Susannah Place (1844)

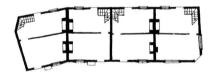

54 R 12

146 Lilyvale Restaurant (ANA Hotel)
Formerly Lily Cottage
176 Cumberland Street, Sydney
1847 architect unknown
GC, V, A

One of the rare surviving examples of a free-standing Georgian house in the inner-city area. The veranda shows the colonial version of the English colonnade with its tapered timber posts, simple details and construction.

Below: Ground floor plan, Lily Cottage (1847)

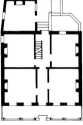

147 Former Congregational Church
264 Pitt Street, Sydney
1840–46 John Bibb
1857–67 architect unknown (galleries & vestry)
GC, V, A

John Bibb brought a similar eye for elegance and proportion to commercial and ecclesiastical buildings as did John Verge to residential buildings. The classical facade with massive Ionic columns clearly states that this church is neither Catholic nor Anglican, since both of those denominations were firmly committed to Gothic Revival. Inside is one of the finest colonial interiors in Australia, even though some of its most distinguished features were later additions to the original sparse interior. The fine galleries over the entry are set on slender cast-iron columns.

●●●

After 1876, plans were drawn up for an awkward centre steeple above the Ionic facade of the Pitt Street church, which was fortunately rejected on financial grounds.

Greek Revival
Following the rediscovery of Italian architecture in England and America during the 1600s and 1700s, Greek architecture was researched and revived as a more ordered and sophisticated system which could be applied to museums, courthouses, police stations and banks (the world over) where authority and gravitas were required. Greek Revival buildings remained remarkably consistent and identifiable through the repetitive use of the temple form, particularly the pedimented porch. Other features included the stepped base, Doric, Ionic and Corinthian Orders, the entablature or cornice, and the pediment roof. In Sydney, these buildings were virtually always made in sandstone and hardly ever in brick.

148 Victoria Barracks
Oxford Street, Paddington
1841–48 Major George Barney (RE)
Open: Thu 10am–3pm
GC, V, A

The home of British regiments until 1870, and still occupied by the Australian Army, Victoria Barracks is the most significant and untarnished example of late Georgian architecture in Sydney.

Begun in 1841 (the same year that the Darlinghurst Gaol was opened), the barracks took seven years to construct under the supervision of the Royal Engineers. Major George Barney, who also designed Fort Denison and the reconstruction of Circular Quay, selected the site and designed the barracks, possibly with some input from the Colonial Architect Mortimer Lewis. The principal colonnaded wing is 230 metres long, with an exquisite Georgian centrepiece. It is one of the finest examples of colonial military architecture in Australia.

149 Royal Australasian College of Physicians
145 Macquarie Street, Sydney
1848 John Bibb (original two storeys)
1910 architect unknown (upper two floors)
1994–95 Clive Lucas, Stapleton (renovations)
GC, V, A

One of a row of five terraces, this building was the home of the owner of the *Sydney Morning Herald*, John Fairfax, until he moved to Bellevue Hill in 1858. The two-storey sandstone structure was enlarged in 1910 by the Warrigal Club, which gave it the current four-storeyed appearance. It was sold by the Fairfax family in 1920 and purchased by the Royal Australasian College of Physicians in 1938. Much of the rich Georgian interior has survived intact.

150

151

23 G 14

150 Richmond Villa
(Society of Australian Genealogists)
120 Kent Street, Millers Point
1849 Mortimer Lewis
1978 (rebuilt on present site)
GC, V, A

This building is interesting as it is one of the
few remaining residential designs by the former
Colonial Architect Mortimer Lewis (1796–1879).
Lewis's work was generally confined to public
buildings such as courthouses and gaols.
Originally sited near Parliament House facing
The Domain, Richmond Villa was carefully
dismantled and rebuilt, stone by numbered
stone, on the present site in Kent Street in 1976.
Its removal made way for a major extension to
Parliament House.

Designing it for his own residence, Mortimer
Lewis chose Gothic outline and asymmetric bay
windows, a thinly veiled cover to what was
essentially a simple colonial home.

Lewis, who had been unfairly disgraced by
government officials and parliamentarians for
underestimating expenditure on the museum
project in College Street (now the Australian
Museum), was forced into early retirement. His
home was repossessed by his financier
GJ Rogers one year after being completed, when
Lewis defaulted on his interest payment.

After relocation, the current tenants were
granted a fifty-year lease in 1978.

25 H 17

151 Commonwealth Bank
11 Barrack Street, Sydney
1847–50 possibly John Bibb
1888 Robertson, Mansfield Bros (third storey)
1981–82 (conservation and refurbishment)
GC, V, A

This Classical Revival building is on the site of
Sydney's first purpose-built bank and
incorporates very high quality materials. Details
include cast bronze capitals and carved marble
columns. The orders of the external colonnade
ascend from the use of Doric columns at ground
level through Ionic to Corinthian at the top. This
building is an excellent example of 19th-century
classical style.

24 L 15

152 Hotel Intercontinental
Formerly The Treasury Building
117–119 Macquarie Street, Sydney
1849 Mortimer Lewis (CA) (corner building)
1896 Walter Liberty Vernon (CA) (Macquarie St)
1916 George McRae (NSWGA) (Bridge St)
1985 Kann Finch & Partners (hotel and tower)
GC, V, A

The conversion of a group of sandstone
buildings which once housed both the Treasury
records and the Premier's Office (before the
State Office Building was erected) into a new
high-rise hotel was regarded as a critical test of
heritage issues during the 1980s. The ambitious
joint venture was between the British
construction group of Sir Robert McAlpine and
the US Intercontinental Hotel Group. The plan
was for a 28-storey tower of 498 guest rooms
above a colonnaded and glazed cortile at the
rear of the building. Despite being opposed by
the National Trust, the development proceeded,
with restoration works carried out by Clive
Lucas and Partners. The project below the tower
is now considered a successful adaptation.

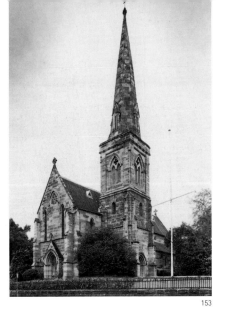

153

154

153 St Mark's Church
Darling Point Road, Darling Point
1848-52 Edmund Blacket (transept)
1864 Edmund Blacket (nave)
1875 Edmund Blacket (spire)
GC, V, A

Edmund Blacket (1817–1883) came to Australia seeking improved living conditions for his wife who suffered poor health. With letters of introduction, he was appointed Diocesan Architect by Bishop Broughton in 1847 and St Mark's was one of his first designs. Despite Blacket's lack of formal training, this church, which is constructed entirely from Pyrmont sandstone, is regarded as one of the most complete and finely proportioned buildings of the day. Other important Blacket designs include St Michael's Church, Darlinghurst (1854) and the neo-classical Presbyterian Church, Palmer Street, East Sydney (1856).

Blacket's rise in Sydney society was meteoric. He was appointed Colonial Architect in 1849, only to resign in 1854 to design the largest Gothic building of the day — the Quadrangle and Great Hall of Sydney University **(158)**.

154 Offices
Formerly Forth & Clyde Hotel
101 Mort Street, Balmain
1850s architect unknown
1890s architect unknown (enlarged)
1978 Mike Blakeney (adapted)
GC, V, NA

Behind the 1890s timber verandas is a traditional stone corner pub of the type found throughout Balmain. This was one of several catering for the many employees of Mort's Dock, which occupied the large wharf site opposite.

155 'Roslyndale'
38 Roslyndale Avenue, Woollahra
1856 Francis Clarke
GC, V, NA

This quaint house is particularly remarkable for its gingerbread Gothic styling with steeply pitched roofs, elaborately decorated bargeboards, bracket posted verandas and external plumbing. It was a precursor to 'The Hermitage' **(212)** and has a similar form to houses in Balmain and Hunters Hill.

Gothic Revival Style

Many styles ran parallel to each other during the 1800s, which is why the choice of the most appropriate style was the first and most important decision by the architect. While Gothic Revival ran parallel to Greek Revival for fifty years, it was clearly the case that the Anglican and Catholic Churches sponsored the Gothic and medieval traditions of England and France, while the gaols, police stations and courthouses were Greek Revival until James Barnet introduced his own version of Italianate which was internationally fashionable during the 1860s and 1870s. Rarely were churches Italianate; the few neo-Classical examples were by the minor faiths who wanted to declare a distinction between themselves and the major denominations.

Gothic style was championed not only by the English clergy, but also by Oxford and Cambridge Universities (in particular The English Cambridge Camden Society), who anointed Gothic the only style for ecclesiastical architecture because it belonged to both 'nature' and to 'England'; a ploy to underplay the existence of Catholic French Gothic. Clearly Pugin and Barry's Houses of Parliament at Westminster (1835–60) influenced the design of buildings such as Sydney University in the 1850s.

157

156 Justice and Police Museum

Former Water Police Court
Cnr Albert and Phillip Streets, Sydney
1852–56 Edmund Blacket (CA)
Open: Sun 10am–5pm
Closed: Good Friday and Christmas Day
GC, V, A

This neo-Gothic style building is the only court-house designed by Blacket, who was better known as a church architect. Commenced in 1853, it was not completed until 1856 (by James Barnet) because of the gold rushes which lured tradesmen away from the city. The museum features a magistrate's court, a police charge room, a remand cell, an array of weapons and forensic evidence from notorious crimes.

157 Fort Denison

Formerly Pinchgut Island
Sydney Harbour
1841; 1855–57 George Barney (RE)
Open: Tours daily (Sydney Harbour Nat. Park)
Closed: Christmas Day
GC, V, A

One of the last Martello Towers to be built in the world, following their proliferation in southern England after the design's defensive capabilities had been proven at Cap Mortella, Corsica, in 1794.

The tower was built to defend Sydney against a possible attack by Russian warships, which never eventuated. Built from 8,000 tonnes of sandstone quarried near Kurraba Point, Neutral Bay, it was named after Sir William Denison, then Governor of New South Wales. By the time the fort was completed, it was redundant.

The tower's gunroom still has three 8-inch muzzle-loading cannons positioned before the stonework was completed in 1857. Due to the narrow passages leading to the gun room, the cannons cannot be removed without dismantling the stone work. The tower is serviced by supply rooms and ordnance stores. When a Japanese submarine entered the harbour in May 1942 (passing through the anti-submarine nets) it was fired upon by the American cruiser USS Chicago. A secondary salvo hit the Martello tower, causing minor, but still visible, damage.

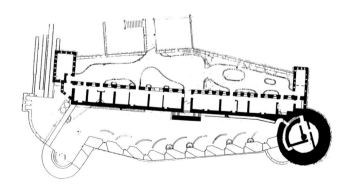

Above: Plan of Fort Denison
(by permission NSW National Parks and Wildlife Service)

158

158 Main Quadrangle Building and Great Hall

Sydney University, Darlington
1854-59 Edmund Blacket
1907 Walter Liberty Vernon
1926 Leslie Wilkinson
GC, V, A

The Colonial Architect Edmund Blacket (1817–83) resigned from his post to accept a commission to establish the centrepiece of Sydney University. Conceiving it as a vast complex, he clung to the Medieval Gothic images of Oxford and Cambridge, the only architectural style considered appropriate. The fact that Blacket was an ecclesiastical architect made him the obvious choice for the job and in 1854 he broke ground on the vast treeless expanse of Grose Farm, to realise his design for the Main Quadrangle and St Paul's College.

The most intricate and medieval element of the building is the Great Hall, perfectly proportioned and enclosed by an open timber roof 21 metres above the stone floor. The hammerbeam ceiling with carved cedar angels bears the motto *'Knowledge puffeth up, Charity edifies'*. Stained-glass windows at the east and west ends represent founders of colleges of the Universities of Cambridge and Oxford, respectively, while the Challis gift of The Royal Window features the young Queen Victoria and her heirs. The cost of facing the building in Pyrmont sandstone was a considerable expense approved by the Auditor General of the day, who declared: 'We must build not for today, or for tomorrow, but for the Futurity'.

159 Bidura Children's Court

Former residence of Edmund Blacket
357 Glebe Point Road, Glebe
1858 Edmund Blacket
1980s NSW Public Works (restored)
GC, V, A

Currently a conference centre run by the New South Wales Department of Community Services, this handsome villa was originally designed by Sydney's great ecclesiastical architect Edmund Blacket (1817–83). The walls are of handmade bricks, rendered to give the appearance of stone coursing, with a slate rather than shingle roof and an attached single-storey veranda of decorative cast-iron. Blacket lived here until 1870, when he moved to a smaller house which he designed for himself in Balmain.

160 The Balmain Watch House

Former Balmain Police Lock-up
179 Darling Street, Balmain
1855 Edmund Blacket (CA)
1880s James Barnet (first floor additions)
Open: Sat 1pm–3pm
GC, V, A

The original building was a simple single-storey sandstone block which was extended during the 1880s. Although a number of lock-ups were built during the 1850s, the Balmain lock-up is possibly the oldest in Sydney and is said by locals to be haunted. It is owned by the National Trust and maintained by the local historical society. The Watch House is open to visitors for a couple of hours on Saturday afternoons.

161 Sydney Observatory

23 H 13

Upper Fort Street, Sydney
1857–59 Alexander Dawson (CA)
1986 (adapted to museum use)
Open: Mon–Fri 2–5pm, Sat and Sun 10am–5pm
Closed: Christmas Day and Good Friday
GC, V, A

Soon after the arrival of the First Fleet, Lieutenant Dawes, under the direction of the British Board of Longitude, established an observatory at Flagstaff Hill on Dawes Point. In 1821, a second observatory was established at Parramatta. In 1858, a new observatory, one of the few buildings designed by Alexander Dawson, enabled regular observations to commence. One feature of the building was a time-ball tower. Each day at 1pm the ball on top of the tower dropped to signal the correct time, while simultaneously, for the visually impaired, a cannon was fired at Fort Denison **(157)**.

The structure incorporates geometric forms related to the housing of telescopes and scientific apparatus. However, by 1892, there was concern that the proposed railway approaches for the future harbour bridge would interfere with the telescope's operation and an astrographic telescope was transferred to Observatory Hill at the corner of Beecroft Road and Pennant Hills Road (Observatory Park) in 1899 until 1930, when the telescope was returned to the main observatory. The site was officially occupied by the Government Astronomer until 1982.

•••

The site was virtually closed down in 1926 when the Government Astronomer WE Cooke requested that the Lang government spend £70,000 for new equipment, otherwise the observatory would be useless. Unwilling to spend the money, Lang terminated Cooke's appointment on the basis that the observatory was outmoded.

162 Campbell's Storehouses

24 J 12

7–27 Circular Quay West, The Rocks
1839–61 (Nos. 9–27)
1854–85 (Nos. 19–25)
1895 (No. 7)
1890s (third storey added in brick)
1975–78 Devine, Erby and Mazlin
(conservation works)
GC, V, A

This early storehouse group was built by John Campbell (1802–86), a son of Robert Campbell Snr (1769–1846), who was one of Sydney's first merchants and original owner of the 'Duntroon' pastoral property near Canberra which is now the Military College. Campbell's Storehouses were originally a row of two-storey gable-roofed stone warehouses, with the present third floor added after the government purchased the complex in 1887, reusing many of the original roof timbers and slates.

In 1891, hydraulic power in the form of high-pressure water was employed to drive hydraulic engines attached to the side of the stores. One of the original engines, known as 'whips' because of the speed with which they lifted goods, is still located in situ. The southernmost bay was demolished to make way for access to the Overseas Passenger Terminal.

Ownership is now vested in the Sydney Cove Authority. The buildings contain several tourist restaurants.

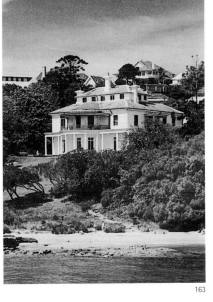

163

164

278 Q 12

54 R 20

163 Strickland House

Formerly 'Carrara'
Carrara Road, Vaucluse
1856 John Frederick Hilly
1933–35 additional buildings
1960s outbuildings and dormitories
GC, V, NA

For more than fifty years, the house 'Carrara'
was known as the Strickland Convalescent
Home for Women (1913–88) after Governor
Strickland. It was one of only two such
institutions run by the New South Wales Health
Department, the other being the Home for Men
located at Denistone.

'Carrara' was originally built for John Hosking,
and the semicircular fronted design marks the
transitional phase between simple rectilinear
colonial designs and more complex shapes of
the Victorian period. There were few bow or
circular fronted houses designed during the
19th century in Sydney. One of the earliest
surviving is 'Fernhill' by Mortimer Lewis **(137)**.

Below: Ground floor plan, Strickland House (1856–1935)

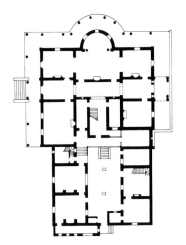

164 Margaretta Cottage

6 Leichhardt Street, Glebe Point
1860 Michael Golden
GC, V, NA

A wonderful and unassuming post-Regency
house set back from the street in a densely
developed neighbourhood. Below the slated
main roof eaves line is a delicate entablature
bearing the house name. The veranda has a
draped metal roof with cast-iron columns. The
property survives with an unusually large front
garden complete with cast-iron fence and
stone gateposts.

The Victorian City
1860–1895

1860–1895

In 1888, celebrating a centenary of colonial settlement, Sydneysiders were proud and optimistic.

The straggling convict outpost had expanded until, as one contemporary guidebook felt constrained to boast, 'the progress of the city and the suburbs is so rapid and the daily improvement in transport so marked that even residents stand in need of a handy reliable Guide'.

Responsible government was achieved in 1856. The gold rushes offered quick wealth and expanding primary industry brought new working opportunities. The population boomed as prospects of a higher standard of living lured thousands of immigrants to the Colony of New South Wales. It seemed a golden age.

Sydney's growth was staggering. In 1851, the population of the actual city was more than 42,000, with another 9,684 people living in the suburbs. By the time of the 1891 census, this figure had increased eightfold – to a total of 383,283 metropolitan inhabitants, of whom three-quarters lived in the suburbs, the rest in the inner city. As the population continued to swell, so did the perimeter of the city, and the pattern for Sydney's sprawl was established.

Growth was unplanned. The metropolis took shape as transport routes converged on the port. Suburban development fanned back out along these routes, to the north along a ridge to Hornsby plateau; along Parramatta Road to the west; along Botany Road to the south and eastwards through Paddington village and Randwick to the semi-rural holdings of the wealthy at Point Piper and Vaucluse. Beyond the built-up areas were pockets of development at Parramatta, Hunters Hill and Manly.

By 1890, Sydneysiders inhabited an area of approximately 150 square miles, linked by a somewhat haphazard transport system.

The government funded the first railway in 1855, with a line to Granville. Initially train travel was unreliable; the railway was primarily seen as a means of opening up the land for development by providing freight transport to country regions. Only later, with the construction of new stations and suburban lines in the 1880s, were trains used by city commuters.

Meanwhile, both passengers and goods relied on horse-drawn vehicles of every variety – from drays to large double-decker omnibuses – to move about town. These contraptions threaded their way through a maze of often unsurfaced roads between Circular Quay and the railway terminus at Redfern and then networked out to the suburbs.

Tramways were the first attempt at a regular urban transport system when, from 1861–66, a horse-drawn tram plied its way the length of Pitt Street. Steam trams were introduced in 1879 to serve the Garden Palace Exhibition, so that Sydney would not appear to be behind the times. This novel form of transport proved as popular as the exhibition, conveying nearly half a million passengers. Once established, the tram system remained in place as a cheap alternative to the much-promised inner city railway line. Trams were conveying nearly 60 million passengers through the city and suburbs by 1890.

Privately operated harbour ferries did more to stretch the city limits than any other form of transport, and were responsible for the development of the north shore and areas such as Balmain and Glebe, Mosman and Lane Cove, Manly and Watsons Bay.

New industries in the expanding metropolis dictated the character of Sydney's suburbs and its housing.

The houses of tradesmen, shopkeepers and the like were built at Paddington, Redfern, Pyrmont, Chippendale, Newtown and the Upper Rocks, all with easy access to the commercial centre. At the lowest end of the social scale, labourers crammed into slum-like accommodation in the inner city, around what is now Darling Harbour, Surry Hills and The Rocks, also home to sailors and wharf labourers. The poor also had to contend with overcrowding and insanitary conditions such as open drains and communal cesspits, common sources of disease.

In the 1860s, south of the city, near the swamps of Alexandria, Waterloo and Redfern, industry attracted a working population. Industries of the more noxious variety, such as tanning, woolwashing, brickworks and metalworks, were often

Horse-drawn omnibus from Sydney Tramway and Omnibus Company, Sydney, c. 1895 (the company built and ran its own buses).

Powerhouse Museum, Sydney

located incongruously between nurseries selling camellias and dahlias. Foundries, flour mills and timber yards also sprang up between the residential pockets close to the railway stations.

The wealthy lived on large plots of land to the east of the city or at Glebe Point or Tempe, and built town villas in Macquarie Street and along Woolloomooloo Hill. The suburbs of Balmain and Glebe combined palatial harbourside residences overlooking their pavilions, sea pools and boat ramps with the smaller cottages of the local workforce, who worked in nearby industries such as timber mills or on the waterfront.

Around the edge of settlement, north and south, were market gardens, poultry farmers and orchards. Botany supplied Sydney's water which prevented settlement in that location, except for Chinese market gardeners. Chinatown was located in the city around George and Argyle Streets, while Australia's indigenous inhabitants had largely been pushed out of the city, to settle at La Perouse.

Parramatta and, further afield, Liverpool remained centres in their own right. Manly was developed in the 1850s by the entrepreneur Henry Smith as a watering place and seaside resort, its picturesque beauty spots being reached by overloaded steamers, whose passengers were entertained by bands. Hunters Hill, the bushland suburb made popular in the 1840s by the Joubert family from France, had many large and attractive stone houses which were serviced by regular steam yachts to the city.

A prize medal of the Sydney International Exhibition of 1879. Of the 7554 prize medals awarded, only 48 were gold, the rest being bronze and silver. The dies for the medals were made by Wyon of London, to designs by Australians S Begg and J Sayers, with production of all gold and silver medals in the Sydney Branch of the Royal Mint. Production of the bronze medals was divided between Sydney and London.

Powerhouse Museum, Sydney

Annandale was established in 1876 by the builder John Young who strived to develop a high-class residential waterfront suburb with 'the finest street in the colony' as its central avenue. On the north shore, development sprang up around the lower reaches of the harbour, and, by the 1880s, with the advent of the railway, small farms and cottages were to be seen around Gordon.

The *Municipalities Act* of 1858 saw many areas declared as municipalities, all requiring town halls, parish churches, post offices and sometimes a courthouse. **Balmain Courthouse and Post Office** (1885) and North Sydney Courthouse (1886) are amongst the grand reminders of colonial optimism.

The city itself was the nucleus of colonial life, a conjunction of industry and governance, culture and housing, serving rich and poor alike. Snubbing attempts at planning restrictions, its streets reflected the vitality of trade and commercial uses; the grandiose intermingled with the shoddy.

Its focus was the shipping trade. Around the harbour from Woolloomooloo Bay to Pyrmont and Balmain, the waterside was alive with activity, the harbour rimmed with masts and a conglomeration of wharves, boat sheds, slipways and bond and free stores. Circular Quay had become a terminal for passenger ships and ferries. Passenger ships from coastal and inter-colonial runs disembarked at Cowper Wharf at Woolloomooloo, which also served the fishing fleet as both moorings and a fish market. Adjacent were sawmills, boat building yards and swimming baths off The Domain. Walsh Bay to Cockle Bay (now Darling Harbour) was the hub of the colonial cargo movement.

Behind Darling Harbour were the wool stores, merchants' warehouses and flour mills. So, too, were engineering works, metal workshops, foundries, wire makers, chemical works, food and drink factories, and even a tobacco factory, all adding to the tumult and outpourings of industry. These areas were usually squalid, with slum-like workers' housing squeezed between industry. Further west, the quarries in Pyrmont supplied much of the building stone used in the construction of the new city.

George Street formed a division between the industrial west and more salubrious establishments to the east. Elizabeth Street was the main thoroughfare for trams, skirting the courts and legal chambers. Macquarie Street was the seat of power, with **Parliament House** established in the old Rum Hospital and a cluster of government buildings spreading down Bridge Street. Nearby were the gentlemen's clubs, such as the **New South Wales Club** in Bligh Street and the Royal Exchange, both within easy walking distance.

Industry intruded nevertheless. Printers were found around Hunter, Pitt and Castlereagh Streets, coachbuilding was located in Castlereagh, Elizabeth and Oxford Streets, and furniture makers in William Street. Clothing and manchester sellers concentrated on George, King, Market and Pitt Streets.

Shopping was diverse with several large department stores, smaller retailers and emporia. Silversmiths and jewellers' workshops; booksellers; sewing machine traders; shops selling scientific instruments such as chronometers, barometers and thermometers; as well as showrooms for imports and agricultural equipment were to be found. In the 1880s, opulent arcades of shops were built. Views of the city show rows of three-storey shops with offices or dwellings above, punctuated by landmark buildings and interspersed with banks, insurance houses, coffee palaces, drinking saloons and a few large hotels for country graziers and visitors from other colonies. Until the advent of the lift in the 1880s, even the tallest buildings only reached four or five storeys.

Strasburg Clock Model made by Richard Bartholomew Smith (1862–1942) from 1887 to 1889; the case is believed to have been made by James Cunningham (1841–1903).

Powerhouse Museum, Sydney

Produce markets provided essential commodities. George Street markets initially provided food and later became permanent shops for bootmakers, butchers and fancy goods. The **Queen Victoria Market Building**, which replaced a jumble of buildings on the site, was conceived in the 1880s, but not completed until 1898. Campbell and Hay Street markets traded in hay and cattle, firewood and fowls — with adjacent vacant land reserved as a fairground and for the circus. The Corn Exchange of 1887 was built on a site in lower Market Street previously used for penning animals, but which later became the official fruit and vegetable markets.

Water and sewerage issues became paramount as the population expanded. Fire was a constant hazard. The City Council was sacked in 1853 over its inability to clean up environmental problems. Open drains swept household waste and sewage through the streets to discharge into the harbour. Roads were impassable; muddy after rain, choking with dust in the dry, with pot holes reportedly so large they could swallow a horse and cart. Following the council's reinstatement, legislation was enacted to remove noxious industries from the city, centralise animal slaughtering and to collect garbage. It also became compulsory for houses to be connected to sewerage and controls were introduced over the use of cesspits.

Adolphus Blau produced this inkstand in about 1870 in Sydney using silver, malachite and an emu egg. The inscription reads: ' Presented to Mr JG Marwick by the Directors of the Pitt Street Congregational Church & School Penny Savings Bank as a grateful recognition of his valuable services as Honorary Secretary for Eight Years, 17th May, 1870.'

Powerhouse Museum, Sydney

The obelisk in Hyde Park, opposite Bathurst Street (1857), serves both as a sewer vent and as a monument to improving conditions. In 1879, the *City of Sydney Improvement Act* was introduced after forty years of procrastination. It established safety standards for new construction and facilitated slum clearance. The upgrading of the roads became a council responsibility and experimentation with road surfaces led to the widespread use of woodblocks with stone kerbing.

The exceptional growth of Sydney created ideal conditions for the building trade. Imported materials flooded in, diversifying the architectural palette. Industrial sophistication ushered in ever greater mechanisation and machinery was soon available to cut stone, shape timber, form bricks and provide ready-made building components to speed up construction. Cast-iron became a wonder material, used for structural columns in large buildings and as decorative panels, friezes and openwork columns to ornament buildings externally.

Architects from Britain and America, or those who had been locally trained in the country's first architectural course (established at the Working Men's College in 1878), followed stylistic traditions. With notable exceptions, Gothic forms dictated the appearance of ecclesiastical and academic buildings such as **Sydney University**, while the classical ideal shaped government, commercial and cultural buildings such as the **Australian Museum**. An unusual conjunction of the secular and religious was the gothic **Mortuary Station** at Redfern (1868), where funeral trains departed for Rookwood Necropolis, the vast 19th-century cemetery.

As the century progressed, both Gothic and Classical styles became increasingly mannered, losing purity until there were instances where the two styles converged. Other exotic styles were introduced, such as the Romanesque or Flemish. By the 1880s, it was not unusual for an architect to 'work up' a variety of different schemes in varying styles for major buildings.

In domestic architecture, the rules were less defined. Italianate houses, with a grand tower, arched windows and a tendency towards cast-iron decoration, were favoured by the wealthy and indicated the pinnacle of success. Around the harbour, Gothic-style residences were well represented with pointed gables and fretted wooden bargeboards. The single-fronted symmetrically designed dwelling, redolent of Georgian times, also lingered into the late 19th century. By the late 1880s, when housing styles had become overblown interpretations of the classical, the Queen Anne style was ushered in, its red brick walls, red-tiled roof and multi-paned windows seeming to suggest a return to domestic simplicity.

This traditional European wedding dress was worn by Emma Oghiltree when she married Francis Robertson in Victoria in 1887.

Powerhouse Museum, Sydney

Urban consolidation and the subdivision of large estates created the terrace house row, a string of identical houses sharing common side walls. They were both economical and quick to erect, and satisfied the whole spectrum of housing needs, from the showpiece of the well-to-do to the single storeyed and cramped workers' rental terrace.

The archetypal terrace was two to three storeys, with upper and lower verandas, a narrow frontage, little or no garden and repeated elements along the row. Its decorative style varied, but typical terraces were lavished with a thick coating of stucco, an ornamental cast-iron balustrade to the upper balcony and a parapet hiding the pitched roof. As the century progressed, their appearance became more elaborate; the cast-iron imitating thick lace, the stucco richly moulded and the parapets ornamented with urns, lions' heads or shapely balustrades. By the 1890s, more Sydneysiders lived in terraces than in any other type of house, giving distinctive form to suburbs such as Paddington and Glebe as they stepped down the hillside.

In the city, the major commercial, religious and public works of this era became the dominant landmarks for the next century. However, only a few commercial buildings from this period remain today. The 1850s Commercial Banking Company facade was re-erected at Sydney University, the **City Bank** (1873) facade is found at Burwood. A number of city warehouses from the 1880s remain on the western slopes of the city.

However, Sydney still enjoys the works of several Colonial Architects. Edmund Blacket's **Water Police Court** (1856) in Albert

Street is now a museum, while Alexander Dawson's **Observatory** (1859) serves a similar purpose on Observatory Hill.

The Scottish-born, London-trained James Barnet, Colonial Architect of New South Wales from 1862–1890, produced more than 1,000 buildings throughout the state. An advocate of the

classical style, his public architecture was accomplished, dignified and fittingly expressed the civic pride of the colony. His **Australian Museum** extension of 1864 changed the scale of the city, with its grand double-height entrance portico. His **Colonial Secretary's Building** on Macquarie and Bridge Streets (1869–1875) is a strong Italianate conception with a domed roof and statues by Fontana. The **Lands Department Building** (1876–1894) in Bridge Street, with an onion-shaped tower, is also by Barnet, as are a host of post offices, courthouses and railway stations across New South Wales. Celebrated amongst his work is the **General Post Office**, the most prominent landmark in the city until the 20th century. To allow the building to be properly sited – it was initially hemmed in by smaller buildings – the architect imagined a grand piazza forecourt. As Martin Place, it now forms the largest civic space in Sydney.

Occasional table attributed to the workshop of William Hamilton, Tasmania, c. 1845. It was exhibited in the Van Diemen's Land section of the Great Exhibition in London in 1851.

Powerhouse Museum, Sydney

Sydney Town Hall – a grand Second Empire conception built to glorify the alternative metropolitan power, the Sydney City Council – was located on the site of an old cemetery, as far as possible from colonial government buildings. The lavishly decorated building with its superb interiors was JH Willson's winning entry in an 1868 competition. With some contributions by others, it was completed in 1889 with the construction of the Centennial Hall.

Major religious buildings also took their place beside the secular. The Catholic **St Mary's Cathedral** was commenced in 1865 by architect William Wardell; the Anglican Cathedral by architect Edmund Blacket was consecrated in 1868 and finished in stages; the **Great Synagogue** in Elizabeth Street was completed in 1878 by architect Thomas Rowe.

The century also introduced a diversity of new building styles. The *Education Act* of 1880 ensured compulsory education and an architect, WE Kemp, was appointed to the education department. His schools at Hunters Hill (1870) and Petersham (1878) were Gothic, while those at Woollahra (1877) and Surry Hills (1883) were classical. Private and secular school buildings also developed, with **St Patrick's Seminary** at Manly in the 1880s, St Joseph's College at Hunters Hill (1883–99) and Newington College, Stanmore, in 1881.

Urban growth brought increasing social problems and wealth encouraged philanthropy. In The Rocks, the Sailors' Home, Mariners' Church and Seamen's Mission were founded to give succour to sailors away from home and to entice them away from the brothels and opium dens found close to all ports. An Asylum for Destitute Children was built at Randwick in 1858; the NSW Institute for the Deaf, Dumb and the Blind (1872) was erected on City Road, near Sydney University. The treatment of the mentally disabled was also a public duty and an **Asylum for the Insane** was commenced at Callan Park, Rozelle, in 1877.

The populace sought their entertainment in theatres, parks and gardens. The Garden Palace Exhibition building was constructed in 1879 in the Botanic Gardens, inspired by London's Crystal Palace Exhibition of 1851. Open for seven months, with a million people passing through its gates, its immense domed roofline dominated the skyline until 1882, when it burnt down in a spectacular conflagration. Today, only the commemorative entry gates remain in Macquarie Street, near the Conservatorium of Music.

A late 19th-century pissoir located beneath the Harbour Bridge in The Rocks was installed by Sydney City Council.

In 1866, the Sydney Common in Moore Park was dedicated for sporting events together with an adjacent zoo; the Royal Agricultural Society was established in the 1870s and the Australian Golf Club in 1882. The nearby park was dedicated as Queen's Park in honour of the Centennial celebrations in 1887, as was Centennial Park, which opened in 1888.

If the Centenary celebrations of 1888 were somewhat self-congratulatory in tone, Sydneysiders felt justified. An impressive city had grown out of the landscape. Serving as a stone backdrop to the thriving waterfront industry and convoys of sailing ships, city buildings emerged with elaborate facades, clock towers and steeples, their golden sandstone walls seeming to reflect the city's prosperity. Its citizens had access to a museum, an art gallery, clubs, theatres and libraries, and Sydney University, founded in the 1850s, emulated English universities with its Gothic Revival spires. Ferries plied the harbour passing picturesque bays and pleasure grounds, workers returned each evening to brand new houses in the spreading suburbs and the wealthy to grand mansions perched above Sydney shores to capture the breezes — all evidence of the prosperity and enterprise of its inhabitants.

MAISY STAPLETON

201

201 Sydney Town Hall

483 George and Druitt Streets, Sydney
1868 John Henry Willson (original design
facing George Street)
1873-77 Albert Bond (mansard roof and
vestibule interiors)
1875-77 Thomas and Edward Bradridge
(clock tower)
1883-89 Thomas Sapsford (Centennial Hall)
1886-88 George McRae with John Hennessy
1934 Entrance portico replaced
GC, V, A

The Sydney Town Hall is possibly the only non-religious city building to retain its original function and interiors since it was built 120 years ago. Accommodation in the 19th-century building includes the Council Chamber, reception rooms, the Centennial Hall and offices for the Lord Mayor and elected councillors.

The building's history is a turbulent one. After decades of unsuccessful negotiations, the city fathers finally secured a land grant from the Crown in the commercial centre of the city — as far away from colonial Government House in Macquarie Street as possible. The site was the old cemetery next to St Andrew's Cathedral, which required careful exhumation and transferral of bodies to other cemeteries. Perhaps envious of Melbourne's lavish Town Hall, built during the prosperity of the gold rush, a competition for its design was held and was won by JH Willson, an unknown architect from Tasmania. After Willson's sudden death, a parade of architects appear to have suffered through their involvement with the project.

When complete, the building had a large *porte-cochère* over the present (rebuilt) steps, and its own ring road inside a stone and iron palisade. Unfortunately, this area was destabilised in 1934 during tunnelling for the underground railway and the formal entry had to be demolished. As a landmark, the tower by the Bradridge brothers was second in scale to Barnet's tower on the General Post Office (203) in Martin Place, while no building to the south or west was taller.

Albert Bond, when City Architect, designed the chamber now known as the vestibule (open to the public) which served as the meeting hall until the larger Centennial Hall was built. The vestibule has elaborately decorated surfaces in plasterwork with stained-glass lanterns and cast metal plaques commemorating royal visits to the city.

The 'Great Hall' by Charles Sapsford — which was officially named the Centennial Hall, but referred to in its day as the Palace of Democracy — was an engineering triumph, involving a highly structured roof system to meet the span. The ceilings are lined with an early use of the Wunderlich metal panel system, chosen to overcome the fear of plaster panels falling on patrons from vibration caused by the immense organ which still functions.

In later periods, the Town Hall was referred to as a wedding cake or lollipop building, but was nevertheless representative of its time, sharing similar Victorian/Beaux-Arts (Second Empire) design concepts with the much grander City Hall in Philadelphia (1871-1901).

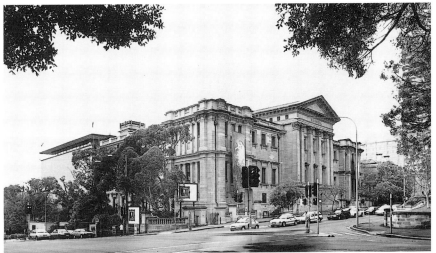

202

56 L 20

202 The Australian Museum

Cnr 6–8 College and William Streets, Sydney
1846–54 Mortimer Lewis (CA)
1864–68 James Barnet (CA)
1897–10 Walter Liberty Vernon (NSWGA)
1959–63 Joseph van der Steen (Design Architect NSWGA)
1987–88 Colin Still (Design Architect NSWPWD)
GC, V, A

The present complex comprises two visually contrasting architectures — that of James Barnet (his first major work after appointment as Government Architect) and Joseph van der Steen (b. 1913), designer of the major modernist addition to William Street. The original, and perhaps unfairly criticised, Mortimer Lewis building (which faced William Street) is discreetly cocooned by the later Barnet-designed wing near the corner of William and College Streets. Although Barnet, at an early stage, planned that the main entrance should be on William Street, the building, as built, faces College Street. The grandly scaled 1864 temple porch was a major public building statement, incorporating an imposing stylobate, 14-metre high Corinthian columns, and column capitals, all carved by the artist Walter McGill.

In absolute contrast, the powerful, yet totally unrelieved William Street extension (1959–1963), by English migrant architect Joseph van der Steen (working in the Government Architect special projects design team under Harry Rembert), was, for its day, an unusual and ground breaking modernist statement. By employing a palette of materials which matched the existing building, an entirely contrasting style was able to sit comfortably side by side with the existing work. The projecting roof-top awning covered a cafe with extensive views to the harbour. A general upgrading of the museum was later undertaken (1989) by the Government Architect (designer Colin Still), providing environmentally controlled collection storage, travelling exhibition space, curatorial workspace, education centre and staff facilities.

●●●

The quality of Barnet's work was exceptional and yet, ten years after completion, it was subject to criticism by the volatile New South Wales Parliament. It was described as being 'crowded with heavy pillars which waste and obstruct light; the internal walls are broken by angles and recesses; there is a useless gallery above the second floor; and there is, in every part of the building, abundant evidence of the architect's desire to subordinate utility to ornament'.

Italianate Style

The Italianate style was largely subsumed under the banner of Victorian architecture because of the curious British (and French) tradition that architecture be known after the ruling monarch of the period. Helped by the English fascination with Romantic traditions and the picturesque, the rural Italian villa, with its asymmetry and tower/wing forms, gave greater flexibility in developing buildings for brand new functions, such as post offices, telegraph offices, public schools and hospitals.

The application of the Italianate style to commercial buildings as they evolved led to the mass production of cast-iron columns and beams. Domestic architecture, too, gained decorative trims and roof and drainage elements, now associated with inner-city suburbs of Sydney. Roofs are usually gable pitched, with verandas attached with bull-nosed iron sheeting. Windows are in pairs or triplets, with round arches or strongly expressed square heads.

1858 New South Wales granted
universal male suffrage

1860 Burke and Wills set out to cross
the continent from south to north

1861 First horse tramway
opened in Sydney

167

203
State Library of NSW (Mitchell Library)

56 J 17

203 General Post Office

Martin Place, George and Pitt Streets, Sydney
1864–91 James Barnet (CA)
GC, V, A

Built at huge expense over the Tank Stream, the General Post Office was constructed in stages from 1866 to 1891. It could well be described as Sydney's Opera House of the 19th century since the relative cost, the time taken in construction and the rejection, then belated recognition, of the architect are all parallels.

The project came to the attention of James Johnstone Barnet (1827–1904) when he was appointed acting Colonial Architect in 1862. The General Post Office was regarded as a building which would come to symbolise Sydney in much the same way as the Houses of Parliament at Westminster symbolise London or the Eiffel Tower Paris. In fact the post and telegraph services of the General Post Office (compared to the Australian Museum or a new Parliament House) were held in such high esteem that the creation of a 'monument' gathered unprecedented support across the full spectrum of politics. The project required the resumption of St Martins Lane for a block between Pitt and George Streets. Barnet's original sketch shows the 100-metre frontage of the building to be without attics, mansard roofs or a clock tower.

At the opening of the first stage, the Post Master General exclaimed that the General Post Office 'will not be surpassed by any other similar structure in the Southern Hemisphere'. Unfortunately, slow progress in the second stage and some adverse comment about his carved figures sparked a controversy in Parliament. The panels over the Pitt Street colonnade depict the following subjects: Telegraph, Literature and the Press, the Professions, Commerce and Mining, Agriculture, Pastoral Pursuits, Science, Art, Banking and the Post Office. The figures were depicted in 'present-day clothing', which led to them being unfairly described by one MP in Parliament as 'tedious abortions'. It was such a contentious issue that a Board of Enquiry was set up, headed by the Gothic architect (and rival) William Wilkinson Wardell (1823–99). The board instructed that the 'grotesque carvings' be immediately removed. Fortunately, the Parliamentary report was ignored by the Post Master General and the 'offensive' carvings remain in all their glory. In the 'Sydney' panel, the architect Barnet can be seen giving instructions to a workman. The tower over the Queen's statue was taken down during World War II because of the threat of air raids and the possibility of the tower collapsing and destroying the trunk telephone exchange located to one side. The mansard roof was added after Barnet's time. The building is subject to a Federal Government redevelopment proposal which may see the erection of a hotel tower behind the original structure, the restoration of the main building and a glass-roofed atrium between the new and old.

•••

The Cenotaph in Martin Place was unveiled on 21 February 1929, and commemorates the soldiers and sailors who died in World War I. It was designed by Sir Bertram Mackennal. The granite base was cut and dressed from a single 17-ton block at the Moruya quarry (which also provided granite for the Sydney Harbour Bridge pylons). It was barged to Circular Quay and dragged by a team of twenty horses to its present location. The bronze statues, based on real servicemen, were cast in Milan. The whole enterprise attracted fierce public criticism, including the choice of military dress, the direction in which the figures faced, and the likeness of the base to a coffin. Traditionally, it is the location of the annual dawn service on 25 April to commemorate Anzac Day.

204

206

65 G 5

204 Former Redfern Mortuary Terminal
Regent Street, Redfern
1868 James Barnet (CA)
GC, V, A

During the 1860s, the colonial government decided to create a large multi-denominational cemetery at Haslams Creek (now called Rookwood) in Sydney's west, as the few existing cemeteries in the city centre occupied valuable space and were nearly full. The Necropolis, as it was officially named, was to be connected to the city by rail on a newly constructed spur line using special funeral trains. These were planned to transport both corpses and mourners via purpose-designed receiving stations at Redfern and Haslams Creek.

The Necropolis Receiving Station at Redfern by James Barnet (1827–1904), featuring carved angels and associated details, was an unusual application of Victorian Gothic — particularly for an architect best known for his Italianate designs. The rail service was discontinued in 1938 after motor hearses were introduced. Subsequently, it became a depot for the Chippendale breweries. Conservation work was carried out on the building in 1985.

•••

The Redfern terminal's non-identical twin, the Rookwood terminus, was dismantled after the rail service was discontinued and re-erected stone by stone as a church in Ainslie, Canberra.

26 L 17
205 Nightingale Wing, Sydney Hospital
Macquarie Street, Sydney
1869 Thomas Rowe
GC, V, A

The Nightingale Wing (named after Florence Nightingale), which sits behind the main building, is a punchy bi-chromatic brick design.

It was originally built to accommodate six British nurses brought to Sydney through the initiative of Sir Henry Parkes, who supported reforms in medical practice.

64 Q 9
206 St Stephen's Church
Church Street, Newtown
1871–74 Edmund Blacket
AC, V, A

A complete English Gothic parish church by Edmund Blacket (1817–83) with bell tower, spire and cemetery enclosed in its own churchyard. Financial constraints of the new colony made it unusual for a church to be so complete.

66 N 2
207 Houses
4 and 5 Darley Place, Darlinghurst
c. 1870
GC, V, NA

The secluded position of these small houses helps them retain their 19th-century atmosphere. Note the cast-iron porch posts on No. 4 and the split cast-iron columns and shuttered doors to the veranda of No. 5.

•••

Darley Street, on top of the Darlinghurst ridge, contains some fine 19th-century terraces and freestanding houses, including 'Stoneleigh' and 'Woolton' (1880s); and 'Novar', 'The Grange' and 'Hilton' (1850–51).

65 B 3
208 Church of St John, Bishopthorpe
Cnr St Johns and Glebe Point Roads, Glebe
1868–70 Edmund Blacket
GC, V, A

Victorian Romanesque design by John Horbury Hunt when employed in Edmund Blacket's office. The tower was completed in 1911 by Cyril Blacket.

209

211

| 294 Q 2 | 275 M 10 |

209 House, 'Holyrood'
Formerly The City Bank and 'Illyria'
The Boulevarde, Strathfield
1873 George and Ralph Mansfield
Re-erected 1893 by Charles Hoskins
GC, V, NA

In 1890, a devastating fire which started in a printing works destroyed valuable buildings between Pitt and Castlereagh Streets, near the city centre (ultimately clearing the way for the future extension of Martin Place). Twenty buildings were damaged, and a good number were dismantled and rebuilt elsewhere, including The City Bank, a lavish Italianate design by George and Ralph Mansfield.

Completed in 1873, it was so admired by the up-and-coming industrialist Charles Hoskins that he bought the ruined front portion, numbered it stone by stone and re-erected the building as the frontispiece of his new family home in the rural and 'healthy' high ground of Burwood. Behind is a large verandahed Italianate house which forms the bulk of the family home with a substantial garage at the rear. Hoskins had a collection of classic cars, starting with the second car imported into Australia, housed in possibly the earliest purpose-built automobile garage in Sydney.

●●●

The Hoskins estate is now part of Santa Sabina College. The banking chamber is used as a Catholic Chapel.

| 43 G 5 |

210 'Wybalena'
Jeanneret Avenue, Hunters Hill
1875 C Jeanneret (builder)
GC, V, NA

A French inspired house.
See the special tour section on Hunters Hill.

211 Abbotsford House
Melrose Crescent, Abbotsford
1878 attrib. George Renwick
GC, V, NA

For a long time enveloped by industry, but now part of a massive residential estate presently under construction, this large mansion is still clearly visible above the shores of the Parramatta River.

The house was occupied by Sir Arthur Renwick, an important administrator who held positions of public trust at Sydney University, with the New South Wales Government and at the NSW Benevolent Society. The building remains in generally good condition. The grand two-storey design, with wrap-around verandas, shows a heavy stuccoed base with lighter iron-work balconies at the upper level.

Below: Ground floor plan, Abbotsford House (1878)

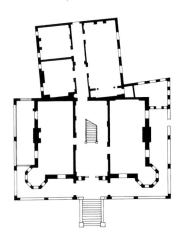

212

214

58 Q 13

212 'The Hermitage'
22 Vaucluse Avenue, Vaucluse
1870s architect unknown
1936 Emil Sodersten (reconstruction after fire)
GC, V, NA

Built over and around the walls of a smaller
1840s house by Alexander Dick, 'The Hermitage'
was built by Edward Mason Hunt some time
between the years 1870 and 1878. The Victorian
Gothic design is a riot of steeply pitched roofs
with intricately carved bargeboards, elevated
gable balconies and secondary balcony roofs.

24 L 15

213 Former Colonial Secretary's Office
121 Macquarie St, Bridge and Phillip Streets,
Sydney
1869–75 James Barnet (CA)
GC, V, A

Second only to James Barnet's General Post
Office **(203)** in design excellence, this complex
served as the workplace of many NSW state
government departments, including the Public
Works Department, for almost 100 years. The
building was completed when Barnet was at the
height of his career, interpreting Victorian
Italianate features within his own rich, arcaded
vocabulary of Sydney sandstone. Evidence of
later work by Walter Liberty Vernon (1846–1914)
is seen in the iron-crested mansard roofs and
the pavilion dome, formerly clad in a very early
version of aluminium, but since removed.

The lavish internal wood panelling is in
Borneo cedar with dados and elaborately carved
door architraves. The Executive Council
Chamber, on the third level at the Bridge Street
frontage, may be one of the finest examples of
a Victorian interior in Sydney. The chamber has
eight bronze busts of significant British figures
including Benjamin Disraeli, Charles Dickens,
William Gladstone and Lord Tennyson.

26 K 19

214 The Great Synagogue
187a Elizabeth Street, Sydney
1878 Thomas Rowe. Partly supervised by Walter
Liberty Vernon
1973 Orwell Phillips and Kevin Gallagher (facade
cleaned, gates restored)
GC, V, A

The merging of two separate Jewish
congregations was the catalyst for building a
new and larger synagogue in Sydney. The
elaborately decorated building is noted for its
fine detail (particularly columns and capitals)
and a high standard of craftsmanship in carved
sandstone. Clearly the design was inspired by
English synagogues in London and Liverpool,
incorporating exotic architectural forms in an
attempt to find an appropriate eclectic style.
The ornate cast-iron gates and detailed
sandstone craftsmanship are noteworthy.

49 F 10

215 Macquarie Lighthouse
Old South Head Road, Vaucluse
1880 James Barnet (CA)
GC, V, A

Set on a verdant carpet of grass, high on the
headland, this lighthouse duplicates an existing
building which stood for sixty years. In 1876,
James Barnet (1827–1904) declared that the old
lighthouse of 1816 by Francis Greenway
(1777–1837) was defective and technologically
outdated, and recommended its demolition.

On 14 March 1880, Sir Henry Parkes laid the
foundation stone of the new lighthouse, with a
larger lamp house, using an electric lantern. In
a display of architectural reverence, the design
was almost a replica of the earlier lighthouse
form, built directly behind it, so that mariners
would not be disorientated by the lighthouse
moving its position.

216

80 P 15

216 Parramatta Post Office
Church Street, Parramatta
1880 James Barnet (CA)
GC, V, A
A handsome and well-proportioned building similar to many others by this architect.

64 L 3

217 'The Abbey'
272 Johnston Street, Annandale
1881 attrib. to CHE Blackmann and/or
John Young
GC, V, NA
John Young was easily Sydney's most important builder during the Victorian period, completing a vast catalogue of structures including St Patrick's (Melbourne), St Mary's Cathedral, St John's College at Sydney University, the General Post Office, and The Lands Department Building, as well as the (since destroyed) Garden Palace Building for the 1879 Exhibition. Young was also a successful politician (Mayor of Leichhardt 1884–85, Mayor of Sydney 1886, Mayor of Annandale 1894–96) and a land speculator who effectively created the suburb of Annandale.

His landmark house in Annandale, 'The Abbey', is a Gothic revival fantasy. The interior is lavish with vaulted hallways, gilt stairs, tiled walls, tessellated floors and traceried windows. At one time it was rumoured to have been built with stonework from the first St Mary's Church (which Young demolished after the fire). However, the stone fabric appears to be contemporaneous with neo-Gothic designs. John Young was one of the highest ranking Masons to have emigrated to Australia (achieving the rank of Thirty-Second Order), which accounts for the presence of Masonic symbols set into the internal walls. Supposedly built for Young's wife, who died before it was finished, there is some doubt that Young himself ever lived here.

In 1885, John Young's neighbour and the original owner of the site of 'The Abbey', Charles H Blackmann, scandalised Sydney by selling a share of his architectural practice to the English architect John Sulman for £3000. Within weeks of the sale, Blackmann absconded with all the firm's money and a well-known Sydney barmaid to San Francisco. Under the partnership agreement, Sulman was left to provide for Blackmann's deserted wife and children.

•••

Curiously, John Young was a great promoter of lawn bowls, which became popular during the 1880s. The City Bowling Club, once the most prestigious in Sydney (next to St Mary's Cathedral in College Street), is a legacy of Young.

Below: Ground floor plan, 'The Abbey' (1881)

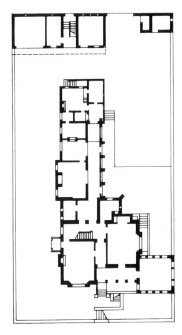

218

220

24 J 14

218 Australian Craftworks

Former Police Station
127–129 George Street North, The Rocks
1882 James Barnet (CA)
GC, V, A

Built as Police Station No. 4, and used
continuously until 1976, this building served as
the local lock-up for the petty criminals of The
Rocks, who frequented its many hotels and bars.
It was unusual for James Barnet (1827–1904) to
depart from his elegant Italianate neo-classical
compositions, but in this design he depicts the
rusticated banding, called *bossage*, made
famous by the French architect Ledoux. Above
the entrance, a lion's head sculpture holds a
police baton in its mouth, while the doors are
patterned with steel studs.

66 Q 2

219 Darlinghurst Public School

Womerah and Barcom Avenues, Darlinghurst
1882 Charles Mayes
GC, V, A

Owing to the large number of schools being
built following the Education Reform Acts, it
became the policy of the Council of Education
and Department of Public Instruction to
commission private practice architects to design
certain schools. In particular, they employed
those architects who shared William Kemp's
commitment to the emerging Arts and Crafts
movement. Charles Mayes, an architect and
quantity surveyor, designed the small Double
Bay Public School (1883) and the unusual
Leichhardt Public School (1883).

The Darlinghurst school, capable of housing
1,000 students, is an excellent example of the
elaborate 'Romanesque' polychrome brickwork
found in Sydney in the period 1870 to 1890.
Schools and technical colleges were frequently
erected in detailed polychrome brick.

66 M 7

220 Bourke Street School

Bourke Street, Surry Hills
1883 William E Kemp
1923 (additions)
GC, V, A

Bourke Street School was designed by the
schools' architect, William Edmund Kemp
(b. 1831), following the *Education Act* of 1880,
which initiated the construction of many new
school buildings. This is an excellent example of
Kemp's preoccupation with bell towers and
detailed brickwork. The thorough design
includes fences, gates and gate posts.

25 H 16

221 Former John Sands Building

62 Clarence Street, Sydney
1882 architect unknown
GC, V, NA

An unusual and playful polychrome facade
represented the business of John Sands.
Although commercial buildings were not usually
decorated so elaborately, Sands was an
exuberant stationery manufacturer and printers'
broker. Note the sandstone bracketed emblems
at the first floor symbolising 'manufacture' on
the south and 'progress' on the north.

222

223

24 J 13

222 Australasian Steam Navigation Co. Building
1–5 Hickson Road, The Rocks
1883–84 William Wilkinson Wardell
GC, V, A

An unusually picturesque and exuberant polychrome brick building by William Wardell (1823–99), the architect of St Mary's Cathedral which was under construction at the time this building was being designed. The Australasian Steam Navigation Co. building, which still retains its timber floors and timber windows, was fitted with an early sprinkler system in case of fire (1894).

Wardell, who was at one time Government Architect of Victoria before moving to Sydney, left a small legacy of carefully studied and detailed commercial buildings including the NSW Club **(231)** and the Grafton Bond and Free Stores (1883) in Hickson Road, The Rocks. The spectacular Flemish gable skyline, emphasised by the siting of the building, fulfils late 19th (and early 20th) century precepts of architecture as a commercial advertisement. It is currently occupied by an advertising agency, the Ken Done Gallery and exhibition spaces.

54 J 17

223 'Kirkbride' — Sydney College of the Arts
Former Rozelle Hospital
Balmain Road, Lilyfield
1877–85 James Barnet (CA)
1880s Gardens by Charles Moore
1995–96 State Projects, Terry King (project architect), Jean Rice (heritage architect)
GC, V, A

On the beautiful harbourside setting of the Callan Park Estate is the Callan Park Hospital for the Insane. It was built by the Henry Parkes Government in response to the short-lived psychiatric program of 'moral therapy' promoted by the American physician Thomas Storey Kirkbride. This mental reform approach, which initially surfaced with the building of the Asylum for Imbeciles, and the Institution for Idiots (1871), both in Newcastle, relies on pleasant surroundings and personal well-being for psychiatric improvement.

The complex was closely modelled on the plans of Chartham Hall by Giles and Gough in the English county of Kent, under the direction of Dr Frederick Norton Manning. Barnet's work adapts the pavilion planning and elevates it into neo-classical sandstone buildings. Despite vocal objections from neighbours, the government of the time built the vast complex, surrounding the whole with sandstone walls, and slippery sloping banks called 'ha-has', an 18th-century device to keep farm animals at bay. The separate yet linked pavilions for male and female patients were designed to accommodate different degrees of lunacy — 'quiet and convalescent', 'noisy and violent', 'recent and acute', and just 'sick'. The overall quality of the project was second to none, with the grounds laid out by the Director of the Botanic Gardens, Charles Moore.

The twenty or so pavilion buildings were recently converted to house the Sydney College of the Arts (now part of Sydney University). The new complex contains studios for painting, sculpture, print media, ceramics, glass, jewellery, photomedia and electronic art.

●●●

The 'bossaged' columns, which Sydney architecture critic Elizabeth Farrelly calls 'poodle-leg' columns (alternating square and round column sections) are rarely seen. Barnet used this column decoration (made famous by London's Newgate Prison) only twice, as seen here and on the entry to his Police Station No. 4 (218) in The Rocks (1882).

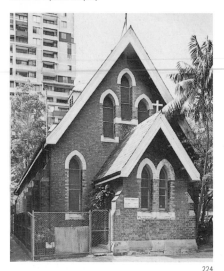

224

225

56 P 18

25 H 18

224 St Columbkille's Church
McElhone Street, Woolloomooloo
1885 architect unknown
PC, V, A

This church is part of social history as, according
to folklore, it was from here that the local priest
Father Edmund Campion wrote the famous
'scrap of paper' letter to the then Lord Mayor of
Sydney, Leo Port, advising him of the existence
of a resident action group (WRAG). This group
fought the massive redevelopment program
which would have turned Woolloomooloo into
high-rise office towers and a transport interchange. The note requested the acquisition of
council and government land for redevelopment
as medium-density housing, foreshadowing a
decision which ultimately overturned the
Federal and State governments' plans for a new
commercial centre in Woolloomooloo. Known as
St Comical's to locals, it is the only remaining
church in the area.

●●●

*It was in 1924, in an address to the NSW
Institute of Architects, that Sir Charles Rosenthal
proposed the redevelopment of Woolloomooloo
as a 'zone for Federal, State and municipal offices
sited around parks and gardens, together with
the removal of the wharves and development of
the shore'. It was this proposal which emerged
in 1969, but was later overturned.*

225 Letraset House
346–348 Kent Street, Sydney
1885 architect unknown
GC, V, NA

The facade of salmon and cream brickwork with
bands of sandstone achieves a simple decorative
rhythm. Two arches at either end of the
building allow cobbled carriageways to lead to
an internal court. The restored interiors retain
the original exposed structural beams and
timber ceilings.

Warehouses and Woolstores
*There are approximately 75 warehouses and
woolstores near the city centre; the highest
concentration is on the west side in the vicinity
of York, Clarence, Kent and Sussex Streets (31),
followed by the Pyrmont/Ultimo area (20). A
few more are spread over five other areas near
the central business district. They were
generally built between the period 1880 and
1920, with the majority erected between 1900
and World War I, a dynamic trade period
following Australia's Federation. The year 1901
was an important turning point, when Australia
moved towards economic self-sufficiency,
rebuilding and taking over wharfage and cargo
handling (Sydney Harbour Trust), and becoming
a more strategic exporter and importer.
Warehouses and woolstores were often located
to take advantage of sloping sites which
enabled a number of levels of vehicle access on
sloping streets. After 1890, most buildings were
face brick, with massive wrought iron or
hardwood timber columns, south light roofs,
internal hoists and herringbone strutted timber
floors capable of carrying heavy loads.*

226

259 J 8   **24 J 14**

226 International College of Tourism & Hotel Management

Former St Patrick's Seminary (until Nov. 1995)
Darley Road, Manly
1885 Sheerin & Hennessy
GC, V, A

John Francis Hennessy (1853–1924) had been trained at Sydney City Council, but departed after conflicts with City Architect Thomas Sapsford during the construction of the Town Hall. Hennessy then went into private practice with Joseph Sheerin. Together they ran a very successful commercial practice, receiving a stream of major commissions from the Roman Catholic Church, including St Patrick's Seminary, Monastery of the Sacred Heart in Kensington, Santa Sabina College in Strathfield, St Joseph's College in Hunters Hill, the Church of Our Lady of the Sacred Heart in Randwick and the completion of St Mary's Cathedral following William Wardell's death.

St Patrick's Seminary is a landmark sandstone building of impressive scale and fine proportions on the northern slopes of North Head. The main staircase, which is entirely of stone, is supported by an ingenious system of vaults and arches. The harsh detailing is distinctly Gothic Revival, and the heavy, dark corridors and some rooms are typically Victorian. The building was recently converted to a hotel management college by Lend Lease Corporation.

●●●

John Francis Hennessy was the only member of both the Institute of Architects and the rival Palladian Club formed by John Sulman in 1886.

227 The Five Bells

Former ES & AC Bank,
The Queen's Wharf Branch
131–135 George Street, The Rocks
1885–86 William Wardell
Extended 1900 and c. 1920
GC, V, A

In 1885, the English Scottish and Australian Chartered Bank constructed their Queen's Wharf Branch in Sydney, which was more or less a miniature version of the ES & AC Bank in Melbourne by William Wilkinson Wardell (1823–99). The Gothic Revival characteristics are rarely found in commercial buildings in Sydney, with the most obvious proponent being Wardell. In 1974, Rothbury Vineyards Hermitage Estate opened a wine outlet and restaurant in the building.

25 H 16

228 Watch House Terraces

GM Laurence & Wherry
105a Clarence Street, Sydney
1886 architect unknown
GC, V, NA

This is the narrowest, if not the smallest, commercial building in Sydney's central business district. The unusually small site may be the result of the building being erected over an earlier laneway which ran behind the adjoining Police Watch House (1827, enlarged 1900). The top floor, with its charming terrace, was a later addition some time this century. It was originally occupied by a fern collector, with later tenants being a fruit seller, chimney sweep, plumber and kilt maker. It is now occupied by a firm of solicitors.

229

229 'Caerleon'

15 Ginahgulla Road, Bellevue Hill
1886 Maurice B Adams and Harry C Kent
GC, V, NA

Perhaps the earliest and most erudite example of the relatively short-lived high English version of the Queen Anne style, despite some clouding over joint authorship. Charles B Fairfax, grandson of John Fairfax, who owned the *Sydney Morning Herald*, commissioned the young architect Harry Chambers Kent (1852–1938), a promising graduate of Sydney University and one-time employee of Horbury Hunt, to prepare a plan for his new home. On one of his many visits to London, Fairfax took the plans seeking appraisal and advice from the fashionable architect and editor of *Building News*, Maurice Adams. Seizing the opportunity, Adams redetailed the entire design in society 'Queen Anne' style using fine Staffordshire terracotta shingles and tiles, Westminster metal casement windows, Hereford paving, carved timber valance work and patterned lead jointed glass. Accepting the inevitable transformation,

Kent agreed to supervise the construction of his made-over design, only to be outraged when it was exhibited in London and published in *Australian Builder and Contractor News* without a single mention of his involvement.

●●●

Harry C Kent later became President of the Institute of Architects of New South Wales between 1906 and 1907.

Queen Anne Style

The English reaction against the importation of European influences such as Greek, Italian and French, regardless of whether they were reheated as Romanesque or Oriental, was highlighted by architect Richard Norman Shaw's so-called 'dishonest' return to the medieval forms of the English countryside. A strong bond formed between this reactionary architectural movement and the concurrent Scandinavian romantic and arts and crafts tendencies of the late 19th century. Large panes of glass were unnecessarily broken down into smaller pieces with lead jointing, and gables were tile-hung, shingled or half-timbered.

Shaw's work appears to have barely influenced buildings in Sydney, although some filtering occurred with later examples in Melbourne. The English Queen Anne Style evolved into a visual presentation of contrasting materials: brick and stone or stucco on the first floor, with closely jointed terracotta bricks above, and shingles or terracotta introduced either before the roof or as a roof form. In Sydney, examples of this style began to appear in 1886, gathering momentum in the 1890s as the northern suburbs expanded from Neutral Bay to Waitara, with developments and improvements in public transport.

Below: Ground floor plan, 'Caerleon' (1886)

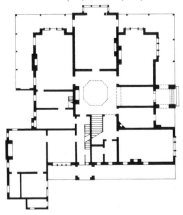

231

65 E 9	26 K 16

230 Former Eveleigh Railway Yards and Workshops

1885 Locomotive workshop
1886 Carriage Workshop George Cowdroy Snr,
Railway Engineer
1907 and 1914 New Locomotive Workshop
GC, V, A

A vast and until recently unused railway site near the city centre is slowly being transformed and put to a variety of uses. Two of the massive brick buildings were purpose built as railway workshops manufacturing the rolling stock for the New South Wales railway system at a time when the two so-called 'generals' of the railways, John Whitton and George Cowdroy, were fierce rivals. These massive buildings (at one time the largest brick buildings in the southern hemisphere) with cast-iron internal structure and gable roofs were later used for storage and maintenance.

Conversion of the Carriage Workshop into a second 300-seat theatre for the Belvoir Street Company by architects David Haertsch and Hill Thalis was due for completion in 1997. The New Locomotive Workshop was converted into the Australian Technology Park by Tom Forgan and Crawford Partners (1996).

Below: Sections through the Australian Technology Park

231 Former NSW Club

31 Bligh Street, Sydney
1884–87 William Wilkinson Wardell
1916 Power and Adams (interior alterations
and fourth floor)
1975–77 McConnel Smith and Johnson
(restoration and upgrade)
GC, V, NA

The New South Wales Club was a relatively late Italianate design by the notable neo-Gothic specialist William Wilkinson Wardell (1823–99). It was described by a newspaper in somewhat high-flown terms as being 'embellished with Palladian and Vignolese details'. There is a striking similarity to the Reform Club in London by the eminent architect Charles Barry. It is an attractive interpretation of English Palladian Revival, although it must have been a conservative work in its day given the state of flux in the architecture profession.

The attic-windowed mansard was added in 1916 to provide a billiards room together with some minor remodelling. Facing demolition in 1972, it was saved through Sydney Council's code for Transferable Floor Space, allowing its development potential to be used on the adjoining site, giving rise to the neighbouring Barclay House project. Lying vacant for many years after the collapse of the Pyramid Building Society, a latter-day owner, it has since been converted into small prestigious offices, one of which is leased by a former Prime Minister.

232

233

54 P 12

24 K 17

232 Balmain Post Office and Courthouse

368 Darling Street, Balmain
1885–87 James Barnet (CA)
GC, V, A

When the Government Architect commenced work on this major civic group, the drafting office consisted of eighty-eight staff divided into three design groups. Both the Balmain Post Office/Courthouse and the Bathurst Courthouse were detail designed by the architect Edward Rumsey, who led one of the design groups. The court complexes at Bathurst and Balmain exude a mannered, almost British Indian flavour, with domes and exaggerated colonnades.

The dual functions of the group are expressed by the clock tower (whose pyramidal roof was restored in 1979 by the Public Works Department after being missing for twenty years) and the metal sheathed dome of the courthouse which dominates the street elevation.

•••

James Barnet's Clerk of Works was Edward Rumsey, who was intimately involved in both the Balmain Post Office/Courthouse project and the rebuilding of Customs House, although the latter was a rather more severe design. He was English-trained and had practised in London before coming to Australia, later proving to be Barnet's most talented assistant. By 1885, Barnet became embroiled with senior public officials who took exception to his stubborn resistance to their often ill-informed requests. Rumsey often appeared on behalf of Barnet to defend the Colonial Architect in front of a Royal Commission or a Board of Enquiry.

•••

Other projects designed in 1885 by James Barnet include Newtown Courthouse, Paddington Post Office, Tenterfield Courthouse, and the University of Sydney Medical School.

233 Customs House, Customs House Square

Alfred, Loftus and Young Streets, Sydney
1887 James Barnet (CA) (major rebuilding and upper floors)
1903 Walter Liberty Vernon (NSWGA) (top floor)
1995–97 Tonkin Zulaikha and Jackson, Teece, Chesterman & Willis
GC, V, A

The present Customs House represents a complete redesign and enlargement of an earlier 1844 building by Mortimer Lewis (1796–1879) by James Barnet (1827–1904). The earlier building had become too small and overcrowded for the expanding customs work in Sydney, and it took six years before the problem was addressed. The original client department occupied the building until 1990, after which the Federal Government made a gift of it to Sydney City Council together with funds for its refurbishment. There was, however, a proviso that the building be put to majority public use.

Tonkin Zulaikha and Jackson, Teece, Chesterman & Willis were commissioned to convert the building into a culture and information centre with restaurants and a large central atrium space. The future of the building had been hotly contested by various interests including music organisations that wished to convert it to a recital hall.

236

237

77 F 19

234 The Royal Hotel

Cuthill Street and Perouse Road, Randwick
1887 John Kirkpatrick
AC, V, A

A delicate country town style hotel which still retains its two-storey cast-iron decorated verandas. These were common features on all country and many suburban hotels built during the 1880s.

54 N 11

235 Millie Villas

41–43 Glossop Street, Birchgrove
1888 architect unknown
GC, V, NA

A small attached pair of houses with tunnel access between the backyards. Also splendid plaster detailing to parapet and pediment, and tiled panels to front window mullions.

64 L 4

236 Hunter Baillie Presbyterian Church

Cnr Collins and Johnston Street, Annandale
1888 Cyril and Arthur Blacket
GC, V, A

The Hunter Baillie Presbyterian Church was designed by the two architect sons of Edmund Blacket, a former Colonial Architect and Gothic Revival specialist. This high street Annandale church is a landmark best known for its cloud-piercing spire. It was selected by Helen Baillie in 1886 from a series of alternative spire designs by Arthur Blacket and commissioned in memory of her husband Hunter Baillie, who had died thirty-two years earlier.

The remarkably slender design gives a dramatic elegance to the otherwise harshly detailed structure. It provides a suitable landmark for Johnston Street, the centrepiece of John Young's suburb (the first wide-street, modern planned suburb in Sydney).

24 K 15

237 The Lands Department Building

Bridge, Loftus, Bent and Gresham Streets, Sydney
1876–88 stage one – James Barnet (CA)
1890–94 stage two – James Barnet (CA)
(design); Walter Liberty Vernon (supervision
of construction)
1938 (clock added)
GC, V, A

A remarkable and lavish interpretation of the Italian Renaissance style for commercial buildings by Sydney's great public architect. This is Barnet's largest building and, when completed, it easily dominated the Bridge Street and Circular Quay area. It exhibits excellent masonry workmanship, particularly in the quality of statuary, which includes royal figures and those associated with the land, such as the explorer Robert O'Hara Burke.

The foundation stone was laid on 7 October 1876 by the Minister of Lands; oddly enough, its location has never been discovered. The design included early examples of emerging technologies such as heating, lighting, ventilation, and a communication system of speaking through tubes and operating pneumatic bells. The builder, John Young, introduced one of the first reinforced concrete floor slabs, with coke concrete vaults to improve fire resistance. This was a particularly sensitive issue in Sydney after the destruction of the massive Garden Palace Building in September 1882. The tower form has a copper 'onion' shape, which is carefully placed to close the vista in Bent Street.

•••

In recognition of his achievements, the sculptor Tomaso Sani was commissioned by the Premier to execute a sandstone bust of James Barnet for the Lands Department Building. However, the new Secretary for Public Works surreptitiously substituted the name of Sir John Robertson for that of Barnet.

238

239

274 R 3

238 Thomas Walker Convalescent Hospital
*Hospital Road, Concord (within the grounds of
Concord Repatriation General Hospital)*
1889 John Sulman
GC, V, A

Following Thomas Walker's enormous bequest of
£100,000 in 1888, an architectural competition
was held and seemingly won by architect John
Kirkpatrick. However, it was suddenly announced
that the project was, in fact, to be awarded to
the architect John Sulman (1849–1934). The
building is considered Sulman's greatest and
most original architectural design, featuring an
axially aligned gatehouse on one side and a
unique turreted watergate on the river's edge.

●●●

*John Sulman's marriage into the Walker family
appears to have accounted for the sudden
change of architect. Yet, in later years, Sulman
was doggedly to accuse his colleague John
Kirkpatrick of using his family connections and
underhand tactics to obtain large commissions.*

55 C 17

239 Pyrmont Community Centre
Former Pyrmont Public School
85 John Street, Pyrmont
*1884 William E Kemp (wing cnr John and
Mount Streets)*
*1891 William E Kemp (main building in
John Street)*
*1993–95 Jones Brewster Regan (conversion
to community centre)*
GC, V, A

The Pyrmont Public School was designed by
William E Kemp (b. 1831) when he was the
architect for schools. Criticised as devoid of
beauty and architectural merit when completed,
it foreshadowed the rejection of Victorian
ornament. As Pyrmont had a relatively small
catchment area for students, it faced dwindling
numbers and closed as a school in 1934. Seen
today, its considerable strength lay in its
revolutionary simplicity and honesty in the use
of quality brickwork. The building has been
recently transformed into a local community
centre with considerable success.

27 F 3

240 Former Sydney Technical College and Technological Museum
Mary Ann and Harris Streets, Ultimo
1891 William E Kemp (college)
1892 William E Kemp (museum)
GC, V, A

This is the first major application of decorative
arts and crafts language to a major public
building in Sydney. While the Arts and Crafts
school in Europe sought to provide alternatives
to classical language for decorating buildings
through subtle references to nature, architects
such as Kemp and Clamp in Sydney translated
this tendency into a pictorial identification of
Australia's unique flora and fauna.

Kemp was able to use the monumental
stature of an educational project to experiment
with terracotta inlay and polychrome brickwork,
creating one of the most significant breaks with
the classically derived sandstone traditions
which existed at the time. Concurrently with
Kemp's design, major classical buildings such as
the Land Department Building were still under
construction (237).

Externally restored, it is now resplendent in
red, brown and cream bricks, decorative terracotta, and stonework detailed with carvings of
Australian flora and fauna (a goanna adorns the
main entrance arch). The former Turner Hall, in
similar style, adjoins the east end. The design is
similar to Kemp's Concord Public School (1890).

243

26 J 18

241 The Strand Arcade

*412–414A George Street and
191–195 Pitt Street, Sydney
1891–92 John B Spencer with Charles E Fairfax
1969 (remodelled)
1978 Alan Lawrence and Stephenson & Turner
(rebuilt after fire)
GC, V, A*

A rare, rebuilt late Victorian arcade from the prosperous 'boom' times when Sydney experienced rapid growth in shopping arcade construction between 1880 and 1900. Inspired by London's successful Burlington Arcade, The Strand was the pinnacle of Sydney's glass-roofed arcades. The roof glass was tinted to provide correct lighting for the upper floor photographers. The recent restoration after fire damage is a true representation of the original craftsmanship. The overhanging gallery is supported independently of the columns so as to obtain a clear and unobstructed view of the full length of the interior. The Strand Arcade originally included a special gas and electricity system and hydraulic lifts.

295 M 10

242 'Ashfield Castle'

*160 Queen Street, Ashfield
1885 architect unknown
GC, NV, NA*

Icing cake Gothic at its thickest. Built by Sir Hugh Dixson of the tobacco family fame, this imposing Victorian mansion has twin gables of stuccoed brickwork, struck to look like ashlar stonework. The ground floor windows have stone tracery and the interior survives with extensive mahogany joinery and an ornate gothic staircase. The main drawing room has an eighteen panel stained-glass window featuring the portraits of six European composers — Weber, Haydn, Mozart, Mendelssohn, Godard and Beethoven.

28 J 2

243 Capitol Theatre and Capitol Square

*Cnr Hay, Campbell and Pitt Streets, Sydney
1892–93 George McRae as New Belmore
Markets
1913–16 RH Brodrick as the Hippodrome Theatre
1927–28 Henry Eli White as the Capitol Theatre
1989–95 Peddle Thorp & Walker as a lyric theatre
1996 Noel Bell Ridley Smith (Capitol Square
hotel and retail centre)
CG, V, A*

The Capitol Theatre seen today is the result of a major redevelopment after a chequered history of rebuilding and additions to the New Belmore Market building erected by Sydney City Council. Completed in 1893, it soon fell out of use, and, after languishing for years, was converted into a circus called The Hippodrome in 1913.

Unfortunately, the Hippodrome was a commercial failure, and the operators soon approached Sydney Council to convert the use from a circus into an 'atmospheric' theatre intended for silent movies and live performances. Henry E White, an experienced theatre designer in Sydney, toured the USA inspecting John Eberson's atmospheric theatres to get ideas. Eberson provided White with a design along similar lines to his Riviera Theatre in Omaha, Nebraska. The interior was meant to create the illusion of sitting in a romantic courtyard under a brilliant night sky, with patrons dazzled by special climatic and lighting effects.

In total, five atmospheric theatres were created in Australia before the Depression, and the takeover by sound cinema. The theatre was restored and extended jointly between the owners Sydney City Council and the developer Ipoh Garden for major musical productions. The adjoining site, including former Watkins Terrace and a new glass vault, was redeveloped by Augustine Chan as a hotel and retail complex.

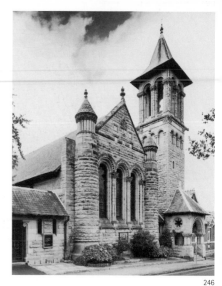

244

246

28 J 1

260 D 4

244 Central Police Court

98-112 Liverpool Street, Sydney
1890 Design — James Barnet (CA)
1892 Supervision — Walter Liberty Vernon (CA)
GC, V, A

The courthouse is an incomplete example of
Barnet's final attempt at neo-Classical Italianate
style for public buildings. In this project, he
turns to a variety of Second Empire architecture
created by the massing of rather heavy and
awkward elements of Beaux-Arts derivation. The
coat of arms above the entrance and the use of
podiums provide interest.

64 Q 2

245 'Montana'

Headquarters of the Sydney Home
Nursing Service
36 Boyce Street, Glebe
1892 Alexander and George McCredie
GC, V, NA

Montana is a modest early example of the
emerging 'Federation Style' which became
fashionable over the next twenty years. It
features fretted timber gable bargeboards with
sunray designs. The carved finials and fretted
valances are interpretations of cast-iron work in
timber. The Italianate brickwork offers a touch
of Victorian detail in a fragrant garden.

Below: Ground floor plan, 'Montana' (1892)

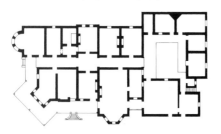

246 St Andrew's Presbyterian Church

56 Raglan Street, Manly
1890–92 Sulman and Power
GC, V, A

One of a number of Romanesque inspired
churches by John Sulman (1849–1934), who had
settled in Sydney and formed the Palladian Club
four years earlier as part of his plan to bring
respectability to the architectural profession.
Sulman kept in close contact with developments
in Europe and his designs mirror contemporary
European thinking.

American Revivals

*During the 1890s in Sydney, the growth in
commercial architecture in the city was directly
influenced by US technological advancements
such as the passenger elevator, large span
girders, electric lighting and fireproof iron
superstructure. Steel-framed buildings were
being coated with a stonemason's veneer which
in time disappeared. With a little help from
some hidden ironwork, the language was more
expressive and derivative of the Orient. With so
many 'revivals' making clients spoilt for choice,
it was not uncommon for architects to prepare
alternative designs for any scheme, perhaps
'American Romanesque', 'Modified
Romanesque', 'Italian Palazzo', 'French
Renaissance' and so on. For the sake of easing
choice for the untutored, permutations were
frequently defined by cost, and often the
'modified' style actually meant a cheaper
version of the 'real' revived design.*

247

| 46 D 5 | 67 D 6 |

247 'Hollowforth'

146 Kurraba Road, Neutral Bay
1892 Edward Jeaffreson Jackson
GC, V, NA

'Hollowforth' was an accomplished design which generated considerable interest. It demonstrates how the architect E Jeaffreson Jackson was able to break the entire mass of the house by dividing the composition into horizontal bands of materials – roof, upper walls, lower walls and base, and then pierce the composition with soaring chimneys.

Jackson was an English-trained architect who practised in Australia for about twenty years before returning to England in 1908. A contemporary of the Canadian-born John Horbury Hunt (1838–1904), Jackson employed the Arts and Crafts palette of brick, stucco and shingles for gables, roofs and walls. He was well regarded by the circle of up-and-coming residential architects (Esplin, Peddle, Joseland, Waterhouse and Hunt), who looked to his work for new materials and arrangements for domestic architecture.

●●●

For other work by Jackson see: House (1905), Cnr Magic Grove and Calypso Streets, Mosman; House (1905), Cnr Magic Grove and Mistral Streets, Mosman.

Below: Ground floor plan, 'Hollowforth' (1892)

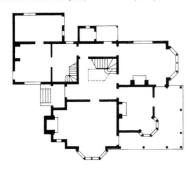

248 'St Kevin's'

117 Queen Street, Woollahra
1893 John Bede Barlow
GC, V, NA

Surrounded by dense vegetation, this is one of the most complete and original Arts and Crafts designs by John B Barlow, a champion of the 'new' architecture, a critic of Victorian ornamentation and a contemporary of the architect John Horbury Hunt. The design reflects Barlow's concern for natural materials and dark, subtle colours and detailing, including bracketed columns and tightly arched narrow windows. In some respects, it is reminiscent of the multi-gabled houses of the US east coast.

275 G 14

249 'St Cloud'

223 Burwood Road, Burwood
1893 EJ Bowen; 1978–82 (renovations)
GC, V, NA

A late Victorian house by the young Balmain architect EJ Bowen, for George Hoskins. The centrepiece tower was used for astronomical observations while the tower's mass provided a suitable entry porch to the house. The estate has been subdivided over the years, resulting in some elements, such as the stone observatory podium, being on adjoining properties.

Below: Ground floor plan, 'St Cloud' (1893)

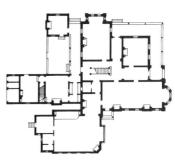

250

215 E 9

250 'The Highlands'
Former AJ Hordern House
Highlands Avenue, Waitara
1891–93 Horbury Hunt
GC, V, NA

The Canadian-born Horbury Hunt (1838–1904) was one of the most important architects of the 1890s working in Sydney. By all accounts, he was a difficult and outspoken man, but a brilliant architect. Hunt produced twenty-two houses during his individualistic career, charac-terised by powerful volumes, strong forms and a distaste for Victorian embellishment. He was an emerging modernist, capable of sculpting the pictorial forms of the international Arts and Crafts movement employing the North American love of stained and painted timber.

'The Highlands' was commissioned by Alfred Hordern, one of the brothers of the Hordern retail dynasty that dominated Sydney department store business for more than seventy years. The emporium families such as those of Hordern, Marcus Clarke, Grace and Farmer often employed important architects and might have built three houses, including a city residence, and summer and winter houses.

Originally commanding a 15.5-hectare estate which extended from Wahroonga to Hornsby, this all-timber house looks deceptively large considering the small scale and darkly illuminated interiors. Divided into two parts and

Below: Ground floor plan, 'The Highlands' (1893)

connected by an enclosed veranda, the conservative room arrangements are clearly dominated by consideration of the two powerful roof forms and, curiously, show little innovation. However the three-dimensional quality of the exterior is exceptional, especially the use of curving, almost peeling wall surfaces to form veranda and balcony areas, and the proportion, design and expression of timber posts, balusters and rails. These predate the 'Federation' bungalow period of the 1900s which returned to timber after rejecting the cast-iron embellish-ments of the Victorians.

●●●

See also E du Faure House, Pibrac Avenue,
Warrawee (1888), by Horbury Hunt, with split
gables and external shingle walls.

26 J 19

251 Former Gresham Hotel
Former Central Hotel and L & I Co. Bank Ltd
Cnr 149 York and Druitt Streets, Sydney
1890–94 Ambrose Thornley Jnr
GC, V, A

Originally designed as a lavish hotel building with a banking chamber on the ground floor for the Excelsior Land and Building Company. The relatively unknown Thornley had previously been a partner of John Smedley who had come to attention during the 1880s for his competition-winning design for the Trades Hall building in Goulburn Street. The upper floor window designs show distinct similarity to the Gresham Hotel. With the recent completion of the Sydney Town Hall and the contemporary construction of the Queen Victoria Markets building, the group established this intersection as the commercial heart of Victorian Sydney. The Italianate styling is vigorous in detailing and composition. The original bank chamber is still intact (now occupied by the Perth Mint).

252

254

25 E 18

252 Former John Taylor Warehouse

Cnr Pyrmont Street and Pyrmont
Bridge Roads, Pyrmont
1893 Arthur Blacket
GC, V, A

Perhaps the earliest of the American-inspired
woolstores in Sydney, this warehouse commissioned by John Taylor broke the tradition of
Gothic or Classical design idioms, where the
masonry was the primary structural material.
The building has cast-iron storey posts
supporting rolled steel main girders with timber
floors. This reduced the external brickwork to a
skin which needed to be stabilised and
animated. The implied Romanesque arches are
shallow and the building is devoid of any
unnecessary ornamentation.

27 H 2

253 The Corporation Building

Formerly The Municipal Building
181-187 Hay Street, Sydney
1893-94 George McRae (SCA)
GC, V, A

Owned by Sydney City Council, this quaint
Anglo-Dutch style Queen Anne building was
built by the City Architect George McRae
(1858-1923) to service the many visitors drawn
to the area by the New Belmore Markets in Hay
Street (present day Capitol Theatre). The building
provided toilets, refreshment rooms and offices
for produce agents and market management.
McRae incorporated a palette of Arts and Crafts
materials of the day, including terracotta panels
and red double pressed bricks. The first floor of
the building is currently used as a branch of the
city library.

26 L 17

254 Sydney Hospital and Sydney Eye Hospital

Macquarie Street, Sydney
1880-94 Thomas Rowe; John Kirkpatrick
1994-96 New buildings by State Projects
Rad Militech and McConnel Smith & Johnson
— Alan Rintoul (Director in Charge)
GC, V, A

Originally named the Sydney Infirmary, this
building was designed to replace the deteri-
orated centre wing of Governor Macquarie's
'Rum Hospital' **(109, 110)**. Three sandstone
buildings and two gatehouses along Macquarie
Street emerged from an architectural
competition held in 1880 and won by Thomas
Rowe (1829-1899). The brief was rewritten (*see
Nightingale Wing* **(205)**). Rowe was heavily
criticised by his peers for the practice of under-
quoting building costs in order to win a
competition, and the Sydney Infirmary and this
project were his *causes célèbres*. Work halted for
some years after partial construction, awaiting
the approval of additional funds from the New
South Wales Parliament. Recent work includes
the relocation of the Sydney Eye Hospital to the
site, the construction of an eight-level car park,
ground floor emergency with eye hospital
outpatients, two levels of wards and an operating
theatre on the top floor. The new work enabled
the demolition of the Travers building, long
considered an eyesore, thereby allowing the
campus to be opened up to The Domain.

•••

*The little pig, Il Porcellino, placed in front of the
Hospital in 1968, is an anatomically realistic
depiction of a wild pig standing over a swamp
with tortoises, snakes, frogs, snails, lizards, crabs
and lilies. It was donated by Clarissa Torrigiani
in memory of her father and brother to raise
money for the hospital and is based on the 1547
original in Florence by Pietro Battiste Tacca.*

255

256

294 Q 2

26 J 17

255 Santa Sabina Convent Buildings

90 The Boulevarde and Jersey Road, Strathfield
1873 George and Ralph Mansfield
1892–95 John F Hennessy, Sheerin and
Hennessy
GC, V, A

This building represents the pinnacle of Anglo-Dutch revivalism during the short period of Queen Anne influence on the Catholic Archdiocese. The Church's architects Sheerin and Hennessy were rarely diverted from large-scale Gothic Revival or monastic Romanesque such as seen in St Joseph's College, Hunters Hill, St Patrick's Seminary, Manly and the Sacred Heart Convent at Rose Bay.

John Francis Hennessy (1853–1924)

An important figure in the development of church architecture in Australia, John Hennessy grew up in Yorkshire and, on completing his apprenticeship, was awarded the Ashpital prize of the RIBA for measured drawings. He attended the architecture school at the Royal Academy of Art in London, after which he had work experience with the noted Gothic Revival architect William Burgess. After a brief period in America, Hennessy arrived in Sydney in 1880.

After a spell as a draughtsman, he was appointed assistant city architect, during which time he designed the Frazer fountain in Hyde Park in 1881 and the Centennial Hall extension to the Town Hall (201).

A genial and popular person, Hennessy went into partnership with Joseph Sheerin in 1884.

Their friendship with Archbishop (Cardinal) Moran helped them receive many commissions, including St Joseph's College, Hunters Hill (1884–94), and St Vincent's College, Potts Point (1886). Sheerin left the firm in 1912 and Hennessy, with his son Jack, completed WW Wardell's plans for St Mary's Cathedral, Sydney.

256 Société Générale House

Formerly Equitable Life Assurance Society of America
348–352 George Street, Sydney
1891–95 Edward Raht; John Reid, supervising architect
GC, V, A

The present day Société Générale House is one of Sydney's most powerful buildings, of a complexity and scale matched by only a few others, such as the Commonwealth Savings Bank in Martin Place. It is an American design by the architect Edward Raht, who sailed to Australia to supervise the construction of two buildings — one in Melbourne and this one in Sydney. Here is a marvellous reworking of the Italian palazzo by the 'American Romanesque' school, although not as stripped and modern as contemporary examples such as The Reliance Building in Chicago (1890–94) by Charles Atwood. However, it is built of fire-proof steel girder construction and clad with heavily rusticated Bowral trachyte.

The building is crucial to the harmony of George Street near Martin Place, an urban atmosphere complemented by the former Bank of New South Wales, the National Australia Bank and the adjoining GIO Building. It is perhaps unfortunate that the entrance doors are so poorly scaled considering the magnificence of the facade.

●●●

James Barnet, a noted Sydney architect of the time, was moved to comment 'recently from the USA has come the Romanesque in an Insurance Office Building (Raht's Equitable Life) and the same style has been applied to Branch Banks, the Technical College (Ultimo), the Queen Victoria Markets Building (George McRae) and no doubt will run its crudities to seed warehouses stores and shops.'

257

26 J 19

257 Queen Victoria Building
George, Market, York and Druitt Streets
1893-98 George McRae (as markets)
1984-86 Stephenson & Turner (Alan Lawrence)
& Rice Daubney in Association (restoration)
GC, V, A

This was the great retailing success of Sydney, despite the jeremiads at the time it was being developed. The massive building was originally designed as a fresh produce market, called the Queen Victoria Markets, and construction commenced in the economically disastrous year of 1893. Architectural styles were in such a state of flux that the City Architect George McRae presented the Sydney City Councillors with four distinct design options: Renaissance, Gothic, Romanesque and Queen Anne.

American Romanesque which is 'now so largely employed by American architects', according to a building journal description of the day, won out narrowly. The construction uses brick vaulting between steel beams with a heavy basalt base quarried in Bowral. The original concept of an internal glass-roofed shopping street was lost with alterations in 1917 and, in 1935, it was converted to office space. A dominant feature is the 20-metre diameter central dome surrounded by twenty smaller copper-sheeted cupolas.

Following proposals for its demolition to make way for a city car park, a restoration proposal was negotiated between developer Ipoh Garden and the owner Sydney City Council. Its feasibility hinged on the provision of a car park under York Street, to which Sydney Council agreed. The building is now an architectural and commercial success, commanding some of the highest retail rents in Sydney.

The lower, mezzanine level (basement) provides one of the city's busiest pedestrian concourses connecting Town Hall railway station to the Pitt Street mall.

At ground level, the gradual rise in George Street has been cleverly absorbed into the design with shops steadily rising in height along the length of the block.

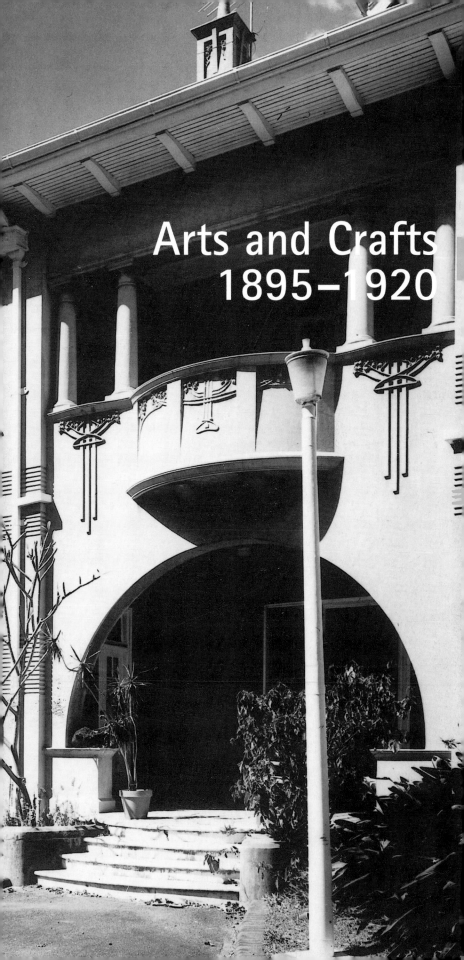

Arts and Crafts
1895–1920

1895–1920

Towards the end of the 19th century, the enduring classical tradition of British and Australian architecture was waning.

In its place emerged an eclectic assortment of styles and ideologies. The rise and fall of the Gothic Revival, confined essentially to the 19th century, helped to establish the enduring influence of the picturesque and a continual search for new forms of architectural expression suitable for its time. The source of inspiration for Australian architecture moved from Britain to North America, where it has largely remained to the present day.

The emergence of the Arts and Crafts movement in Britain in the late 1880s was a reaction to the aesthetic, social and political crises caused by the ills of the Industrial Revolution. Its founder, William Morris, and other like-minded craftsmen railed against the architectural sterility or outright stupidity of thoughtless historicism in architecture and the decorative arts, where a railway hotel such as George Gilbert Scott's St Pancras Hotel impersonated a Gothic cathedral, or a hallway heater masqueraded as a medieval suit of armour. Morris stood against the demeaning exploitation of the working classes in factory production where traditional noble craftsmanship was replaced by the repetitive labour of automation.

Morris and his proto-socialist friends were predominantly well-to-do upper middle class worthies on a crusade to save the poor labouring classes from moral, philosophical and aesthetic squalor, by establishing an 'Earthly Paradise'. The Arts and Crafts movement denigrated the artifacts made of imitation materials in mock Gothic, recycled Renaissance or overblown Baroque, and declared a profound belief in 'simplicity, truth-to-materials and the unity of handicraft and design', advocating the importance of comfort over style and a return to native vernacular traditions as suitable sources for inspiration.

The impact of the movement's aesthetic theory and practice reverberated around the English-speaking world and far beyond, laying the foundations of Modernism and Functionalism in architecture and industrial design. The emergence early this century of the German Deutscher Werkbund and Bauhaus drew heavily on Arts and Crafts aesthetic principles (appropriateness of use to function, honesty of design, use of materials, for example) through the application of industrial technology. In Australia, however, the movement's influence was little more than a superficial, if fashionable, taste in surface decoration.

Earlier in the 1860s, young English architects such as Richard Norman Shaw, JJ Stevenson and William Eden Nesfield rebelled against the strictures of rule book Gothic and developed the so-called Queen Anne Revival. Borrowing freely from a wide array of sources, the style, as Mark Girouard so aptly put it, 'was a kind of architectural cocktail with a little genuine Queen Anne in it, a little Dutch, a little Flemish, a squeeze of Robert Adam, a generous dash of Wren and a touch of François'. Essentially, the eclectic and irregular form, plan and outline, the delight in rich materials and 'prettiness of details' of Queen Anne houses represented the last significant flourish of 19th-century picturesque principles. Like the Arts and Crafts movement which developed in its wake, the Queen Anne Revival was the popular manifestation of well-to-do middle classes of London and the Home Counties seeking to define their position in society through art and architecture. In Sydney, prominent mercantile families such as the Fairfaxes also used it, in houses such as **Caerleon**, to define their position in society.

'Red flowering gum' silk fabric designed by Olive Nock (1893–1977). The design won a competition established by Henderson's Silk Company for 'an Australian design to be printed by Liberty of London'.

Powerhouse Museum, Sydney

Bernard Smith economically described the Australian version of Queen Anne as being 'pre-eminently of terracotta roofing tiles and exposed bricks of a deeper red'. The style is now widely known by the term 'Federation' in New South Wales, although the other states had significant regional variations, especially discernible in subtropical Queensland, conservative Adelaide and flamboyantly showy Melbourne.

The period of great economic buoyancy and activity of the 1880s, which gave birth to the Italianate Boom style, was built on crooked land speculation, bullish markets and widespread commercial and political corruption. A significant portion of the architectural profession was deeply involved in fraudulent practice, bilking their clients and each other. The conduct of architectural design competitions, then much more widespread than today, was notoriously corrupt and corruptible. As the century drew to a close, Australia's artificial prosperity crumbled overnight. By 1890, Australia's population had grown to approximately 3,100,000 people. In July of that year, the financial crash of Argentina prompted English financial institutions to withdraw their capital from the Australian banks they had founded. As a consequence, the economy plunged, bringing to a halt most building construction in the country and financial ruin to the many architects. By 1892, and during the following year, a series of Australian banks collapsed as the economy sank into a serious depression with widespread economic hardship.

Vase by L H Howie (1876–1963), Adelaide 1910, with the application of Australian flora to an imported porcelain blank.

Powerhouse Museum, Sydney

The infrastructure of Australia's primary produce export economy is still clearly visible around Sydney's harbour foreshores. With trade expanding and a significant growth in Sydney's population to 377,300 by 1901, pressure mounted for the redevelopment of the port and wharf facilities. Carried out by the Sydney Harbour Trust in the first two decades of the 20th century, the rebuilding of almost all of the city's maritime infrastructure was a public work of unprecedented scale: the grandest surviving legacies of this are evident in the **Woolloomooloo Deep Sea Wharf** and the **Walsh Bay Finger Wharves** (1907–22). Here, engineer Henry Deane Walsh pushed timber marine building technology to the extreme, using pure, if unconscious, Arts and Crafts ideas of honesty of materials and directness of design to function.

In adjacent Pyrmont and Ultimo, the city's largest buildings — the woolstores — enjoyed a frenzy of construction in the two decades from 1890. Ironbark post and beam internal structures wrapped in muscular load-bearing and unpainted face brickwork expressed the nobility, simplicity and genius of functional architecture.

As in Victorian England, engineering and technical innovation rather than architectural ideology captured the real spirit of the age. Spain and Cosh's **Culwulla Chambers** (1911–12) so alarmed the city fathers with its dazzling height of 170 feet (52 metres) when completed, that the *Height of Buildings Act* was passed that year to restrict construction to a maximum of 150 feet (46 metres). The act, which was not repealed until the late 1950s, had the effect of suppressing commercial development in the city until the early 1960s.

Architects such as John Sulman and writer–publishers such Florence Taylor expressed a deep concern for the planning of urban growth, the development and integration of public transport and the redevelopment and improvement of the city. Sulman wrote many newspaper articles in 1907 advocating city improvements, including the extension of Martin Place from Darling Harbour to Woolloomooloo. In 1907, a Royal Commission for the improvement of Sydney was set up after agitation by Sulman and the Town Planning Association. The Commission's Report of 1911, which proposed the extension of Martin Place only as far as Macquarie Street, resulted in its current configuration.

The expanding public transport — ferries, suburban trains and trams — was a critical factor in the growth of the city and caused the emergence of the garden suburb as the accepted pattern of urban living. The opening of the underground City Railway in 1926, anticipating the completion of the **Sydney Harbour Bridge** in 1932, caused the commercial focus of Sydney to shift from the Railway Square precinct with its array of department stores (Grace Bros, McDowells, Marcus Clarke and Anthony Horderns) to mid-town. Farmer & Co (now Grace Bros) opened near Town Hall Station, **Mark Foy's** was virtually on top of Museum Station and David Jones Elizabeth Street store was right opposite St James Station.

The Victorian pattern of crowded inner-city terraces for the poor and commodious villas for the well-to-do gave way to the acceptance of the free-standing house or bungalow in a garden as the model for all new residential development. Before the opening of the Sydney Harbour Bridge, the upper middle class residents of harbourside suburbs such as Mosman, Cremorne and Neutral Bay, who lived in substantial Federation and Arts and Crafts houses such as **Hollowforth** and **Brent Knowle**, commuted to the city by ferry; the lower middle and working classes caught the tram to work from Haberfield and Dacey Gardens Estate (now Daceyville).

If the 'Federation Style' was in fact the most popular style, other architectural languages flourished to varying degrees in this hopeful and expansive era. The Romanesque Revival took its principal inspiration not so much from English architects such as Alfred Waterhouse, JF Bentley and John Oldrid Scott, but rather from the full-blooded work of Chicagoan Henry Hobson Richardson. Although George McRae's magnificent design for the **Queen Victoria Building** (1893–98) is the most notable example of what has been termed 'American Romanesque', his alternate designs for the building in Italianate, Queen Anne and Gothic were typical of the stylistic eclecticism of the times. New York architect Edward Raht's design for the offices for the **Equitable Life Assurance Society of America** (1893) (now Société

Sideboard by woodcarver Lewis J Harvey (1871–1949) and cabinet maker John Merten (1861–1932). Made of silky oak and leadlight glass, Brisbane c. 1925.

Powerhouse Museum, Sydney

Générale House) represents Sydney's most forcefully realised piece of Richardsonian Romanesque design with its huge, rough-faced trachyte rusticated base.

Arts and Crafts ideas became more pervasive in the popular domestic style that succeeded Federation after World War I, the California Bungalow style. By now the focus of American architectural influence had deserted the East Coast for the West. Until the appearance of the California Bungalow, perhaps the principal contribution of the English Arts and Crafts movement was the idea of a 'free' style. John Sulman's masterpiece, the **Sir Thomas Walker Convalescent Hospital** (1893) in Concord, combines diverse classical elements drawn from Italianate, Classical, Palladian and Queen Anne styles in a highly successful, if eclectic, axial composition of plan and form. Despite its fall from popularity, the classical style continued to be employed on a small but significant number of public buildings (**Central Railway Station**, 1904–08; **Art Gallery of New South Wales**, 1904–09; **State Library of New South Wales**, 1906–09) designed by the New South Wales Government Architect Walter Liberty Vernon. His preference for a vernacular-inspired Arts and Crafts language, evident in lesser public buildings such as **Darlinghurst Fire Station** (1910), could not overcome the innate conservatism that dressed major official buildings in classical clothes up until World War II.

Although the first appearance of architectural elements of a functionalist character, such as the flat roof in the work of George Sydney Jones, occurred just before World War I, their general impact on architecture was very limited at that time. After the war, the California bungalow gained immediate and widespread popular approval. Alexander Stewart Jolly's **Belvedere** (1919) in Cremorne drew direct inspiration from the work of prominent Los Angeles architects Greene and Greene, in whose work 'timber was used with an almost Japanese expressiveness, together with "earthy" materials such as rough clinker bricks and smooth river stones'. Low, spreading roofs with deep, overhanging eaves and the use of dark varnished or oil-stained internal joinery inside and out embodied the Arts and Crafts idea of honest and truthful expression of materials in a manner that found widespread and immediate appeal in Australia. This was particularly true of Sydney with its subtropical climate.

In domestic architecture other movements were afoot. Walter Burley and Marion Mahony Griffin introduced revolutionary ideas to Sydney, embracing the relationship of buildings to their sites, a reverence for native flora, open planning and a decorative language anchored in imagination rather than historical precedent. Few of their Sydney buildings survive apart from a small cluster of seven houses in Castlecrag, the harbourside suburb they planned and developed, and few architects followed their precepts. William Hardy Wilson's advocacy of a return to the Australian colonial Georgian and Regency styles made a splash with the design of his own house **Purulia** (1916) at Warrawee. The direct simplicity of its single-storeyed form, its elegant Georgian details, its egalitarian placement of the servantless kitchen to the right off the entrance hall outraged its neighbours in their large Federation mansions who feared that their property values were under threat and the tone of the neighbourhood was at risk. The real impact of Wilson's magnum opus, his magnificent, self-published *Old Colonial Architecture in New South Wales and Tasmania* (1924), the finest quality architectural tome ever published in Australia, was not felt until many years after his death in 1955.

By 1925, the population of greater Sydney had swelled to more than 550,000, and the age of the automobile was firmly established. The Arts and Crafts period witnessed a struggle between the innovative and forward-looking thinkers keen to embrace a new world and century and the traditional conservatism that periodically reasserts itself in all aspects of Australian culture.

TREVOR HOWELLS

301

307

23 H 15

301 St Patrick's Convent

145 Harrington and Grosvenor Street, Sydney
1840 Original, 1896 attrib. Sheerin and
Hennessy (street facade)
GC, V, NA

The crispest example of tight-jointed red
brickwork in Sydney. This building barely uses
mortar. A building of mixed styles including
ecclesiastical Gothic, English Queen Anne
Revival, and Arts and Crafts.

215 M 16

302 'Ingleholme'

17 Boomerang Street, Turramurra
1896–c. 1910 Sulman & Power
1930 and later (additions)
GC, NV, NA

In stately Old English style, 'Ingleholme' was
designed by Sir John Sulman (1849–1934) for
his parents, who decided they would rather stay
at his own house 'Blytheswood' at Warrawee.
Consequently, Sulman moved there himself for
fourteen years. The two-storey mansion of nine
bedrooms, library and two studies, with slight
Tudoresque overtones, was later occupied by the
Pymble Ladies' College Preparatory School.

Sold to developers in 1978, it was saved from
demolition and land subdivision by former Lord
Mayor of Sydney, Jeremy Bingham. This large
home was designed ten years after the Sulman
family's move from London to Sydney, and was
described as an 'artistic residence'.

Below: Ground floor plan, 'Ingleholme' (1896)

26 J 17

303 Colonial Mutual Life Assurance Society

Former MLA Insurance Co. of New York
10a–16 Martin Place, Sydney
1893–96 John Kirkpatrick
1976 Joseland & Gilling (office tower and
remodelling)
GC, V, A

The1890s brought an influx of North American
insurance companies that left a legacy of steel-
framed fire-proofed landmark buildings. This
trachyte and sandstone design was built for the
Mutual Life Assurance Co. of New York, on part
of the development site sold by the Sydney City
Council during the depression of the 1890s. The
council, strapped for cash because of its building program (Queen Victoria Markets Building,
Haymarket etc), sold off a 30-metre wide strip
of Martin Place opposite the Post Office, the
present-day sites of the GIO, Challis House and
CML. The building was extended by three floors
in 1929 by Hennessy and Hennessy.

A later proposal for a super block redevelopment was put forward in the early 1970s,
amalgamating twelve building sites and extending
200 metres along both Pitt and George Streets.

Abandoning this scheme, CML proceeded
with a new tower design specifically to rehouse
their Sydney office, including demolition of their
original landmark building. Despite approval by
The Height of Buildings Committee and Council,
a public backlash supported by Building Union
Green Bans caused a redesign incorporating the
old building. The system of bonuses set up by
the City Plan encouraged retention of the
historic facade and led to the extraction of a
higher floor area than the planning instruments
permitted. At the time of its completion, the
twenty storey glass-walled tower was
considered to be one of the best examples of
contrasting new and old architecture.

306

215 H 11

304 Ewan House
Knox Grammar Preparatory School
Formerly 'Innisfail'
Cnr Billyard Ave and Cleveland St, Wahroonga
1897 Herbert Wardell
GC, V, A

Using a design just as suitable for a golf club as a large house, William Wardell's son Herbert loosely based this scheme on Norman Shaw's Old English style. The vast mansion for the JT Toohey family attempts to merge American Romanesque, Anglo Dutch and English Revival themes at a time when architectural influences were moving away from Europe to America.

25 H 19

305 Former Edwards Dunlop Warehouse
414–418 Kent Street, Sydney
1897 Robertson & Marks
GC, V, A

Robertson and Marks ran a very successful practice specialising in large commercial buildings. They are generally considered pioneers of the Federation style of warehouses which ran from 1895 to 1915, and was only extinguished by World War I. The cart dock retains the original granite setts and steel tracks.

55 A 13

306 'Concertina Terrace'
5–13 Colgate Avenue, Balmain
1898 attrib. Benjamin Backhouse
GC, V, NA

Until about 1920, this street was named Broadstairs Street and these set-back houses had good water views over Mort Bay. The stepped arrangement produces a lively design against the street frontage. Each narrow front is dominated by a bay window surmounted by an attic balcony.

24 L 14

307 The Ritz–Carlton Hotel (portion of)
Former NSW Board of Health Building
93 Macquarie Street, Sydney
1896–98 Walter Liberty Vernon (CA)
1990 (converted into a portion of the hotel)
GC, V, A

The former Board of Health Building makes overtures to the Arts and Crafts architecture of the Scot Charles Rennie Macintosh. It marks a significant change in style within the Government Architect's department when Walter Liberty Vernon (1846–1914) took charge. His designs consciously contrasted with his long-term predecessor, James Barnet (1827–1904), who had been accused of expensive formal Italianate architecture and 'living in the past' by his jealous peers and the Public Works Minister. The Phillip Street elevation reveals a further signature Arts and Crafts detail in the form of a carved medallion piece on the eastern chimney showing the Board of Health's seal. Today, the building is part of the Ritz Carlton Hotel, which also occupies the adjoining site.

25 H 17

308 CW Foley & Co.
230–232 Sussex Street, Sydney
1899 architect unknown
GC, V, A (courtyard)

Viewed from the internal courtyard, the Foley & Co. building is now regarded as the most intact and original representation of a small-scale manufacturing complex from the 19th century. It has undergone little, if any, external change. The open courtyard enabled goods to be hoisted by hand from horse-drawn carts to the upper floors through opening doors and hoist bars which are still visible. Original tenants included small businesses as varied as a bootmaker and grocer. The complex is currently occupied by an advertising agency.

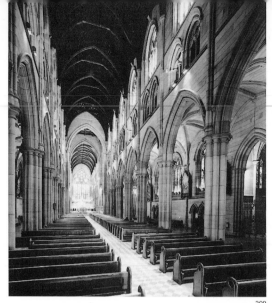

309

309 St Mary's Cathedral
College and Cathedral Streets, Sydney
1865–99 William Wilkinson Wardell (transept dedicated 1900)
1913–28 John F Hennessy (supervised nave, towers, rose window)
1961 (crypt completed)
GC, V, A

The cathedral occupies land granted in 1820, when the nearest building was Hyde Park Barracks and the Sydney archdiocese was Australasia. Immediately after the old St Mary's Cathedral was burnt down on 29 June 1865, the Anglican architect William Wardell (1823–1899), then Inspector of Public Buildings in Victoria, was asked to draw up plans. He had earlier gained widespread recognition for St Patrick's Roman Catholic Cathedral in Melbourne (1858–1939) and St John's College (1859–1935) at Sydney University.

The style is 13th- to 14th-century Gothic, mixing French and English precedents between interior and exterior, and from one to end to the other. Costing in excess of £300,000, the church was built in stages as funds became available. It faithfully reflects Wardell's design (spires are yet to come), except for the lengthening of the nave foundations by 12 metres. After Wardell's death, this created a crisis when it was realised that the entry staircase landed in Cathedral Street. In 1915, the church solicitors negotiated a resumption of Cathedral street from Sydney Council to complete the building, which explains the unusual street pattern.

Built from yellowblock Pyrmont sandstone, the stone louvres in the main tower ironically came from a site called Purgatory, and the flagstones from a site called the Hell Hole — names quarrymen gave to the difficult rock strata from which the stones were cut deep in the Pyrmont quarry.

310 Apartment Building
73 Windmill Street, Millers Point
1900 architect unknown
GC, V, NA

This walk-up apartment building, possibly the earliest of its type in Sydney, is closely related to similar American examples of the same era. The brick and cement rendered 'block' has a central balcony space on each level which projects from the facade.

311 Burns Philp & Co Building
5–11 Bridge Street, Sydney
1898–1901 AL and G McCredie & Anderson
GC, V, A

The exuberant sandstone facade is the only one of its type in Sydney capturing the neo Romanesque tendencies of American corporate architecture rather than the Art Nouveau developments of European domestic architecture. It was designed by Arthur and George McCredie, who were the same architects for the white ceramic-faced Mark Foys building; they clearly demonstrate their versatility and eclecticism. This is a composite stone, brick, steel, cast-iron and timber structure with rusticated plinth, arched openings and vaulted entry vestibules.

•••

Burns Philp & Co erected their new head office in 1897, on a site across the road from their existing Victorian office building (now demolished) designed by Mark Cooper Day.

•••

The McCredie Brothers were significant urbanists (along with WL Vernon, the Government Architect; John Sulman and JJC Bradfield) during the 1890s, debating transportation, tunnel and bridge schemes across the harbour, as well as designing successful commercial buildings.

311

314

26 J 17

312 Government Insurance Office
Formerly The Bank of Australasia
Cnr 2 Martin Place and 354 George Street
1901–04 (interiors 1908) Edward E Raht
GC, V, A

Built of the same materials by the same visiting architect who designed the adjoining Equitable Life Assurance Building (1895), this five-storey building has two large basement levels which extend 5 metres under Martin Place. The structure is a composite of load-bearing external walls with wrought-iron columns and rolled steel girders. The facade is of a broad Italian Renaissance influence with some forms drawn from early Renaissance models, while others appear to be of Baroque derivation. The interior is lavishly decorated with extensive use of bronze, marble, cedar, fine wrought iron and gold leaf dominating the main banking chamber. On its completion, Raht closed his architectural office in George Street in 1904.

•••

The roof area behind the parapet (not open to the public) affords one of the best internal views of the city, taking in Martin Place and the GPO building and George Street to the Town Hall.

25 H 19

313 Warehouse Offices
Former WP & SJ Dunlop Stores
435–441 Kent Street, Sydney
1901 Robertson & Marks
GC, V, A

With sixty-five privately owned wharves in Darling Harbour, nearby Sussex, Kent, and Clarence Streets were filled with warehouses. This is a well-preserved example of a face brick and sandstone warehouse built at the turn of the century. One of the four bays had a cartway at street level to provide access to the centre of the building where goods were hoisted above.

25 H 17

314 Forbes Hotel
30 York and King Streets, Sydney
1901 Sheerin & Hennessy
1980s extensive internal remodelling
GC, V, A

Designed by architects better known for their ecclesiastical designs, the Forbes Hotel features red face brick in the Federation Anglo Dutch style. It survives with terracotta detailing, vertical brick strapwork and timber-framed arched head windows with projecting keystones. Interior details include pressed metal and plaster panel ceiling, timber staircase and cast-iron columns.

24 J 12

315 The Earth Exchange
Former Electric Light Station
18 Hickson Road, The Rocks
1903 Walter Liberty Vernon (NSWGA)
1908 Walter Liberty Vernon (NSWGA)
GC, V, A

Erected as an electric light generating station for the government housing at Millers Point, the Electric Light Station was never fitted out or used. By the time it was completed it was considered too small to house the required generating plant. In 1908, it was tripled in size and converted into a Mining Museum and Chemical Laboratory displaying rock and mineral specimens dating from 1875. In 1991, the institution was revamped as the Earth Exchange (now closed). The relatively utilitarian design by Walter Liberty Vernon (1846–1914) is notable for its tall circular brick smokestack, which has never been used.

•••

In 1903, Vernon's son Hugh Vernon went into partnership with Howard Joseland (1860–1930). Joseland had won a competition to design a model suburb with WL Vernon in the 1880s.

316

28 J 4

316 Central Railway Station — Terminal and Viaduct
Railway Square, Sydney
1904–08 Walter Liberty Vernon (NSWGA)
1995–96 NSWGA (alterations and renovations)
GC, V, A

An important landmark building bringing the countryside to the city by an extensive railway network which once reached deep into the country's interior. The new terminal, which had previously been located at Redfern, was made possible by exhuming corpses and building over the old burial grounds near Belmore Park.

The strangely transitional design features heavily rusticated sandstone piers and viaducts in front of a relatively austere neo-classical building. The twin ramps once brought the tram service to the upper concourse level, which is currently being reinstituted as a light rail service with modern cars. The large steel-roofed booking hall has traces of Art Nouveau decoration amid the complexity of hip trussed steelwork resolved with a reasonable degree of elegance.

Recently, the interstate bus terminal was moved to Central to provide a transport interchange. The forgotten lower levels have also been refurbished, and there are plans to upgrade and restore the external stonework and viaducts.

54 Q 20

317 Sze Yup Temple (Joss House)
Edward Street, Glebe Point
1904 architect unknown
GC, V, A

This temple was built by emigrants from Sze Yup, a region near Canton, who settled and became market gardeners in this vicinity. It is dedicated to Kwun Ti, a third-century Chinese hero who was the epitome of brotherly love, loyalty and charity. The temple roof is guarded by 'Keelins', who are benevolent mythological figures.

28 J 2

318 Chamberlain Hotel
420–428 Pitt Street, Sydney
1904 architect unknown
1936 Copeman, Lemont and Keesing (major renovations)
GC, V, A

This is one of three Anglo-Dutch style hotels surviving in the city.

●●●

So-called Federation architecture (coinciding with changing attitudes after the federation of Australian states in 1901) was a collection of styles which rejected the lacework and frills of Victorian cast-iron in favour of timberwork, face brickwork, metal sheet and terracotta.

Art Nouveau
The Art Nouveau style climaxed in Europe with the work of Victor Horta (Brussels), Antonio Gaudi (Barcelona) and Charles Rennie Macintosh (Glasgow). CR Macintosh was particularly idiosyncratic, taking a 'whole of building approach', which included not only the exteriors and interiors, but the internal furnishings, furniture, light fittings and signage. This architecture incorporates the slender curves of foliage, flower stalks, waves, flowing hair and flames. The ubiquitous forms are rendered in opalescent colours set against a crisp, often pure white background or framework.

Very little of this influence emerged in Sydney, except perhaps for the broad, piercing chimney lines found in Walter Liberty Vernon's work (The Health Department Building, 307). A few notable exceptions did occur, with the most important being Babworth House by Morrow and de Putron.

319

319 Babworth House
Mount Adelaide Road, Darling Point
c. 1909 David Morrow and William de Putron
GC, V, A

Built by Sir Samuel Hordern, Babworth House is one of the two mansions which still occupy large estates on Darling Point. Situated on the highest land, with panoramic views over the Harbour, Babworth House is an architectural curiosity. It is a perfect example of decorative Art Nouveau detailing echoing the designs of CR Macintosh, who worked in Glasgow at the time. Motifs animate both internal and external surfaces, and the delicacy and consistency is considered to be the most sophisticated example of this style in Australia.

Following the death of Hordern in 1957, the trustees of the estate released Babworth House for sale and lodged plans with the local council to subdivide the property into lots for small apartment buildings. Woollahra Council decided that larger lots, which would allow tower buildings, made 'better town planning sense' and attempted to amend the intended approval while simultaneously resuming the land at the asking price of £145,000. This caused a local stir and a stalemate resulted.

The issue became a major controversy when the wealthy Queensland grazier-cum-philanthropist, Major H de V Rubin offered to donate the sum of £300,000 to buy the property and refit it as an after-care centre (nursing home) for St Vincent's Hospital. The story flooded the newspapers of the day and brought more than 300 people to a Woollahra Council meeting. Through the intervention of the Government Architect and the Minister for Local Government, the nursing home plan went ahead and the the site was saved from destruction.

320 'Elim'
1 Church Street, Burwood
1905 John Sulman
GC, V, NA

A large home in Queen Anne Style, with highly defined edges to openings and broad chimney.

●●●

Unfortunately, many of Sulman's non-residential buildings have been demolished. They include: St James Church in Turramurra, The AMP Society headquarters in Sydney, the Australian Joint Stock Bank and Sargood's warehouse in Sydney. His 1896 concept for a privately financed harbour tunnel was finally built 100 years later.

321 'Logan Brae'
24 Louisa Road, Birchgrove
c. 1905
GC, V, NA

The vestigial tower, tuck-pointed brickwork, florid fenestration and curlicue veranda timber mark this small house as typical Art Nouveau.

The ornate design is quite exceptional for Balmain, even though the area was experiencing a building boom at the time.

322 Fire Station
St Johns Road, Glebe
1906 Walter Liberty Vernon (NSWGA)
GC, V, A

Handsome idiosyncratic 'Federation Style' design by Walter Liberty Vernon (1846–1914) reminiscent of the work of CFA Voysey in England. Fire stations are one of the few types of building which survive commercial pressures and remain relatively intact. Compare with Vernon's other Fire Stations – Pyrmont, 1907, of Edwardian design (325); Darlinghurst, 1910, showing Mackintosh influence (340).

323

325

26 L 16

323 The State Library of New South Wales
Shakespeare Place and Macquarie Street, Sydney
1905–10 Walter Liberty Vernon (NSWGA)
(Mitchell Collection)
1929 RMS Wells (NSWGA) (Dixson Collection)
1934–42 Cobden Parkes (NSWGA) (main reading room)
1988 Andrew Andersons (NSWGA – Design Architect) (new wing)
Mitchell Library: Open Mon–Fri 9am–9pm; Sat 11am–5pm; Closed Sundays and public hols. (Reading Room: Open Sun 11am–5pm)
GC, V, A

Possessing the last 'Greek Temple' portico (symbolising a public institution) to be erected in Sydney, The State Library has a formal elegance backed by the intrinsic quality of materials. The site has been subject to a rolling building campaign since its inception in 1905.

The State Library of NSW was designed to be constructed in stages according to available funding. The first stage to house the Mitchell collections was constructed in 1906; the Dixson wing followed in 1929 and the great reading room was built during the 1930s. The Mitchell and Dixson wings share a large daylit basement area, made possible by perimeter excavation against the building face protected by a stone balustrade.

The entry foyer floor has a marble inlay map of Australasia, with polished marble stairs leading up to the gallery. The moulded door panels to the main reading room were donated by William Dixson and sculpted by Arthur Heishmann; they feature Australian explorers and Aboriginal life.

A major extension was undertaken in 1988. The new building comprises stack space, a new reading room, administration offices and a theatrette, with a considerable portion of the building (five storeys) built underground.

25 H 18

324 W Horace Friend Warehouse
197–199 Clarence Street, Sydney
1906 Robertson & Marks
GC, V, NA

Robertson & Marks were perhaps the best exponents in Sydney of HH Richardson's American Romanesque. Their extensive range of warehouses was built on the wave of optimism following Australia's federation.

25 E 18

325 Pyrmont Fire Station
Gipps Street and Pyrmont Bridge Road, Pyrmont
1907 Walter Liberty Vernon (NSWGA)
GC, V, NA

The Pyrmont Fire Station is an idiosyncratic Edwardian design by Walter Liberty Vernon (1846–1914), taking advantage of design freedom permitted by fire stations. The brickwork is of high quality and the fanciful corner tower is particularly notable.

•••

This building has been recently reopened as a functioning fire station.

•••

Walter Liberty Vernon (Liberty was his mother's maiden name) was both a professional soldier and an architect. In England, he had served in the 4th Battalion of the Oxfordshire Light Infantry.

In January 1855, after his arrival in Australia, Vernon joined the NSW Lancers and gained his commission in March of the following year. In 1893, he was promoted to captain and, four years later, he commanded the contingent of NSW Lancers at Queen Victoria's Diamond Jubilee.

Vernon's military ascendancy continued as he became lieutenant-colonel of the 1st Australian Light Horse Regiment (originally the NSW Lancers) and finally colonel of the 2nd Light Horse Brigade from 1907–10.

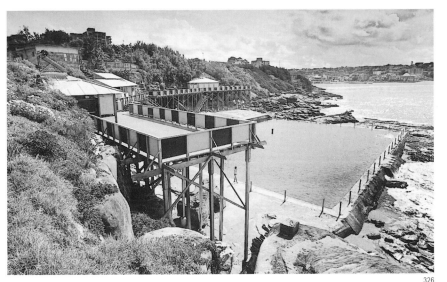

326

326 Wylie's Sea Baths
Neptune Street, Coogee Bay
1907 HA Wylie
1993–95 Allen Jack + Cottier (repairs and renovations)
GC, V, A

The Sydney area has many harbour and sea baths, but none with such a spectacular setting as Wylie's Baths at South Coogee. The elevated timber sun decks are of special interest, erected by local carpenters under Wylie's direction to inch out valuable space above the pool. It was one of the earliest pools in which mixed sex bathing was allowed, following the breaking down of rigid Victorian mores. A serious swimmer's pool, it was the home of the first Australian Swimming Championships held in 1911, and was for many years a training venue for some of Australia's international standard swimmers including Mina Wylie, Fanny Durack and Annette Kellerman (who lived at No. 7 Neptune Street).

By the 1980s, the pool structures were in a state of dilapidation and decay. A plan for reconstruction and repairs was commenced by Randwick City Council in 1993.

The council's architects, Allen Jack + Cottier, were able to salvage the structural posts, but almost all of the remaining timberwork was rotten. The design intention was to evoke the atmosphere of the baths during the 1950s, which is how most of the locals still remember them. The chequerboard colour scheme of the timber cladding was used as a design reference point, together with the pyramidal roofs from the original 1907 design, in an effort to retain the flavour of the baths' colourful history.

•••

Interestingly, a similar new structure, if conceived today, would be unthinkable on environmental grounds.

327 The Royal Sydney Golf Club
Kent Road, Rose Bay
1908 Maurice B Halligan
GC, V, A

Established on what is now a particularly valuable site, The Royal Sydney Golf Club has distinct Scottish overtones in the design of the pyramid-roofed tower and adjoining building. It was designed by Maurice Bernard Halligan (1862–1926), who had completed about twenty works in private practice from 1888 to 1907, including The Surrey Hotel, the IOOF Building in Elizabeth Street and the wonderful Tooths malt houses at Mittagong next to the southern railway. This was his last major design commission before forming a partnership with FHB Wilton, with whom he later designed the Dymocks Building in George Street.

328 'The Crossways'
50 Martin Road, Centennial Park
1908 Waterhouse and Lake
1990s Espie Dods (major alterations)
GC, V, NA

This large house from the early days of the Waterhouse and Lake partnership breaks away from overt decoration and presents the then voguish 'stylessness'.

Below: Living level plan, 'The Crossways' (1908)

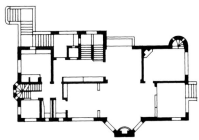

329

329 The Downing Centre

Former Mark Foy's Department Store
*Cnr 143–147 Liverpool, Elizabeth and
Castlereagh Streets, Sydney*
*1908 McCredie & Anderson (first two floors
and plaza)*
1928 Ross & Rowe (top four floors)
1991 NSWGA (conversion to law courts)
GC, V, A

Before closing for business in 1980 after the drift of retail to the northern CBD, the Piazza store of Mark Foy's was one of Australia's most famous shopping landmarks. It was the show-piece of Mark Foy's three emporiums and showrooms, all located along Elizabeth Street. This building was the first opulent department store with natural lighting and lavish finishes in Sydney, making the project a great success. The architects Arthur McCredie (1852–1926) and Arthur Anderson (1869–1942) toured Europe to inspect retail stores, choosing Bon Marché in Paris as their model. The original three-storey facade featured terracotta panels and glazed bricks imported from the United Kingdom. The names of various departments such as millinery, hosiery and gloves were set in mosaics which can still be seen along the Elizabeth Street elevation. The original plan called for these mosaics to reach as far as Goulburn Street.

Major extensions by Herbert Ross (1868–1937) extruded the walls a further four floors, rebuilt the turreted mansards and re-erected the glazed tile details at roof level. The new fire-proof reinforced concrete structure was technologically advanced, with large spans and hexagonal columns. Unfortunately, the old interior structure, delicate glass roof, ornamental ceilings and glazed dome were lost as a result, and replaced with a ballroom and exhibition area at the new roof level. The store was a fabulous social and financial success until World War II. It is connected to the underground railway at Museum Station by a tunnel which still bears the Mark Foy's name set into the subway walls in ceramic tiles.

330 House

58 Murdoch Street, Cremorne
1908 HA Wilshire
GC, V, NA

An example of early two-storey flat roof along the lines of philanthropist George Sydney Jones.

*Below: Ground floor plan,
58 Murdoch Street, Cremorne (1908)*

331

332

55 D 16

331 Royal Australian Navy establishment

Former Royal Edwardian Victualling Yard and
Ordnance Stores
Wharfs No. 17 and 18 Darling Island, Pyrmont
1903–08 Walter Liberty Vernon (NSWGA)
1995 Jackson Teece Chesterman Willis
(conservation and refit)
GC, V, NA
Soon after the complete revamp of Darling
Harbour in 1901, these large brick buildings
were constructed to keep stores for the
Australia, India and China stations of the Royal
Navy. Built partially on rock and partially on
hardwood piles, they were designed with electric
lifts and had access to road and rail. Still
retained by the navy, the buildings are best
viewed from Point Street **(409)**.

20th-Century Revivals

After the collapse of Victorian ornamentation,
architects returned to a variety of traditional
languages in a much more stripped down form
in an effort to simplify what had become a
rather complicated art. Neo-Classical Revival
and Greek Revival continued in Government
work, while the commercial image was
momentarily reconstructed through Late Gothic
Revival. During the 1920s, this style was seized
upon for churches and colleges, cinemas and
high-rise office buildings, but not for warehouses
and other utilitarian structures. The style was
loosely based on English Perpendicular,
embracing sculptured surfaces either in stucco
(State Theatre, **417***) or, in the case of stone*
(Scots Church, **416***), in pre-carved panels which*
were attached to the face of the building.   *JH*

26 M 17

332 Art Gallery of New South Wales

Art Gallery Road, The Domain
1904–09 Walter Liberty Vernon (NSWGA)
1971 Edward Herbert Farmer (NSWGA)
1980s Andrew Andersons (NSWGA) (extensions)
GC, V, A
At Sydney's great International Exhibition of
1879–80, a building was set aside for a fine arts
display. When the exhibition closed, the exhibits
became the nucleus of a government collection.
The Governor, Lord Carrington, opened the
original building by WH Hunt just before 1885.
It has since been demolished.

After Federation, the National Art Gallery (as
it was then known) was rebuilt in The Domain
by NSW Government Architect Walter Liberty
Vernon (1846–1914). This was the penultimate
example of the long established, but by then
overdone, use of the neo-Greek temple as a
portico for a major public institution in Sydney
(the final application of the Greek Temple front
was the State Library of NSW **(323)**). The
conservative design demanded by the Sydney
arts establishment must have challenged
Vernon's strong Arts and Crafts sensibilities.

The 1971 addition almost doubled the
exhibition space, from 2000 to 4900 square
metres. Flexible spaces were created using a
system of movable screen walls and lighting,
relating to ceiling modules. A grey-toned rough
mixture of concrete was used to blend with the
sandstone of the old building.

Completed in 1988, the Captain Cook
Bicentenary Wing creates a sense of light-filled
open space. Glimpses of the outside address the
problem of museum fatigue by redirecting
viewers' concentration by momentarily
distracting them. More recently, and as part of
the Open Museum, sculptures have been
positioned along the entry road.

91

333

26 L 16

333 'Wyoming'

175–181 Macquarie Street, Sydney
1909–11 John Burcham Clamp
GC, V, NA

This is one of the earliest examples of a 'high-rise' speculative building. It was specifically designed to provide medical suites for the growing number of practitioners associated with the Sydney Hospital in Macquarie Street. 'Wyoming' was commissioned by John O'Brien, a grazier who had sold his property of the same name near Junee in central west New South Wales, allowing him to invest in a number of city projects (see 'Astor', **403**). Initially a six-storey building (as exhibited at the Third Biennale Exhibition), it was revised to eight storeys; a reflection of the economic prosperity of the period from 1901–14.

The building was designed by John Burcham Clamp (1869–1931), a gold medallist of the Institute of Architects (NSW) who was a prominent Freemason and the Building Surveyor for the Anglican diocese of Sydney. He was regarded as an efficient planner and sound constructor with Arts and Crafts leanings, which were established during his training under Harry C Kent. Clamp bridged the romantic styles of the late 19th century with the rational and functional approach of commercial 20th-century architecture. Elegantly conceived, the sandstone-trimmed brickwork, with its alternating balconies and oriels facing Macquarie Street, has Art Nouveau decorative touches which avoid the 'functionalist' brick banding which appeared over the next few years.

The first tenants of 'Wyoming' included an occulist, an orthodontist, pharmacists, dental surgeons, physicians, opthalmic surgeons, orthopaedic surgeons, dermatologists and a laryngologist. Except for some upgrading of essential services and the conversion of the basement to a car park, the building is largely the same today as it was eighty-five years ago, anticipating a building of the same height to be built to the north.

•••

'Wyoming' is owned by the Albert family of music industry fame, who built 'Boomerang' (408) at Elizabeth Bay. The top floor is the Albert Group Headquarters.

25 H 17

334 RTA House

Warehouse offices
Cnr 120–122 Clarence and 44 King Streets, Sydney
1909 Spain & Cosh; 1912 (two floors added)
1981 Allen Jack + Cottier (internal refurbishments)
GC, V, NA

Colonel Alfred Spain and Thomas Cosh (with Rupert Minnett) were fortunate in being appointed architects for the Board of Fire Commissioners of New South Wales. From about 1895, 'fireproof' construction was introduced worldwide, which either took the form of terracotta shielded steel or reinforced concrete, in which the firm was able to claim special expertise. Externally, their designs were articulate and well engineered. Warehouses built in the city from 1895 to 1920 often incorporated large-scale facade compositions using loadbearing brickwork with sandstone trim or sandstone arches, and this building is no exception.

336

335 'Rochester' ('Lorne')
63 Beecroft Road, Beecroft
1909 George Sydney Jones; 1970s (repairs by Peter Cook)
GC, V, NA

This is one of three surviving houses in the Pennant Hills area (another being 'Barncleuth', The Crescent, Pennant Hills) by the philosopher architect George Sydney Jones (1865-1927), who experimented with the first examples of modern house architecture in Sydney. Both a naturalist and a nationalist, Jones promoted a social theory of architecture, in which the very design of buildings would change society by suggesting a new way of living.

He proclaimed the technological virtues of the 20th century — the century of the flat roof, reinforced concrete and glass — as a means of escaping the social decay of the 19th century. Like the modernist architects to follow, such as Sir Arthur Stevenson, he also became involved in new hospital design and sanatoria (Women's Hospital, Paddington, Melbourne Hospital) preaching the values of functionalism, clean mind, clean spirit and environmental goodness.

Perhaps way ahead of his time, he imagined interiors of entirely smooth glass — which he

Below: Ground floor plan, 'Rochester' (1909)

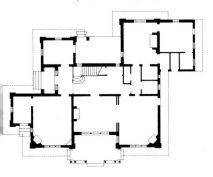

called 'sanitary architecture'. Jones published his own version of the 'ideal house' in 1906, with room sizes determined by the fresh air volumes worked out in hospital design, and flat roofs that were entirely roof gardens with pergola structures. Surprisingly Jones's ideas were widely accepted at the time — and he became a president of the Institute of Architects in NSW and later designed Australia's first administrative building in Canberra.

●●●

Born in Sydney, George Sydney Jones was the son of the Chancellor of the University of Sydney. Following Sydney Grammar School, he attended University College in London, studying architecture under Professor Roger Smith. His extensive world travels took him to India, the Middle East and Europe, which he put to good use on his return. He devoted his practice almost entirely to charitable and human causes such as asylums, children's homes and hospitals.

23 G 13

336 High Street Housing
High Street, Millers Point
1906-17, 1910 (kindergarten) Henry Deane Walsh
GC, V, NA

One of the earliest social housing projects in Sydney, it was built as part of the major Sydney Harbour Trust reconstruction to provide housing for local residents and waterside workers following slum resumptions. High Street is designed to fall from both ends to the centre, where a bridge over Hickson Road provided upper level access to timber wharves in Darling Harbour (since demolished). The brick and timber housing, consisting of two flats above reached by a centre stair, and two below, retain their original use today. Some descendants of the earliest tenants still occupy the buildings.

337 Travellers Rest Hotel
Former City Markets Building
9 Ultimo Road, Sydney
1910 George McRae
c. 1990 (converted to a hotel)
GC, V, A

The so-called 'Haymarket area' generally proved to be a far more successful location for market activity than previous siting attempts such as the Belmore Market (the Capitol Theatre) and the Queen Victoria Markets. George McRae (1858–1923), who had designed virtually all market buildings erected by Sydney City Council, produced a handsome polychrome elevation to Ultimo Road, with loading bays to the street at the upper level, in a style of projecting parapets which remained in use for about ten years.

338 National Cash Register House
Cnr York and Barrack Streets, Sydney
c. 1910
GC, V, NA

The freely interpreted classical ornamentation is typical of the early 20th century. The form of the building follows the American Beaux-Arts model of vertical division into the base, shaft and capital of the classical column.

339 Culwulla Chambers
Cnr Castlereagh and King Streets, Sydney
1911–12 Alfred Spain, Thomas Cosh &
Rupert Minnett
GC, V, A

Culwulla Chambers was Sydney's tallest building when built (excluding the AWA tower structure in York Street), and remained so until 1956. At 170 feet (52 metres), it challenged the structural ability of the engineers and inadvertently challenged the as then untested questions of

how tall a building should be, what it should look like and what were the appropriate sources. Both Spain and Cosh, who had travelled widely, drew on American precedents from personal experience. The up-to-the-minute inclusions listed were fireproof construction, high-speed lifts, ducted vacuum cleaning, postal box system, internal fire escapes and roof-top water storage.

The project was built by Dr Herbert Marks, a surgeon with offices in the recently completed medical tower 'Wyoming' in Macquarie Street (333). Investing in speculative buildings suddenly emerged as a fashionable and profitable pastime in a Sydney central business district which had hitherto been mainly owner/occupier or government buildings.

The height controversy following its completion led to the Heights of Building Legislation of 1912, which limited all buildings to 150 feet above the pavement (which lasted until 1956). The legislation divided approval powers between the State Government (controlling buildings over 100 feet) and the Sydney City Council (controlling buildings under 100 feet).

●●●

'Culwulla' was the name of a family property at Jamberoo on the New South Wales south coast, owned by Herbert and Walter's father, James Marks. A keen yachtsman, Walter Marks named his house in Darling Point 'Culwulla', and won many Australian sailing trophies in his successive yachts Culwulla I *to* Culwulla IV.

340

342

66 P 1

55 E 16

340 Darlinghurst Fire Station

Cnr Darlinghurst Road and Victoria Street, Darlinghurst
Designed 1910 Walter Liberty Vernon (NSWGA)
Completed 1912 George McRae (NSWGA)
GC, V, A

This stylised brick and stone fire station is by Walter Liberty Vernon (1846-1914), who was heavily influenced by the Arts and Crafts movement and the Glaswegian architect, Charles Rennie MacIntosh. It is interesting to compare Vernon's earlier Pyrmont Fire Station of 1907 **(325)**, which draws on more Edwardian vocabulary, and Vernon's Randwick Fire Station in The Avenue which is a different composition again. An attempt was defeated in recent years to convert the building into a nightclub and restaurant, and it retains its original function, with fire officers in readiness, reading newspapers or polishing their engines.

26 K 19

341 Banking House

Former Bank of New South Wales
226–230 Pitt Street, Sydney
1910-12 John Reid
1937 Bruce Dellit (ground floor alterations)
1981 (offices upgraded)
AC, V, A

The banking chamber of Banking House was built specifically to serve the horse racing bookmakers of the nearby Tattersalls Club, who had a 'tendency' to handle large amounts of cash. A feature of the bank was the large strong room at the lower level designed to hold large amounts of cash on the premises. In addition, this was possibly the first recorded bank project to include speculative office space at the upper levels. The trachyte, sandstone and brick exterior conceals a steel frame with fireproof terracotta floor system.

342 Former Ordnance Stores

Darling Island, Pyrmont
1909-12 Walter Liberty Vernon (NSWGA)
1994 Jackson Teece Chesterman Willis; Lend Lease Interiors; Philip Cox, Richardson, Taylor and Partners (Conservation Management Report)
GC, V, NA

Being the exception rather than the norm, this large, heavy brick building has an affinity with Venetian palaces in that it has a masonry superstructure supported by hardwood timber piles over water. It was designed by the NSW Government Architect to accommodate Commonwealth department needs, such as those of the military and postal service.

A remarkable and rare building, it makes no concession to its location, pretending to be situated firmly on land, right down to the provision of Victorian bluestone slabs on the floor. The building contained the first electrically driven internal lifts in New South Wales and its Italianate tower once held a water tank at its top, which served as a revolutionary sprinkler system.

The new work was controlled by Burra Charter conservation principles, which meant a high degree of respect was paid to the original building fabric while ensuring that the work could be reversed. The accommodation requirement for the conversion necessitated a transformation of the stores into a modern, serviced office space for more than 400 occupants, while retaining an exposed and open structure internally. This was achieved by channelling services behind 'clouds' of perforated metal, suspended from timber floors above, leaving the original massive timber beams and columns with cast-iron capitals visible. Some of the old machinery has been restored and is on show in the building.

1911 Royal Australian
Navy established

1911 Construction began on the
Trans–Continental Railway line

1912 American architect Walter
Burley Griffin designed Canberra

343

23 G 13

343 Palisade Hotel
Cnr Munn and Bettington Streets, Millers Point
1912 Henry D Walsh (Chief Engineer – Sydney Harbour Trust)
GC, V, A

This powerful looking hotel was built on the site of an earlier pub called Armstrong's Palisade Hotel. Before the massive building clearances began after the outbreak of bubonic plague, there were originally eleven pubs in the Sydney Harbour Trust area. They were replaced by just two, designed by the chief engineer Henry Walsh; The Palisade in Millers Point and the Big House Hotel in Sussex Street. The Palisade remains one of those rare hotels built before World War I which is wholly intact, both internally and externally. In 1920, when the rebuilt wharves were in full swing, the after-hours trade must have been something to behold, in strong contrast to the more genteel patronage of today. The slight art nouveau-ish period interiors include decorative glass and tiles, timber bar and a motifed staircase. The building is a prominent landmark in the Millers Point area, commanding clear views to the Harbour and beyond.

344 'Kingsclere'

56 Q 19

1 Greenknowe Ave and 48 Macleay Street, Potts Point
1912–13 Halligan & Wilton
GC, V, A

The matriarch of Potts Point apartments, 'Kingsclere' was the first Manhattan-style apartment building erected in Sydney. Built by

Sir Alexis Albert of the Albert Music fame, it was often temporary home to musicians, conductors and divas visiting Sydney. As one of the first examples of high-rise accommodation, and built before co-operative housing schemes (company title) and strata titling were introduced, it survived in remarkably original condition as a rental building until the 1990s.

The nine-storey building, featuring 250 square metre four-bedroom apartments, was fitted with the latest technology, including two automatic passenger lifts, 'telephonettes' (intercoms) for tradesmen to each flat, and possibly the first installation of electric lighting and power throughout. Many of the original bakelite light switches and power points survive, as do the original parquet floors. This is because individual flats were not in private ownership until 1995, when a strata plan was drawn up and each sold off. It may have no car parking, but it does have individual storage rooms for each apartment under the slate roof, where a cinema had been originally proposed (it was refused on the grounds of it being a fire risk). Its vigorous form and bold, simple detailing show the transition from the heavily ornamented 19th century building to the more functional modern structures. When completed, it was the tallest building on the Potts Point ridge, commanding views of the city and the harbour.

•••

Potts Point apartment buildings to follow Kingsclere include 'Manar' in Macleay Street (1919), 'Byron Hall' (1929), 'Wychbury' (1934), 'Birtley Towers' (1934), 'Wyldefel Gardens' (1935) and 'Macleay-Regis' (1939).

345

236 G 8

345 'Eryldene'
17 Macintosh Street, Gordon
1913 W Hardy Wilson
Conservation work by Clive Lucas & Partners
GC, V, A

Described as Australia's first architectural historian, W Hardy Wilson (1881–1955) was an exponent of colonial Georgian architecture (he closely studied the buildings of Sydney's first architect, Francis Greenway), which he fused with 'a technique gathered from the masterpieces of Italy and the magnificent modern architecture of the USA'. In the summer house and in the garden, he tried to combine Chinese and Greek cultures as well, making him a modern multiculturalist! The garden surrounding 'Eryldene' is outstanding, with its Chinese pavilion and study building, dovecote, fountains and camellias. The client, Professor EG Waterhouse, was a renowned camellia expert. Hardy Wilson's own much-criticised house was 'Purulia' **(354)**.

•••

Other houses designed by Hardy Wilson include: the Lionel Lindsay house 'Meryon', named after the French etcher Charles Meryon, 7 Burns Road, Wahroonga, and the Thomas W Garrett House, 34 Hastings Road, Warrawee (1919).

Below: Ground floor plan, 'Eryldene' (1913)

26 L 18

346 Registrar General's Department
Prince Albert Road, Sydney
1913 Walter Liberty Vernon (NSWGA)
GC, V, A

Inspired by the neighbouring cathedral, this Tudor Gothic design could nevertheless only belong to the 20th century when subjected to close examination. Behind the sandstone walls and slate roof are fully reinforced concrete floors and steel framing, and functionally organised interiors.

26 K 17

347 Castlereagh Chambers
Formerly Usher's Hotel
64–68 Castlereagh Street, Sydney
1914 attrib. to Wilson Neave & Berry
1925 Ross & Rowe (alterations)
1961 (converted to offices)
BC, V, A

This was once one of Sydney's small and elegant boutique hotels, designed by a conservative firm who preferred the gentle Georgian architecture often referred to by W Hardy Wilson.

24 K 15

348 Education Department Building
35–39 Bridge Street, Sydney
1912–14 George McRae (NSWGA)
GC, V, A

George McRae (1858–1923) had been Sydney City Architect between 1889 and 1897, designing a considerable number of council buildings including the Queen Victoria Markets **(257)**. By this stage, the Greek temple and the Italian palazzo had finally disappeared as symbols for government buildings, leaving the French-inspired Beaux-Arts style to influence composition. Although bulk overwhelms detail, the massing and use of materials contribute significantly to the Macquarie Place streetscape.

349

350

| 26 J 17 | 65 F 6 |

349 Commonwealth Banking Corporation Head Office

Cnr Martin Place, Pitt and Rowe Streets, Sydney
1912–16 John Kirkpatrick (Martin Place frontage)
1929–33 EH Henderson & F Hill (CDW, Pitt Street frontage)
GC, V, A

This is one of the first buildings to utilise a fully steel frame structure in Sydney. References are made to the lavish interiors of New York style skyscrapers, and little expense was spared on surface decoration or the quality of polished stones. The exterior, traditionally styled and heavily detailed, was later immortalised as the Commonwealth Bank money box issued to every school child who opened an account. It is monumental both in character and materials, and a key building in the Martin Place streetscape, previously established by Barnet's General Post Office **(203)**.

•••

John Kirkpatrick was one of the most commercially successful architects in Sydney, but was much despised by the local architectural fraternity. He was the cousin of the Governor of the Commonwealth Bank, Denison Miller, and employer of his cousin's son in his own architectural practice.

•••

In 1912, John Kirkpatrick was not only appointed architect for all new Commonwealth Bank buildings throughout Australia (a vast commission), he was also appointed in 1918 sole architect for the homes of all returned servicemen. Since the Returned Servicemen's Commission was funded and directed by the Commonwealth Bank, needless to say, he was derided by both his peers and the Institute of Architects for exploiting family connections.

350 Strickland Flats

Cnr Meagher, Balfour and Cleveland Streets, Chippendale
1913–14 Robert H Broderick
GC, V, A

Named in honour of NSW Governor Strickland, this is the first example of purpose-built workers' housing provided by Sydney City Council designed soon after the New South Wales government enabled council-built social housing. The design was exemplary for its day, achieving an extremely high population density within a relatively compact plan. The original design was for two buildings, providing 134 flats. However, only one building was completed before the outbreak of World War I halted the project. The sanitary provisions included private bathrooms, lavatories, rooftop laundries and garden areas, generally not found in the terrace slum resumptions which this design was intended to replace.

A second building went to an open architectural competition, won by Reid and Sons, but was never built.

•••

It was not until 1912 that the New South Wales State Parliament finally acquiesced and passed the long overdue legislation which enabled the City Council to build social housing. Although considerable slum clearances had already taken place, the council did not have the power, until 1912, to actually build housing in their stead.

352

194 P 20	23 H 15

351 'Mount Wilga' (Hospital)
Rosamond Street, Hornsby
1913–14 H Marcus Clarke & John Thomas Day
AC, V, A

'Mount Wilga' was the grandest of three houses built by the department store magnate Henry Marcus Clarke. The city residence was at Dulwich Hill, the summer house at Mt Wilson and this, the winter residence, was situated on 95 hectares of land on the 'upper paradise' of the North Shore.

The owner worked directly with a draftsman and the foreman, fusing Italian materials with the grand villa style of US east coast houses. Interiors are oak lined with a variety of plasterboard and panel designs, including native flowers and musical instruments. Materials include Italian tiles, pottery and marble, and sandstone quarried from the site. Unfortunately, Clarke died just prior to the building's completion.

352 St Patrick's Hall
133–137 Harrington Street, Sydney
1914 Hennessy & Hennessy
AC, V, NA

Following on from Sheerin & Hennessy, the father-and-son practice of Hennessy and Hennessy was still favoured for Roman Catholic buildings. This brick hall is an eclectic amalgam of contemporary trends in architecture, while their churches were predictably Gothic Revival. Attempting to incorporate the 'stylessness' of its period, this building adopts the asymmetrical massing of the Queen Anne Revival, striated masonry of Gothic Revival, Romanesque arching and Art Nouveau details.

Unfortunately, this building may be demolished to make way for a high-rise development.

Below: Ground floor plan, 'Mount Wilga' (1914)

353

355

46 P 3

353 'Brent Knowle'
31 Shellcove Road, Neutral Bay
1913-14 Waterhouse & Lake
GC, V, NA

Neutral Bay and Cremorne were developing alternative 'society' suburbs at the turn of the century, connected to the city by ferry. Romantics and humanists with Arts and Crafts tendencies found a strong bond in the distant and relatively heavily landscaped settings around the northern bays of Sydney Harbour. 'Brent Knowle', perhaps referring to Brent Knoll in Somerset, was commissioned of Bertrand James Waterhouse (1876-1965) and John Hamilton Lake (1872-1924) by the broker and financier, Major Joseph Henry Booker, only one year before his death from a longstanding paralytic illness. The design recognised both the automobile and the horse and carriage, with servant areas looking out onto an enclosed south court. Perhaps conscious of his ailing health, Booker requested a fully self-contained apartment on the ground floor, leaving the

remainder of the house for parties and entertaining. The references to English Arts and Crafts, particularly the work of Charles FA Voysey (1857-1941) are unmistakable, and it established a design trend which continued in the Neutral Bay area for at least another fifteen years.

●●●

See also 10 Bertha Road and Claudea Ave (1920) — stucco with exposed timber detailing; 26 and 35 Milsons Road, Cremorne (1920) — bay windows, shingle walls and false roof lines;

215 G 15

354 'Purulia'
16 Fox Valley Road, Wahroonga
1915-16 W Hardy Wilson
GC, V, NA

The architect W Hardy Wilson's (1881-1955) own house represented a romantic return to colonial times in its symmetrical form and detail, against popular taste. In 1916, its stark simplicity caused an outcry, and was described by critics as a 'tram shed' with 'pokey' rooms. Neighbours strongly opposed any obvious deviation from the 'Federation' style of the day and petitioned the council to have it demolished claiming that it would lower the value of their houses.

●●●

'Purulia' was described as 'a maidless flat.... the maid is only in the process of vanishing ... the kitchen becomes more and more a family room ... the kitchen adjoins the living room and the front door ... as the walls arose square, bleak and factory like, consternation filled the souls of neighbours dwelling in multangular villas ... their indignation could not be contained. They foresaw depreciated values all along the road.'

Below: Ground floor plan, 'Brent Knowle' (1914)

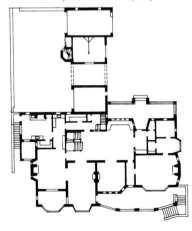

357

| 76 Q 11 | 56 P 17 |

355 'The Bungalow'

39 Robertson Road, Centennial Park
1915 John Burcham Clamp and
Walter Burley Griffin
GC, V, NA

John Burcham Clamp (1869–1931) and Walter Burley Griffin (1876–1937) were partners for one year after a chance meeting in the United States of America in 1914. This is one of their very few collaborations (1915 was a year of turmoil for Griffin) and the design is more Griffin than Clamp with its stylised Arts and Crafts treatment of fences, gates and a spacious columned veranda.

●●●

See also JB Clamp's (& McKellar's) 'Babington', 2 Martin Road, Centennial Park (1919), with its Queen Anne curved bay front, and Clamp's earlier 'Kirkoswold', 22 Warrawee Avenue (1906), built for John Meloy.

| 26 K 18 |

356 The Trust Building

Formerly The Daily Telegraph Building
72 Castlereagh Street, Sydney
1916 Robertson & Marks
1934 Samuel Lipson (interior remodelled)
GC, V, A

One of the first of the new type of offices for daily newspapers. It reflects the composite influences of Beaux-Arts and Renaissance design principles on a reasonably compressed site by one of the city's foremost architectural firms. Compositional facade features are strongly emphasised, including the high elliptical and semicircular fenestration.

The refined banking chamber was a later interior remodelling by Samuel Lipson, who was considered one of the up-and-coming modernists having just completed the Anzac Memorial in Hyde Park (**427**).

357 Woolloomooloo Deep Sea Wharf

Cowper Wharf Road, Woolloomooloo
1910–14 Henry D Walsh
1925 (additional building)
PC, V, NA

The largest timber wharf of this variety in Sydney (and possibly the world), belonging to a family of heavy timber wharves designed by the chief engineer of the Sydney Harbour Trust. All of those in Darling Harbour and one in Walsh Bay have been demolished. This structure and four piers in Walsh Bay are all that remain. The massive hardwoods came from extensive first growth northern New South Wales forests, while the 1000 spliced piles which support the structure are up to 30 metres long, driven by pile drivers into the soft mud. At one time, the pier was used by the Navy for departing troops, while more recently it was used for unloading imported cars.

The wharf's future has been hotly debated, attracting comment in 1994 from the Prime Minister of the day that the building was an eyesore and should be demolished. It is currently part of a redevelopment proposal controlled by the Walker/Multiplex consortium employing architects Peddle Thorp and Walker and the Buchan Group from Brisbane. The tender proposal includes redevelopment of the adjoining land on Lincoln Crescent for apartments, together with a marina and a hotel/apartment complex on the water.

358

361

46 P 3

358 'The Cobbles'
49 Shellcove Road, Neutral Bay
1918 Peddle & Thorp
GC, NV, NA
Completed for the 'trustees of the estate of Captain Craig', the whimsical and rustic design by Peddle and Thorp featured an organically shaped fireplace of naturally rounded stones. The handbuilt fireplace occurs in a few examples in both Sydney and Melbourne. It echoes a 'return to nature' movement of home-made bungalows built between 1900 and 1940 on the northern shores of Sydney, and shows the direct influence of American architects Greene and Greene in the rustic timber detailing. Unlike a number of similar houses which have been demolished in recent years, 'The Cobbles' has survived in good condition.

●●●

Other houses by James Peddle from this period include: 'Grosvenor Cottage' for FE Bartholomew, 8 Grosvenor Street, Wahroonga; and 'Mount View' for Frederick Fleming, 102 Grosvenor Street, Wahroonga.

46 R 1

359 'Egglemont'
11 Cranbrook Avenue, Cremorne
1919 Esplin & Mould
GC, V, NA
An interesting version of the Californian bungalow by a firm of established architects in a builder idiom.

67 J 3

360 'Fenton'
8 Albert Street, Edgecliff
1919 Robin S Dodds
GC, V, NA
A modest stucco house influenced by Colonial Revival.

46 R 1

361 'Belvedere'
7 Cranbrook Avenue, Cremorne
1919 Alexander Stewart Jolly
GC, V, NA
This house was commissioned by the wealthy pastoralist Christian Stockman to be built on the recently created Cremorne Heights Estate. AS Jolly, a member of a timber milling family from Armidale in the northern tablelands district of New South Wales, was influenced by the Californian bungalow, especially the published reworkings of the architecture of Greene and Greene. His use of their designs was tempered by an appreciation of Frank Lloyd Wright's interest in materials. The twin brick gable end piers, wide overhanging roof lines, and *porte cochère* closely resemble the feel of Wright's early prairie houses, which are sensitively and skilfully executed. This is an architecturally significant house which predates the revival in Sydney of Wright's work some thirty years later.

●●●

See also House (1918), 18 Lavoni Street, Balmoral — romantic and picturesque use of rough stonework.

Below: Ground floor plan, 'Belvedere' (1919)

362

46 M 2

362 'The Gables'
16 Spruson Street, Neutral Bay
1920 Bertrand James Waterhouse
GC, V, NA

Perhaps the best-known of Waterhouse's shingle designs which were developed in the Cremorne and Neutral Bay area from 1908. It expands on the 'shingle style' of the Sydney architect Horbury Hunt (1838–1904), who had worked as a young architect in Boston and established the style in Sydney by the early 1890s. 'The Gables' takes its name from the steep pitched roof, shingled gables and picturesque forms. As the house was built in 1920, its shingles are actually terracotta and the dark walls are of matching brickwork. Built on the crest of a hill and surrounded by streets on three sides, with a flowering garden and ornamental garage, "The Gables' is probably the last example of its type, but no less for it. For other Waterhouse villas, see also 'Brent Knowle' (1914), 31 Shellcove Road (353), 'Ailsa' (1908), 33 Shellcove Road, and 37 Shellcove Road (1920) in Neutral Bay.

In 1919, the east coast of Australia suffered a devastating outbreak of influenza. To contain the outbreak, the New South Wales government prohibited all gatherings of more than three people, preventing the RAIA annual general meeting in February which would install the new president elect Charles Slatyer. An application in March to install the new council was refused by the Minister for Health. Permission was finally granted to hold the Annual General Meeting on 29 April 1919, when Slatyer was elected to office. Within a week (5 May 1919), Slatyer died from influenza.

•••

Surviving 90 years, BJ Waterhouse was a well-known and highly regarded figure in the architectural circles of Sydney. He was born in Leeds and travelled to Australia after completing his schooling in England. He commenced his part-time studies at Sydney Technical College while working for the architect John B Spencer, who had just completed the glass-roofed Strand Arcade (1891) between George and Pitt Streets. With his artistic eye and humanist approach, BJ Waterhouse, of the 1908 partnership Waterhouse and Lake, emerged as the gifted designer, with JH Lake securing the clients.

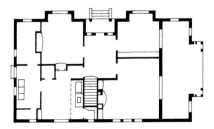

Left: Ground floor plan, 'The Gables' (1920)

The Moderne City
1920–1940

1920–1940

There was no clear line of demarcation between the Art Deco style, the Classical Revival style and Avant-garde Modern.

'Modern' was the label applied to buildings of all styles. 'Functionalist' was also used to describe the oft-stated demands of the style's adherents that every designed object should be 'functional' above all else.

In the 1920s, numerous styles were developed in parallel, with architects adopting different styles for different building types. The late 1920s were characterised by a revival of classicism which paralleled a general worldwide phenomenon. This classical revival continued in Sydney, particularly in residential work, through to the 1940s. It was strongly promoted by such key practitioners and theorists as Morton Herman and Leslie Wilkinson. By the 1930s, the classical decoration gradually began to leave the surface, revealing simple masses with fenestration puncturing the facades.

The shift between early 20th-century classicism, Art Deco and Avant-garde Modern was essentially related to the extent and literal use of decoration, and was a direct response to the perceived tradition of a building type. Where no tradition existed, the range of stylistic interpretation was varied.

The development of high-rise and low-rise occurred, as in America, along quite different parameters. The high-rise building is certainly a building type associated with the modern era, because it is only during this period that technological advances enabled its construction. In Sydney, the building of **Culwulla Chambers** was a catalyst for the 1912 *Height of Buildings Act*, which set the Sydney height limit at 150 feet (46 metres). As part of a general international trend, disdain for the skyscraper was common among the conservative architects and critics who believed that the commercial nature of the tall office building was incompatible with the art of architecture.

Some significant attempts were made in the 1920s to express the steel-framed structural system which was replacing the load-bearing external wall. The fireproofing requirements, however,

Resch's DA Dinner Ale Painting.

RB Coleman Signs

required that steel columns and beams be clad with stone, brick or terracotta, with the result that many facades continued to adopt a traditional expression. Technological modernity, symbolic of progress, was not always paralleled by the glass tower aesthetic normally associated with high-rise modernity. The **Royal Assurance Building** by Seabrook and Fildes was the first glass facade in Sydney, a trend that was not readily adopted until after World War II.

Banks, insurance companies and those well-established, conservative financial institutions preferred the continuity of classical styles. The stripped classical style, in which detail such as the column capitals were removed, was appropriate to the image they wished to create.

Some individual houses and group housing assumed a new Modernist appearance and adopted its progressive socialist ideals. William Crowle's units at **Wyldefel Gardens** were described as examples of Continental modern home planning and the 'most modern building of its kind in Australia'. Its arrangement promoted a community spirit considered to be one of the best aims of modern civic planning.

The social agenda of the Avant-garde Modern was generally adopted as part of the 'expressed positivism' of the housing reconstruction of the post-World War II period. The Commonwealth Housing Commission, the RAIA NSW Chapter Study Groups and the War Service Homes Commission were some of many organisations formed at this time. The architect assumed an important role in planning the suburban expansion of new subdivisions, using the principles espoused by Walter Burley Griffin in the 1930s and the MARS Group in the 1940s.

The 1920s, prior to the Depression, were characterised by the optimism of progress. The development and accessibility of technology reduced the traditional barriers of time and distance. Improved media for communication, the wireless, the gramophone and the motion picture increased knowledge of world events. In the 1930s, a greater awareness of European Modernism occurred. The development of the cinema and the dramatic increase of this building type led to the adoption of a modern style which included translations of both French Art Deco and German Expressionism. With increased accessibility, overseas influence on Australian architectural design came chiefly from three areas: architects who migrated to Australia, Australians who travelled to Europe and the United States, and the increased circulation of both lifestyle magazines and professional journals which provided indirect exposure to overseas trends.

Walter Burley Griffin, Leslie Wilkinson and an influx of European migrant architects, including Samuel Lipson and Aaron Bolot, were major influences in increasing the knowledge of Modern architecture from beyond Australia.

It was Walter Burley and Marion Mahony Griffin who introduced the Prairie School of architecture to Australia when they began practice in Sydney and Melbourne in 1914. Their arrival from Chicago, as the successful entrants in the Canberra competition, had increased the professional and popular exposure to American architecture, particularly that emanating from Chicago. In 1929, the Griffins established the Sydney harbourside suburb of Castlecrag, which incorporated modern planning principles and promoted a community spirit.

The introduction of the more genteel Mediterranean style owes

Evening dress in gold rayon by Lucy Secor c. 1938.

Powerhouse Museum, Sydney

a great deal to one man, Professor Leslie Wilkinson, who arrived in Sydney in 1918 to take up the first chair of architecture in an Australian university. Wilkinson, who had travelled extensively in Spain and Italy, recognised that Sydney had a Mediterranean climate, bright sunlight and a water-orientated topography, all of which were conducive to an architecture of simple shapes, light and shade, bleached pastel colours and accents of classical detail. His influence as a teacher, critic and juror of the prestigious Sulman Award resulted in the continuation of Mediterranean and classical architecture throughout the Modern period and into the 1940s.

Greater ease of transportation, the standardisation of professional qualifications and the lack of work resulted in an increase in overseas travel. By the early 1930s, approximately 20% of the architectural profession had obtained work in England and the United States. This departure was prompted by the Depression, which reached its nadir in 1932. However, the introduction of travelling scholarships, which encouraged recent graduates to work and travel overseas, was another incentive. Holland was a source of great interest for many travelling Australian architects and developments there were often reported in contemporary journals. Between 1921 and 1929, every state except Queensland had passed Acts of Parliament requiring architects to become registered and to meet specified minimum standards before being recognised. The rise of university courses in architecture further assisted the regulation of the profession and put it on a par with the British system.

Australians who travelled did not initially go in search of Modern work, because they were uniformly in ignorance of it. Arthur Baldwinson's original intention in departing for Europe in 1930 was to study at the Ecole des Beaux-Arts in Paris, but by the time of his departure his plan was to seek employment in London, which resulted in his encountering a radically different set of Avant-garde Modernist influences. Sydney Ancher departed Sydney in 1929 for a five-year period in Europe and England. Despite working in England, Ancher was quite unaware of Mies van de Rohe's work until he took a travelling holiday in Europe. He visited the 'Berlin Building Exhibition' in 1931 when, as he recalled, 'I was bowled over by it, I thought it quite marvellous ... we'd never heard his name before'. After the Berlin experience, he sought work in the office of the architect, Joseph Emberton, in London. Other noted Australian architects such as Walter Bunning also worked at this office while in the United Kingdom. In 1930, Morton Herman made contact with one of the original Modernists,

HS Goodhart-Rendel. Herman's interest in the historically significant architecture from England paralleled his interest in modern design. In 1937, on his return, Herman actively promoted both modern architecture and the protection of the historical architectural heritage.

Perspective of Bruce Dellitt's competition-winning design for the Anzac Memorial in Hyde Park, 1929

Mitchell Library, State Library of NSW

The Melbourne firm of Stephenson and Meldrum, which in the 1930s became Stephenson and Turner, was a particularly influential office. Arthur Stephenson made extensive trips overseas, encouraged and financed members of his firm to do likewise, and gave an excellent training to young aspiring architects. His hospitals gained him an international reputation and it was after his trip to Russia and America in 1932 that his designs shifted towards a Modern style. In recognition of his work, principally the Royal Melbourne Hospital, Stephenson was awarded the Gold Medal of the Royal Institute of British Architects, in 1954. It was an honour which had been bestowed on only a few architects, such as Frank Lloyd Wright and Walter Gropius, and the first to an Australian.

Emigrants from New Zealand, Canada and Australia were well established in London in the 1930s. One Englishman was to remark that it was their lack of English tradition that allowed them to accept the Modern Movement so completely. Architects such as Connell and Ward from New Zealand, Wells Coates from Canada and Raymond McGrath from Australia were all active in the English Modern Movement. Some, like Arthur Baldwinson, had direct exposure to the Modernist philosophy during his period of employment with Gropius in England in the 1930s.

Ancher returned to Sydney in December 1935, and formed a partnership with RA Prevost in 1936. Baldwinson returned in 1937 and was offered a position at Stephenson and Turner. Both architects, with other travellers such as Eric Andrews and Walter Bunning, were actively involved in the Australian formation of the Modern Architectural Research Society (MARS). This group consisted of Australians who had experienced Modernism first hand in Europe and through work experience in London. The group was based on the English Modern Movement group of the same name, which was associated with the CIAM Association. It was established in 1938 and continued until 1943. The Sulman Award was established in 1932, and its winners from 1938 on were dominated by Modernist style. A preference for design solutions with strong parallels to the contemporary work of Dutch, Scandinavian and German architects was particularly noticeable.

The increased circulation of magazines provided indirect exposure to overseas trends. Most publications arriving in Australia prior to 1914 were English, while there was a fair balance between British and American publications after 1918. After the 1918 armistice, and during the 1920s, the number of pamphlets or books about the bungalow and the American high-rise tower was quite considerable. These publications and the images prevalent in American movies reinforced knowledge and acceptance of American styles. The bungalow fused many ideas about the nature of housing and lifestyles during the period from 1913 to 1927. It reached its zenith in both style and popularity during the 1920s and lasted well into the next decade.

From 1934, the journals began to feature European modern houses consistently, and *Art in Australia* regularly featured 'modern' work. The publication of *Dutch Architecture of the 20th Century*, in 1926, and its availability to Australian architects, encouraged this interest. FRS Yorke published his *Modern Homes* in 1934 and Australian expatriate Raymond McGrath published his text *Twentieth Century Houses* in the 1930s, which included Australian examples. Sheldon Cheney's work *The New World*

Architecture, and *International Style*, both published in 1930, were available to Australian readers.

The work and publications of the mid-1930s show a growing acceptance towards European Modernism. While numerous examples from the 1930s exist, Modernism remained very much a minority movement until after World War II, when it became widely accepted, and Modernism or International Style dominated the architectural scenes until the 1960s. Discussions on Avante-garde Modernism, motivated by progressive social ideals, were rarely heard in Australia or written about in British architectural magazines in the late 1920s. The occasional articles that did appear were critical of the freakish quality of European Modernism. The first Australian Exhibition of International Architecture, which included a portion devoted to modern architecture, was opened in June 1927 in Sydney. The two reviews of the display, one by Wilkinson in the journal *Architecture*, and the other in *Australian Home Beautiful*, mentioned this modern work only in passing.

Painted breakfast set by Olive Nock (1893–1977).

Powerhouse Museum, Sydney

The concept of Modernism as a break with the past was not adopted until the mid-1930s, when returning Australian architects began to promote it. While houses of varied styles were described in terms of their free-flowing plans and large areas of glass, it was the flat roof that confirmed them as being modern, as Morton Herman's text *Building the Ideal Australian House* clearly indicates.

The concept of Modernism was generally applied to building types, construction, planning and aesthetics, and included a wider range of issues than normally associated with those examples illustrated in texts of the 1930s. The application varied such that Modernist technology was often sheathed in traditional facade or avant-garde aesthetic of traditional construction. Many practitioners had first-hand experience of the wide range of Modernist work. A specifically Australian response could be seen in much of the work, and strong parallels were drawn with the regionalist approach of the Scandinavian countries.

JENNIFER HILL

401

257 N 8

401 Walter Burley Griffin Houses, Castlecrag

*GSDA No. 1 Dwelling, 136 Edinburgh Road 1921
(seen in photo above)
GSDA No. 2 Dwelling, 140 Edinburgh Road 1921
Johnson House, 4 The Parapet 1921
Grant House, 8 The Parapet 1922
(Griffin's home)
Moon House, 12 The Parapet 1922
Cheong House, 14 The Parapet 1924
Mower House, 12 The Rampart
Guy House, 23 The Bastion 1925
Wilson House, 2 The Barbette 1930
Creswick House, 4 The Barbette 1926
Duncan House, 8 The Barbette 1934
Felstead House, 158 Edinburgh Road 1924
Fishwick House, 15 The Citadel 1929
Castlecrag Hospital (O'Malley House),
150 Edinburgh Road
Rivett House,148 Edinburgh Road
Griffin Centre Shops, Edinburgh Road 1924*

In 1912, having won the Federal Capital Competition for the town plan of Canberra, the Griffins came to Australia. Walter was appointed Federal Capital Director of Design and Construction. Both Walter and his wife, Marion, had practised in Chicago and worked with Frank Lloyd Wright.

Between 1894 and 1909, Marion had been Wright's chief designer and was held in high regard by him, while Walter had also worked with Wright in an associate capacity from 1901 to 1906. After problems arose in Canberra, the Griffins took the opportunity to put their ideals to the test in a model community in Sydney. Griffin formed a company, The Greater Sydney Development Association (GSDA), which purchased 650 acres at Middle Harbour in 1920 to create just such a community. He laid out the streets, designed the houses and established a pattern of behaviour to which the residents should subscribe. The buildings listed to the left are the surviving legacy of Griffin, his wife Marion and his partner Eric Nicholls in the creation of the suburb of Castlecrag.

●●●

The philosophy and political ideas of Walter and Marion Griffin were dominant factors in the architectural development of Castlecrag and its community life. The suburb had a social centre, a neighbourhood circle which met every month (in which everyone participated), and an open-air theatre which used a stone outcrop as a stage. Plays were produced by the residents, some of whom were influenced by the anthroposophical concepts of the theatre as an important aspect of spiritual communication. There were drawing and dancing lessons and, in the 1930s, Mr and Mrs Eric Nicholls and Marion Griffin started a school based on the writings of Rudolph Steiner.

Below: Plan of the Moon House by Walter Burley Griffin 12 The Parapet, Castlecrag (1922)

294 M 3

402 'Brookby Lodge'
*127 Homebush Road, Strathfield
1923 AL Buchanan
GC, V, NA*
A fabulous Arts and Crafts mansion inspired by the English architect CF Voysey.

403

404

24 L 15

403 'The Astor'

123 Macquarie Street, Sydney
1922–23 Donald Thomas Esplin and
Stuart Mill Mould
GC, V, A

The Astor is the grande dame of elegant high-rise apartment living in Sydney. In addition to the relatively large area devoted to each apartment over the 13 floors, the lower levels included a convenience store, hairdresser, patisserie, liquor shop and florist. The basement restaurant, The Macquarie, was connected to the upper apartments by internal dumb waiters for those residents wishing to dine in.

The scheme was devised by John O'Brien, former grazier turned Macquarie Street property developer (see 'Wyoming', **333**). He used the building as an example in his campaign to legitimise apartment ownership by company title, and targeted the well-to-do. The company, Astor Ltd, with O'Brien as chairman launched the 'Co-operative Homes Scheme' which enabled apartment ownership with prices ranging from £1,541 to £2,177. After a number of sites had been amalgamated, an architectural competition was held and won by Sydney architects Thomas Esplin and Stuart Mould Snr, of whom Mould was the well travelled design partner.

Conservatively modern, the building melds two architectural idioms. The window openings show an obvious expression of the simple concrete framework. This relatively 'modern' interpretation is topped with a traditional neo-Classical cornice and three Ionic columns for good measure. Semicircular windows on the third floor aim to divide the appearance of the structure into 'base' and 'tower', like a column shaft. The roof incorporates a garden terrace for residents. A favourite accommodation of early feminists, the Geach family (Portia, Florence and Miriam) were often seen in their Buick driven by a uniformed chauffeuse. Other famous owners include SH Ervin (after whom the National Trust gallery is named), Ruby Rich (an early women's activist), Dame Edith Walker, and the author and actor Barry Humphries.

48 R 10

404 'Greenway'

24 Wentworth Road, Vaucluse
1922–23 Leslie Wilkinson
1951 Leslie Wilkinson (three-storey addition)
GC, V, NA

The architect Leslie Wilkinson (1882–1973) came to Australia from England in 1918, having been appointed Australia's first professor of architecture at Sydney University. He developed a regional approach whereby the style and details of Georgian and Mediterranean architecture were blended, taking into account the site, the landscape and the climate. Wilkinson was well respected as a teacher and was affectionately known as 'the Professor'. This is his own house, 'Greenway', built four years after his arrival and named in honour of the early Sydney architect Francis Greenway, whom he much admired.

Below: Ground floor plan 24 Wentworth Road (1922)

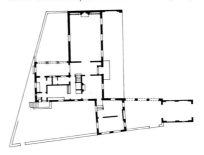

● 1923 Work commences on
the Sydney Harbour Bridge

● 1923 A savoury yeast spread called 'Vegemite'
is created and becomes popular

● 1924 Andrew 'Boy' Charlton wins
Olympic gold medal and sets new world
swimming record for the 1500 metres

405

65 A 6

405 Physics Building
University of Sydney, Darlington
1926 Professor Leslie Wilkinson
GC, V, A

This long, symmetrical building reflecting
Beaux-Arts circulation planning and Spanish/
Florentine Classical proportions and details is by
the university's first Professor of Architecture,
Leslie Wilkinson (1882–1973). When completed,
it presented a powerful new image to the
university, which until then consisted of
compact courtyard buildings with strong neo-
Gothic overtones. Its design embraces many
details of Wilkinson's architectural language
which were used in various ways during his
lifetime. Of particular note are the plastered and
colour-washed external walls, which he was
promoting to become the standard for all
university buildings. A frieze is positioned across
the lowered central section of the building. Two
plaques on each tower by the sculptor Raynor
Hoff commemorate the works of Archimedes,
Galileo, Newton and Maxwell.

406 National Australia Bank
26 J 17

Former Commercial Banking Co of Sydney
(Head Office)
343 George Street, Sydney
1920–25 Kent & Massie
GC, V, A

The head office of the Commercial Banking
Company of Sydney was completed just prior to
the adjoining Bank of New South Wales. As a
pair, they terminate the western end of Martin
Place at George Street. The design, by Harry
Kent (1852–1938) together with his third partner
HH Massie, was the most important of the 185
buildings completed by the partnership (which
lasted until 1930). The construction employs
both steel and reinforced concrete while the

neo-Classical trachyte facade produces a strong
civic presence with the adjacent Bank of NSW.
The ground floor banking chamber features a
coffered ceiling, massive marble columns and an
elaborate balustraded staircase with an elliptical
landing overlooking the chamber.

407 Rookwood Crematorium
294 H 2

Barker Road, Strathfield
1925–27 Frank I'Anson Bloomfield
GC, V, A

Convincing applications of the Mediterranean
style to crematoria may be seen at Woronora
(430) and Rookwood. The semicircular arched
arcade with circular decals, masonry tower
and shallow pitched roof of the Rookwood
Crematorium give the building a calm mosque-
like appearance that inspires contemplation.

Mediterranean Style
*The circular arches, pastel tones and terracotta
tiles of Spanish architecture slowly appeared
in Sydney through the work of architects Hardy
Wilson, Leslie Wilkinson and Neville Hampson.
Their arrival came at a time when academic
arguments were being put forward for an
'Australian architecture' based on Mediterranean
styles which were 'gentle, romantic and
timeless'. After the 1930s, the Spanish style
became a popular middle-class idiom alongside
neo-Tudor, and it is frequently seen in the
eastern and northern suburbs of Sydney. An
early application of Mediterranean design to
non-residential buildings occurred in the
crematoria, introduced after World War I. The
restful arcades and soft rounded forms provided
an atmosphere of tranquillity and peace.*

407

408

56 R 18

408 'Boomerang'

42 Billyard Avenue, Elizabeth Bay
1926 Neville Hampson
GC, V, NA

'Boomerang' was a highly publicised mansion commissioned by the music publisher Frank Albert, who lived there until his death in 1962. It was named after his company's famous trademark — the 'Boomerang' — which was the brand name of his popular songbooks and a range of mouth organs. The large pressed metal 'professional boomerang', the 'large boomerang' and the 'miniature boomerang' reeded mouth organs were very popular at home and an intimate companion for virtually every Australian soldier and sailor during World War I.

Prior to drawing up plans for 'Boomerang', the little-known Neville Hampson, an English architect, travelled extensively in search of inspiration in Europe and California. Hampson brought the much-publicised Spanish hacienda style to Sydney, with the epic stylisations of Hollywood movie moguls. A popular myth of the time was that 'Boomerang' was a reflection of Randolph Hearst's Castle at San Simeon in California, designed by Julia Morgan. Inspired by the example of 'Boomerang', the Spanish style was soon adopted as an alternative to the Italianate or Florentine forms of Leslie Wilkinson. It was fashionable, flamboyant and thought to be climatically suitable for harbourside suburbs.

The house has a strong axial plan which leads from the *porte cochère* to the water's edge. The interior is lavishly decorated. Each bedroom has its own suite of bathroom, dressing room and balcony, while the master bedroom has folding panels and concealed robes. The guest bedroom has its own private cloister balcony. The large compartmented basement level has a cinema seating 40, originally fitted with two 35-mm arc projectors, film storage and film processing rooms, with a separately accessed marine workshop for the Albert yachts.

●●●

Hampson also designed a smaller single-storey house in Spanish style for the well-known local retailers, the Grace family, in Victoria Street, Watsons Bay.

●●●

Boomerang, which has no further subdivision potential, is one of Australia's most expensive city houses, trading in October 1996 for a record $15 million.

●●●

The Spanish style soon appeared in public buildings, with Robertson and Mark's Bondi Surf Pavilion (1930), Balmoral Bathers Pavilion and the Sacred Heart Catholic Church (1934) on the Pacific Highway at Pymble.

Below: Living level plan, 'Boomerang' (1922)

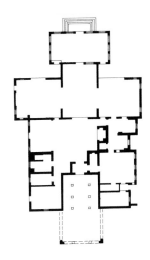

1927 Charles Kingsford Smith and Charles Ulm create a new round–Australia flight record of 10 days 5 hours and 15 minutes

1927 Federal Parliament meets for the first time in the Australian Capital Territory

409

55 C 16

26 J 18

409 Point Street Flats

Former 'Way's Terrace' Workers Housing
12–20 Point Street, Pyrmont
1923–26 Leslie Wilkinson (with JC Fowell)
AC, V, NA

An unusual Mediterranean style apartment building in the form of a continuous terrace house block built for Sydney City Council on a distinctive rock eminence. Its Mediterranean character derives from the use of arches, balconies, exposed rafters, decorative valance boards, tiled roofs and cement rendered walls. Built as social housing, the execution of the design is less than Leslie Wilkinson's (1882–1973) more typical work for private clients. The original design included valanced timber 'Juliet' balconies. The apartment building, which enjoys stunning views over the city, is a rare component of Sydney's building history.

●●●

Wilkinson joined with Joseph Fowell, an architect at Sydney University, to undertake this project.

Below: Perspective watercolour, 'Ways Terrace' (1923), by Leslie Wilkinson (Courtesy David Wilkinson)

410 'The Block'

Dymocks Building
424-430 George Street, Sydney
1926-28 FHB Wilton
1928-32 (additions)
GC, V, A

Unlike its namesake in Melbourne, 'The Block' in Sydney is the antithesis of the retail arcade and the one-stop department store.

The interior was designed to house numerous small boutique businesses in a similar manner to New York and Chicago tower buildings, with continuous vertical access for the public through the building via open staircases and lifts. Conceived and commissioned by John Forsyth, who had purchased the Dymock family book business in the early 1900s, the scheme was aimed at middle- to low-rent paying tenants who were being displaced by the growth of the city centre. The project was delayed for some years as finance was difficult to obtain without a substantial number of committed rent-paying tenants. It is a credit to Forsyth's perseverance that the project was completed, particularly as the architect, FHB Wilton, was dismissed during construction for drunkenness. Dymock's bookshop still occupies the main ground floor of the building.

The facade is known as inter-war Commercial Palazzo style based on a tripartite vertical composition. Notable elements are bronze windows and giant Doric columns with bronze spandrels. Decorative features include Greek key balustrade and a lapidez central cartouche.

1928 Kingsford Smith and Ulm make the first trans-Pacific flight in *Southern Cross*

411

412

411 House

12 Ginahgulla Road, Bellevue Hill
c. 1928 Wilson, Neave and Berry (Hardy Wilson in England)
GC, V, NA

Classicism Revisited

The late 1920s were characterised by a revival of Classicism which paralleled a general phenomenon in Europe and the USA in the early years of the 20th century. Numerous styles were developed, with architects adopting whichever would suit a particular building. The beginning of what is generally perceived to be contemporary architecture therefore drew strength from the Classical tradition which was not perceived to be based on an inviolate set of rules.

The establishment of a university degree in architecture influenced by the teaching of English academics reaffirmed the connection between Classicism and the upper middle class residential clientele. An awareness of European classicism came second-hand through architects such as Lutyens, Richardson, McKim Mead and White, who were graduates of the Ecole des Beaux-Arts in Paris. Information about the 1925 Exhibition 'Arts Décoratifs et Industries Modernes' in Paris was provided through English and Australian Journals.

In the 1930s, the Classical motifs gradually began to leave the surface, revealing simple masses with fenestration puncturing their surfaces. Ornament took on new subjects related to a particular building type. Triangles rather than squares or circles, or corn rather than acanthus, or a nude rather than a clothed figure. Their position on the facade, whether allegorical or purely decorative, remained part of the Classical tradition.

JH

412 Commonwealth Savings Bank

48–50 Martin Place, Castlereagh and Elizabeth Streets, Sydney
1928 Ross & Rowe
1983–91 Australian Construction Services – Barry McGregor, Project Architect (restoration and conservation)
GC, V, A

A sumptuous Beaux-Arts building of immense civic presence. The base is faced with red granite and the four massive Ionic columns and pilasters are clad with pink-glazed ceramic tiles rather than the traditional masonry materials of sandstone or brick. These materials foreshadowed the rise of glazed terracotta which was used extensively throughout the Art Deco period. The building at roof line has a two-storey attic and dentilated cornice.

The interior at the lower levels is largely intact. The grand hall and banking chamber are overly detailed in a lavish neo-Classical style featuring the extensive use of marble and scagliola on massive stylised columns. Of particular interest are the northern stairs and lift lobby connecting Castlereagh and Elizabeth Streets, with a barrel-vaulted stained-glass ceiling.

The plan is 70 metres by 50 metres, with a central light well which was converted to a glass atrium during the extensive conservation works. In the original design the light well illuminated the ceiling of the two-storey high banking chamber.

•••

The excellent conservation works, which were supervised by Barry McGregor, took eight years to complete.

415

27 H 4

413 Sydney Institute of Technology
Former Marcus Clarke Emporium
827–837 George Street, Sydney
1928 Spain & Cosh (earlier building, 1910 James Nangle)
AC, V, A

Next to an earlier store by the noted architect and academic James Nangle (1868–1941), the prestigious architectural firm of Alfred Spain (1868–1954) and Thomas Cosh (1868–1947) erected one of the largest retail emporiums in Sydney for the Marcus Clarke firm. It was one of the last decisions by a retailer to locate near Central Railway, the majority of other retailers having drifted northwards to the retail district around St James and Wynyard underground stations.

The exterior is of robustly detailed brickwork in stripped Classical idiom, completed about ten years before the first streamlined modern showrooms appeared. The ground floor featured elegant display windows (since removed), high ceilings and a vertical movement provided by six lifts. In the centre of the facade is a square tower surmounted by a squat octagonal spire. The old Marcus Clarke motto, 'Bound to Rise', is just discernible on the stonework of the tower base and remains as an inspiration to the students who now occupy the building.

26 J 16

414 Wales House
Formerly The Sydney Morning Herald Building
Cnr Pitt & O'Connell Streets, Sydney
1922–28 Manson & Pickering
GC, V, A

The downtown 'prestige' office building for Fairfax & Sons, the proprietors of the *Sydney Morning Herald*, was erected during the boom of the late 1920s. The design exaggerates the tight corner with a circular porch and ornamental cupola, similar to intersections in New York. The intact stone-faced steel-framed structure reflects modern building practice. Much of the interior has been altered, with the exception of the oval boardroom with its acoustic dome.

26 K 17

415 Legal Offices
Formerly 'The Sun' Building
60 Elizabeth Street, Sydney
1926–29 Joseph Alexander Kethel
GC, V, A

Completed just before the economic crash of 1929, *The Sun* newspaper building was one of the last headquarters buildings of the major daily newspapers to be constructed in the CBD. It was also the first commercial neo-Gothic office building in Sydney, possibly in Australia.

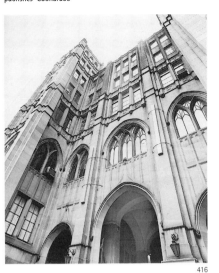

416

417

25 H 16

26 J 18

416 Scots Church
2 York Street, Sydney
1927–30 Rosenthal, Rutlidge and Beattie
GC, V, A

This was the winning design from the architectural competition for a new Presbyterian church to replace the one removed to make way for the approaches to the Harbour Bridge. Despite its curious commercial Gothicised appearance (high-rise church of the 1920s), the exterior and interior contain elements of high quality, particularly the unique auditorium design.

The original design proposed a steel-framed commercial tower on top of the church, to the maximum height permitted of 150 feet (46 metres). After the economic crash of 1929, construction of the tower was deferred, although all the foundation structure is in place. The external stonework was attached to the steel frame with concealed fixings, making this a very early use of dry-jointed cladding. The project was a commercial failure, with the huge debt a continued financial burden on the church.

•••

The architect, Major-General Sir Charles Rosenthal (1875-1954), was a well-known and admired military officer, an oratorio singer and a persuasive public speaker as well as an active architect. He was president of the Australian Museum (1926–30) and suffered bankruptcy twice, in 1898 and in 1930.

In an address given in 1924 to the NSW Institute of Architects, Rosenthal argued that Woolloomooloo should be redeveloped as a zone for federal, state and municipal offices surrounded by parks and gardens, with the timber wharves removed and development of the shoreline at the water's edge.

417 State Theatre
49 Market Street, Sydney
1929 Henry White & John Eberson (NY)
GC, V, A

This is a glorious fantasy palace from the 1920s built specifically to show 'talking pictures'. When opened, it was billed as 'The Empire's greatest theatre', which referred both to seating numbers and interior treatments. This was perhaps the most prestigious project for Sydney architect Henry Eli White, who had recently introduced the 'atmospheric theatre' to Sydney through the Capitol Theatre in the Haymarket **(243)**. However, White's work was only a reflection of the vast theatres designed in the USA by John Eberson, whose worked White had visited, researched and brazenly copied. For this project, Eberson was invited to work in association with White, giving the State Theatre extra shades of originality.

The lobby, crush spaces, foyers and mezzanine foyer are gold and red, lavishly animated with cast plaster figurines, statuary, foliage patterning and concealed lighting. Grand stairs lead from the foyer to the galleries, adding to the pomp and occasion associated with a good night out on the town. Externally, the building has weak Gothic detailing in painted plaster surfaces, caught between the baroque extravaganza of the Plaza Theatre in George Street (now Planet Hollywood) and the sombre repetition of the Gothic Scots Church **(416)** built in the same year. The State Theatre is home to the Sydney Film Festival. The Wurlitzer organ is still in working order and is the only Wurlitzer still to be found in its original location.

•••

Henry White designed more than 150 theatres, including the recently restored Civic Theatre in Newcastle.

418

24 L 15	25 H 17

418 BMA House

135–137 Macquarie Street, Sydney
1928-30 Joseph Fowell & Kenneth McConnel
GC, V, A

The result of a high-quality competition, this design ushered in a new approach towards high-rise city buildings. While certainly modern at the time of its construction, it was not too avant-garde for its clients. The Art Deco transition from stone and brick to vitrolite glass or glazed terracotta with integral decoration could be found in Britain and the USA at the same time. The curious, almost fussy level of detail of woven terracotta to the bay windows and spiral cords is balanced by Australian and medical iconography, including snake and sword shields, gargoyles, lions and representative Australian fauna.

•••

BMA House is the only building in Sydney to be topped by koala sculptures.

419 Grace Building

77–79 York Street, Sydney
1930 DT Morrow and PJ Gordon
GC, V, NA

Inspired by the concept of an underground railway delivering commuters to the city centre, this was built by Grace Bros as a purely speculative venture. Based on the much-publicised Chicago Tribune Building (1922), it reflects the American hybrid of fusing perpendicular Gothic (complete with decorative turret buttresses) with the machine manufactured glazed tile of Art Deco. A Grace Brothers department store occupied the ground floor for a short time, with offices above.

It was requisitioned by the Government during World War II as a command centre for General MacArthur's Pacific operations, and has been used as offices and a post office since. Plans have been approved for the conversion and refurbishment of the building as a hotel.

420

58 N 20

420 Plumer Road Shops

Cnr Plumer and O'Sullivan Roads, Bellevue Hill
1930s architect unknown
1994 Roger J Thrum (renovations and new work)
GC, V, A

Not an original Art Deco shopping street,
although it looks like it. One side dates from the
1920s, the other from the 1930s. Over the years,
the shops had become an eclectic hodgepodge
of styles, until it was decided in 1994 to
renovate the shops by re-creating the look and
feel of a 1930s group. The designers worked in
sympathy with the original 1930s tile-fronted
design, on the advice of Anthony Rowan at
Woollahra Council. An amicable collaboration
between architect and heritage planner
followed, which led to a design drawn from Art
Deco examples from the 1930s in Australia and
England for colour scheme, tile patterns and
insignia. Some tilework is original and as much
as possible of the original shops was retained,
e.g. footboards. The cafe/restaurant was a new
addition for the 1990s cafe society. The complex
now evokes an agreeable village atmosphere.

24 K 15

421 'Kyle House'

27–31 Macquarie Place, Sydney
1931 C Bruce Dellit
GC, V, A

This building represents an early attempt to
discard historical stylism and search for forms
relevant to the 20th century. The 'arch', which
was to become Dellit's trademark, together with
his use of ceramics and decorative brickwork,
anticipates 'Art Deco' skyscraper development
in Sydney.

26 J 17

422 Westpac Bank

341 George Street, Sydney
1927–32 Robertson & Marks
GC, V, A

During the first half of the 20th century, banks
became increasingly competitive, particularly in
their claims about which had the most impressive and up-to-the-minute banking chambers.
For banks in particular, the building itself had
become a sign of prestige and monumentalism,
thinking which was only finally rejected in the
1960s as being stolid and inflexible.

Both the adjoining Commercial Banking
Headquarters and the former Bank of New
South Wales Headquarters are important
landmarks in defining Martin Place — although
at one stage Martin Place would have been
extended to York Street, but for the stubborness
of the banks in refusing to move. With obvious
well-mannered Beaux-Arts stylism, both banks
echo the wave of commercial confidence during
the 1920s following World War I. The ground-
floor banking chambers are magnificent,
including extensive counter areas which the
computer-aided banking industry now finds
hard to utilise. The building is steel-framed,
exhibiting the usual rusticated base, decorative
balconies and cornice, and is clad with grey
granite and sandstone. It complements the
General Post Office **(203)**, although the conception of the design is different. The interior
is notable for the range of marbles and use of
scagliola (marbling effect), particularly in the
boardroom which has an Art Deco interior.

423

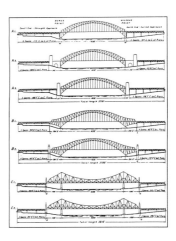

24 K 11

423 **Sydney Harbour Bridge**
Design 1922–24; construction from
1923 (approaches)
1929–32 John Job Carew Bradfield (E) (bridges)
Construction by Dorman & Long, Ralph Freeman
Consulting Engineer
Sir John Burnet & Partners Consulting Architects
GC, V, A

Although the concept of a harbour crossing was entertained fifty years earlier, it was not until 4th January 1900 that tender designs and financial proposals were sought for a 'North Shore' bridge to span the harbour. This was despite Sir John Sulman's suggestion that a tunnel was a better option. All of the twenty-four schemes were criticised and thought unsatisfactory. By 1903, the firm of J Stewart and Co. had submitted one design (of many) for a single arch bridge without pylons, which is very similar to the one built today. However, this too was rejected as being 'too huge' and 'objectionable' from an artistic point of view.

Over the next fifteen years, under the guidance of one of Australia's greatest civil, structural and transport engineers, JJC Bradfield (1867–1943), the bridge project took shape; finally, an international competition was held, with Bradfield suggesting that the design should be an arch bridge with granite-faced pylons at either end. The winning design tender by Dorman and Long (recommended by Bradfield himself) proposed the single arch design No. A3 (one of six alternatives) be built from both ends (using cable supports) and joined in the middle. The contract was let in March 1924. The structural calculations were supervised by Ralph Freeman in London who had left the Cleveland Bridge Company in the USA. As it was an arch design, any design change required a recalculation across the entire structure, and the calculations for the

bridge both in tension (cable supported) and compression (as an arch) filled twenty-eight books of transcribed calculations. An impressive but high maintenance design, it kept the Dorman and Long factory in Britain busy producing steel, having agreed to an attractive payment plan with the NSW Government. The social impact of the bridge, its construction areas, and its connecting highways involving the demolition of 800 houses, would be inconceivable today. Built between the wars, the project reduced the unemployment created by the Depression and was the greatest labour intensive project to employ 19th-century work practices of sledge and cold chisel.

The span is 1,650 feet to allow unobstructed passage for ships in Sydney Harbour. Of sixteen deaths, seven were workers on the bridge structure itself (139 died during construction of the Brooklyn Bridge). Families living in its path were displaced without compensation. Rural taxpayers saw 'the vampire city, of which the bridge is so complete a symbol ... sucking the life blood of the suffering country'. The mythology of the bridge being a 'symbol not only for the city, but for the aspirations of the nation' blinded most people to the injustices.

•••

The first motor car to cross the bridge was a
Model A Ford carrying the Bradfield family
on the Sunday before the official opening.

•••

In 1924, an editorial in the British journal
Engineering referred to the Sydney Harbour
Bridge's pylons as 'meaningless masses of
masonry', while a number of libel suits over
various engineers' claims about structural
integrity came to nothing.

● 1932 Bodyline controversy
begins in Test Series cricket

● 1932 Memorial to The Dog on the
Tucker Box unveiled at Gundagai

● 1933 First edition of The
Australian Women's Weekly

424

425 & 426

56 Q 18

424 'Wychbury' and 'Werrington'
5 and 7 Manning Street, Potts Point
1934 Emil Sodersten
GC, V, NA

'Wychbury' has interesting Art Deco motifs at its summit and is of considerably higher architectural quality than 'Werrington'. Sodersten popularised the use of face and texture brick with a number of high-rise residential blocks in this area.

57 E 19

425 and 426 Houses
4 and 6 Wiston Gardens, Double Bay
1932–34 Leslie Wilkinson
(6 Wiston – RAIA Sulman Award 1935)
GC, V, NA

Both the Sweetapple House (No. 4) and the Parkinson House (No. 6) are built in simple Mediterranean style with walls of cream-washed stucco, pale emerald green shutters and red-tiled roofs. They exhibit typical Wilkinson Mediterranean detailing with intricate plans.

Below: Living level plan, 6 Wiston Gardens (1932)

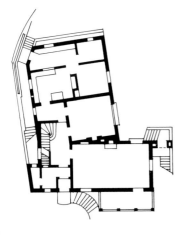

Art Deco

A strong influence on Sydney architects' designs came from the United States skyscraper style of the 1920s and 1930s, through the work of Raymond Hood, William Van Allen and Shreve, Land & Harmon. The Chicago Tribune Tower had an influence on Sydney architects and was closely emulated in the Grace Building of 1930 (419). Raymond Hood's first Art Deco skyscraper, the American Radiator Building of 1924, predates the 1925 Paris Exposition, but draws heavily on Hood's Ecole des Beaux-Arts training and Saarinen's modern second-placed entry in the Chicago Tribune Competition. The three main sources which influenced the development of Art Deco in Australia were the decorative pavilions of the 1925 Paris Exposition, the intricate patterned brickwork of the Amsterdam and German School, and the Art Deco American skyscrapers. By the late 1920s, there were many designs for Art Deco buildings, but the Depression delayed most of these, with the majority being constructed between 1934 and 1940.

The first major Art Deco building to be erected was the professional chambers tower built for the New South Wales Branch of the British Medical Association, which was designed by the architects Fowell and McConnel (418). The Sydney Harbour Bridge was symbolic of the economic recovery of the 1930s and was a fine example of science and technique, and a lesson in what human labour could accomplish. When The World's Wonders was published in Britain in 1938, the bridge, along with the Battersea Power Station and the Empire State Building, was considered one of the 'seven wonders of the modern world'. By the 1930s, a geometric and streamlined aesthetic in which florid ornaments were constrained within an overall vertical massing replaced the more Gothic mode of the late 1920s.

427

427

26 K 20

427 Anzac War Memorial
Hyde Park South, Sydney
1929–34 C Bruce Dellit; exterior restored 1979
Sculptor: Raynor Hoff
GC, V, A

The Anzac War Memorial was designed by
C Bruce Dellit (1900–1942), winning first prize
in one of the most prestigious architectural
competitions of the day. Twenty-nine years old,
in his second year of practice, the young
architect imagined a monumental and highly
sculptured design which broke away from
revivalist traditions. It caused an uproar in the
local architectural fraternity.

Located on the central axis of Hyde Park
South (missing the underground railway), the
Memorial was made possible after a protracted
fund-raising program initiated in 1919. Dellit's
design in Bathurst granite is highly symbolic,
with representational sculptures depicting
events and personnel involved in World War I.
The memorial can be approached from four
directions; the north and south approaches
consist of grand staircases which lead to the
upper circular 'Hall of Memory' (with its unique
wreath-like balustrade). The east and west
entries lead to the lower circular 'Hall of Silence',
featuring the sculpture representing the
'Sacrifice'. In the upper space, the visitors are
compelled to look downwards, causing their
heads to be reverently and naturally bowed.

The statuary, sculptures and bas-reliefs were
the work of English-born artist Raynor Hoff.
Above the east and west portals are bronze bas-
relief panels which depict the activities and
campaigns of the Australian Infantry Forces
(AIF). Eastern Front campaigns are represented
on the east portal, including Gallipoli, laying of
railway, Army Service Corps, Army Medical
Corps, Light Horse, Camel Corps, Signal Units,
Infantry, Artillery, Machine Gunners and the

Pioneers. The record of the AIF on the Western
Front shown on the west portal includes the
Air Force, Cycle Corps, Artillery, Army Medical
Corps, Bombers, Engineers, Tank Corps, Pioneers
and Infantry.

Each of the sixteen granite buttresses is
surmounted by cast granite figures, saddened
and reflecting the loss caused by war.

North elevation, from left to right:
Ammunition Carrier, Bomber, Pioneer, and Lewis-
Gunner
East elevation, from left to right:
Naval Signaller in winter kit, AB Seamen with full
landing gear, Light Horseman and Driver of the
Field Artillery
South elevation, from left to right:
Air Force Mechanic, Nurse of the Army Medical
Corps, Air Force Pilot, Naval Wireless Operator
West elevation, from left to right:
Surgeon, Tunneller, Field Telephone Mechanic
and Infantryman

The four standing figures set into the corners
near the stepped apex represent the Army
(north-east); the Army Medical Corps (north-
west); the Air Force (south-west) and the Navy
(south-east). The two internal spaces, the upper
'Hall of Memory' and the lower 'Hall of Silence'
are lined with lists of famous battles and
campaigns in which Australians took part.
Within the dome of the 'Hall of Memory', lit by
the amber glass windows piercing the side walls,
is a constellation of 120,000 golden stars, one
for each Australian who perished in the conflict.
Outside, to the north, is the black-lined
remembrance pool.

•••

The design shares a similar design philosophy to
Sodersten and Crust's Canberra War Memorial,
not completed until 1941.

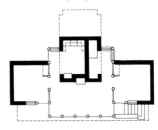

428

56 R 19

428 'Birtley Towers'
8 Birtley Place, Elizabeth Bay
1934 Emil Sodersten
GC, V, A

When completed in 1934, 'Birtley Towers' — designed by Emil Sodersten (1901–61) — was reputedly Australia's largest block of flats. Together with the 1936 block 'Hillside' **(435)**, it did much to popularise red texture brick, brickwork detailing and Art Deco motifs. Described by one critic as a 'voracious sponge', 'Birtley Towers' was designed soon after Sodersten's earlier texture brick precedent 'Wychbury' **(424)** but well before his 1936 overseas study trip which gave rise to new design directions exhibited in the CML Building **(434)**.

Approached by a rising entrance driveway, 'Birtley Towers' commands high ground. The 'U'-shaped arrangement of six flats per floor shows innovative and sophisticated planning, which maximises surface area (and cost). Few equivalent examples were built internationally at the time. The transitional face brickwork, graded from darker shades at the base to lighter shades towards the top, is a common Art Deco treatment found, for example, in Earle and Calhoun's 55 Central Park West apartments (1929) in New York. Less common perhaps was the use of such unevenly textured brickwork. The Art Deco sunrise motifs exploding over window arches had equivalent examples in the South Bronx and Murray Hill areas of New York. With small balconies (often glazed in) facing four different orientations, it takes little advantage of the temperate Sydney climate.

The stiff yet decorative interiors of 'glossy "piano finish" veneer, etched fountain mirror, black glass mantel and finned metal windows' are somewhat dated when compared with the more flowing forms of the 'Macleay Regis' **(460)** built five years later.

180 B 16

429 'Burley Griffin Lodge'
Former Estelle James House
32 Plateau Road and 5 Palmgrove Road, Avalon
1934 Walter Burley Griffin
1960 Sydney Ancher (alterations)
GC, V, NA

Designed by the American emigrant architect Walter Burley Griffin (1876–1937) in the 1930s, this house has a strong kinship with his earlier designs from 1910 created soon after his arrival in Australia. The plan, which is free of corridors, is small, symmetrical and simple, sitting below the garage at street level. It is one of the finest surviving examples of Griffin's domestic work, exemplifying his organic approach in its use of site and natural materials.

Below: Typical plan, 'Birtley Towers' (1934)

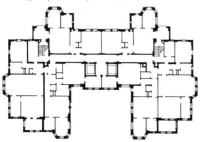

Below: Living level plan before additions,
32 Plateau Road, Avalon (1934)

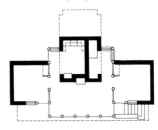

431

354 B 12

430 Woronora Crematorium
Linden Street, Sutherland
1934 Louis Robertson and Sons
GC, V, A

During the 1930s, the general practice of plot
burial began to be overtaken by cremation.
There was a proliferation of crematoria in
Sydney cemeteries adopting either Art Deco or
Mediterranean styles as the simple dignified
languages of the day. The Woronora facility,
described in a 1930s booklet as a place where
'beauty softens grief', consisted of east and west
chapels (300 and 200 mourners, respectively),
an open court of remembrance with a lotus pool
(now a garden), the cremation chamber and the
campanile-like chimney. Many original details
have survived the sensitive alterations.

57 E 17

431 'Craigend'
86 Darling Point Road, Darling Point
1935 Frank L'Anson Bloomfield & Roy McCulloch
GC, V, NA

This is an early International Style house which
one might expect to find in Haifa or Jerusalem
during the 1930s. It attempts to merge Moorish
elements, horseshoe arches on diagonal
embossed columns, pointed arches, cupolas
and decorative tiling with the horizontality and
glazed walls of a white Modernist house.

Bloomfield, son of Edward L'Anson, RIBA
President (1886–87), worked in Australia with
BJ Waterhouse after studying at the
Architectural Association in London. He was a
talented modernist who later designed the
Spanish style Northern Suburbs Crematorium.
He also designed the 'streamlined' Top Dog
Men's Wear Centre in Dee Why with John
Spencer, which won the Sulman Medal in 1950.

'Craigend' was tailored to the whims and
memories of its owner James Patrick, who
owned a successful shipping business. Patrick
was a local yachtsman who mixed with the
wealthy.

In 1938, the phosphor bronze cupola made
from melted-down yachting hardware previously
owned by Cornelius Vanderbilt was added. After
the war (1948), the house was purchased by the
US Government as the official residence of its
Consul-General, thereby preserving much of the
interior from unnecessary alteration.

Below: Living level plan, 'Craigend' (1935)

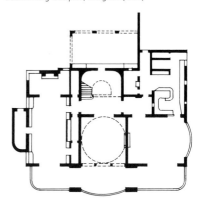

432

432 'Wyldefel Gardens'
8a Wylde Street, Potts Point
1935-36 WA Crowle and John Brogan
GC, V, A

At the time of its completion in 1936, 'Wyldefel Gardens' was arguably the most modern and striking example of residential architecture in Australia, certainly unrelated to any local precedent. The design predates the modern-based but Moorish-styled 'Craigend' of 1935 at Darling Point by Frank L'Anson Bloomfield (431), and Sydney Ancher's Prevost House of 1937 at Bellevue Hill (441).

'Wyldefel Gardens' consisted of twenty terraced garden apartments in two cascading wings separated by stepped gardens. The gardens contained landscaping, free-form pathways, tennis courts and swimming baths where the site met the foreshores of Sydney Harbour. It was a thoroughly integrated concept, combining interior with exterior, building with terrain, yet ensuring privacy from adjoining buildings with the openness of the 'democratic' and communal central gardens.

It was as much an experiment in living as it was a town planning or architectural project; its social objectives formed part of the news commentary of the day.

The driving force behind the promotion of these ideas was the socialite philanthropist William Alfred Leopold Crowle (d. 1959), who travelled extensively for half of each year and held dinner parties in Sydney for the other half. He was Sydney's greatest private collector of art and artifacts. These were held in Crowle's 1888 mansion 'Wildfell', which had extensive harbour views — views he was determined to protect by a modern terraced housing scheme. As an avid collector and reader, it is possible that Crowle had seen FRS Yorke's publication *The Modern House* (1934) and set about looking for a

suitable example of multiple terraced apartments, not documented in Yorke's book. While travelling in Germany, Crowle discovered a housing scheme just completed in the hills outside Oberammergau, which he extensively photographed and recorded.

Back in Sydney, Crowle engaged an architect of his acquaintance, John R Brogan, who had achieved some notoriety by winning a 1926 competition for the Ideal Home in Sydney. Later as author of *101 Australian Homes*, he indicated an awareness of housing issues. However, there was little evidence of this concern in his work, which largely consisted of stockbroker's Tudor Revival texture brick homes on Sydney's upper north shore, built both before and after this commission.

Brogan's drawings were a lifeless version of his client's wishes, and required many modifications. Crowle added three further units to the scheme and a house and boatshed building on the harbour for his own residence, called 'Once Upon a Time'. The concrete flat-roofed units were originally designed with square glass windows, but later fitted with curved windows and cantilevered awnings. They step down the hillside as a series of two-storey elements, the roof of a projecting block forming the garden of the next, higher unit, contrasting against the outcropping rocks.

The life of the realised project was brief. Four years later, the Navy resumed the foreshore to build the Captain Cook Graving Dock, one of the largest dry docks in the southern hemisphere. This removed the views and made the site effectively land-locked. The timber, steelwork and glass of the foreshore building were dismantled in late 1941 and transported on barges and motor trucks across the harbour. It was rebuilt on a similar site at Kurraba Point, Neutral Bay in 1942, again with space to

433

36 Q 20

accommodate the motor yacht under the building. Today, design insiders queue to buy or lease apartments in the complex, and continue the vision of Crowle's democratic Modernism.

●●●

William Crowle, a former Adelaide-based bicycle enthusiast, made his fortune from the motor industry as the first local importer of Citroen and Buick cars.

●●●

The Crowle collection of antiques and fine arts was gradually dispersed over many years. In 1935 almost 2,300 lots were auctioned; in 1968, another 669 lots were submitted; in 1979, 304 lots were offered and, finally, in 1985, the last 384 lots were sold.

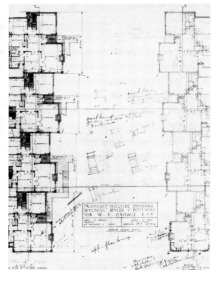

433 **Hayden Orpheum Picture Palace**
Former New Orpheum Theatre
380–386 Military Road, Cremorne
1935 GN Kenworthy
GC, V, A

An excellent and rare example of an Art Deco cinema, foyer and auditorium designed by GN Kenworthy and painstakingly restored by the current owner. The 1,735-seat Cremorne Orpheum landmark was built in 1935 by Italian immigrant Angelo Vergona, who was also responsible for the first Orpheum Picture Show in North Sydney. During the 1940s, it was run by his son Bob Vergona, who used to sit in his chair in the cinema foyer to welcome guests, and was known for driving the last patrons home from late-night movie sessions.

When opened, the project was praised for the 100-foot uninterrupted width of the dress circle, supported by 130 tons of steelwork. The street elevation was sensitively treated with the inclusion of black 'Carrara' glass shopfronts at ground level, even though the main body of the theatre runs parallel to the street.

Restoration of the cinema began in 1987 by current owner and television personality Mike Walsh, who was fascinated with the golden era of cinema. He added a fourth cinema, appropriately named 'The Vergona', which is more streamlined and less decorative in keeping with the Moderne style of the 1940s, based on the Odeon Theatre in London. Two fibreglass sculptures of ballet dancers, named Myrtle and Shaz, built by Melbourne sculptor Laszlo Biro, are well known to Vergona cinemagoers, as are the Saturday night movies which are preceded by an organ performance on the Wurlitzer which rises from beneath the stage in the Orpheum.

Left: Original design plan, 'Wyldefel Gardens' (1935), by John Brogan (State Library of NSW)

434

26 K 16

434 Former City Mutual Life Building

60–66 Hunter Street, Sydney
1934–36 Emil Sodersten
1989 Travis and Partners (conservation work)
GC, V, A

One of the most impressive and innovative inter-war Art Deco buildings in Australia, this was designed by Emil Sodersten (1901–61) after he had completed an important tour overseas. At thirty-three years of age, when CML was designed, Sodersten (like C Bruce Dellit one year his senior) was a young architect pioneering modern design in Sydney, with considerably more impact than his conservative and more established peers.

The 'V'-shaped plan addresses Richard Johnson Square, on the corner of Bligh and Hunter Streets, with a strong chamfered entrance which rises the whole height of the building. Behind the entrance is a courtyard and full-height lightwell which provides good natural light to each floor. The serrated or 'zig-zag' window treatment to the street (also found on the Queensland Insurance Building in Pitt Street by Sodersten, 1940) allows much greater control of direct sunlight from one direction, while still allowing a view from the other. This was also the first private office building in Sydney to be fully air-conditioned. Fine interior features and finishes appear in seven types of stone with original fixtures. The polished stone entrance features bronze sculptures by Rayner

Hoff who had just completed his tour-de-force at the Anzac War Memorial **(427)** in Hyde Park.

67 F 3

435 'Hillside'

412 Edgecliff Road, Edgecliff
1936 EC Pitt and AM Bolot
GC, V, A

A landmark building near the ridge in Edgecliff, 'Hillside' is related in style to 'Birtley Towers' **(428)**, with its powerful expression of red textured brick. Like 'Borambil' in Manly, 'Hillside' extends the stairwell and lift shafts through the centre of the building to become a major flagstaff.

A typical floor has a pair of symmetrical apartments of three bedrooms, with separate living room, dining room and kitchen arranged around an entrance hall. Approximately nine cars can be squeezed into a tight basement using two turntables and radial parking.

Below: Ground floor plan, 'Hillside' (1936)

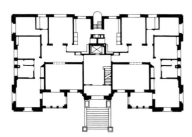

436

25 H 16

179 Q 13

436 'Transport House'
Former Railway House
19 York Street, Sydney
1934–36 HE Budden & Mackey
GC, V, A

In 1936, Railway House was lauded as Sydney's
most up-to-date and prestigious office building,
all glass and tile, and all air-conditioned — a
declaration about the government's position on
quality. Built for and by the Railway Department
to house all their office requirements, it was
constructed by day labour (somewhat contro-
versially). The steel and bronze components
were manufactured at the New South Wales
Railways' own Chullora workshops, which were
established to produce rolling stock.

Sitting directly above Wynyard railway
station, this 12-storey building has a series of
connections to the underground, including an
early use of escalators, tunnels and lifts.
Transport House combines both the horizontal
lines of the Moderne skyscraper with the
vertical lines of the Art Deco tower. The exterior
includes trachyte at street level and green
faience tiles to the upper levels, with inset
bronze windows. It is decorated with quality
metalwork. The building was awarded the Royal
Australian Institute of Architects' Sulman Medal
in 1936, and the Royal Institute of British
Architects Bronze Medal in 1939.

437 'Hy Brasil'
62 Chisolm Avenue, Avalon Beach
1936 Alexander S Jolly
GC, NV, NA

During Scottish-born architect Alexander Jolly's
(1887–1957)eventful career, he spent a period
living on the northern peninsular as a land
speculator, real estate agent and organic
architect. 'Hy Brasil', is one of only a handful
of houses by Jolly which survive and it was
commissioned by a North Sydney dentist named
Wilson as a holiday cottage. The design is a
fantastic fusion of natural materials, including
hand-dressed timbers and rusticated stonework.
The present owners, who purchased the
property in 1958, open the grounds to artists
during the Pittwater Festival each year.

●●●

*For other houses by Jolly, see also Careel House
(1931), Rayner Road, Whale Beach, and Loggan
Rock (1930), 111 Whale Beach Road*

*Below: Ground floor plan, including later additions,
'Hy Brasil' (1936)*

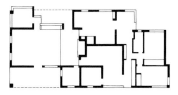

439

59 A 13

438 House (Roberts)
11a Gilliver Avenue, Vaucluse
1936 Guy Crick and Bruce Furze
GC, V, NA

One of the first houses to reflect the curvilinear and streamlined forms of Art Deco, more often found in cinemas and pubs. It was commissioned as a speculative demonstration house of the 'new architecture' by the builder GJ Wells. The clean-lined design by Guy Crick and Bruce Furze, who were well-established Art Deco cinema architects, incorporates the recessed planes, plasterwork and steel window details found in their designs for the King's Theatres. The building was purchased by Herbert Roberts, part-owner of the King's cinema chain and a client of the architects. It survives today in excellent original condition both inside and out.

58 J 15

439 House
1 Wolseley Crescent, Point Piper
1937 Eric M Nicholls
GC, V, NA

An exciting composition of sharp angular geometry, cream texture brick, stone and concrete.

215 H 13

440 'Maiala'
7 Warrawee Avenue, Warrawee
1937 Leslie Wilkinson
GC, NV, NA

Commissioned by Beresford Grant, chairman of the real estate firm Raine and Horne, 'Maiala' is one of Professor Leslie Wilkinson's (1882–1973) larger Mediterranean mansions, tentatively reminding the viewer of his neo-Georgian sensitivities.

•••

Other architect-designed houses in Warrawee Avenue include: 'Harwood' by HV Vernon (1912); the Mackerras House by James Muir (1979); the Hornery House by Glenn Murcutt (1982); 'Audley' by F Glynn Gilling for the Gowing family and 'Kirkoswald' by John Burcham Clamp (1906) for John Meloy.

P&O Streamline Moderne Style
During the mid-1930s, European developments which rejected all ornamentation and embraced reinforced concrete and the latest technological developments were regarded as economical, streamlined, dynamic and slick. Before World War II, examples of this dynamic look were very slowly introduced into Sydney, almost always through new building types, such as those associated with the motor car, cinema, healthcare and the production line factory. Originators of the style were influenced by changes in technology, construction methods and materials. Visually, the Streamline Moderne Style stressed the use of glass, the expressed horizontal line, glass blocks, the port hole and the absence of a pitched roof.

441

68 J 1

441 House (Prevost)

Cnr 65 Kambala Road and Rupertswood Avenue, Bellevue Hill
1937 Prevost & Ancher
GC, V, NA

One of Sydney's most important prewar designs by architect Sydney Ancher (1904–1978), for the family of his partner Reginald Prevost (d. 1942). The well-travelled Ancher had worked in Britain for the 'nautical' Modernist Charles Emberton. Ancher's design was selected by Prevost from an in-house design competition among the staff. It reflected his recent experiences in Britain and also drew on Mies van de Rohe's Tugendhat House (1930), in particular the curved dining area projecting into the living space. The front door is opaque glass surrounded with clear blue glass bricks, balanced by one red post at the entrance. The external design has nautical themes with port hole style windows, ship's railing and sculptured parapet.

The house was openly claimed to be the first functionally designed house in Australia — 'where function was hampered by tradition, tradition was scrapped'. Forgotten and uncelebrated during the 1960s and 1970s, the property was purchased by a real estate agent in 1987, with the intention to demolish and redevelop. After a protracted campaign by the National Trust, the RAIA and members of Prevost's family, the case was decided by the Land and Environment Court in January 1989 under Justice Noel Hemmings. He ruled that the Prevost house, was a convincing exemplar of the radical International Style and must remain standing.

Ancher had turned down a job with Stephenson and Turner to work with Prevost. This was an important practice which produced a number of Modernist pubs, including the Civic Hotel (1940–41) in Pitt Street, Sydney, and the Art Deco 'Golden Sheaf' Hotel in Double Bay.

●●●

The hearing in the Land and Environment court which prevented demolition of the building produced some interesting comments.

Reasons given to the court why this house must be demolished included: the bedrooms are located on the street side; the bathroom has opaque windows which face the courtyard; the dining enclosure is too crowded; the sunroom is too small; the access to the garage is highly inconvenient; and the open decks are exposed to the public and do not offer privacy.

Below: Living level plan, 'Prevost house' (1936)

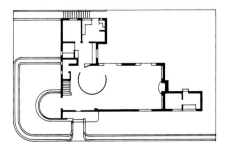

442

444

442 Sydney Dental Hospital
Former United Dental Hospital
Cnr Chalmers and Elizabeth Streets, Surry Hills
1936–38 Stephenson, Meldrum & Turner
GC, V, A

Designed just before ACI House **(446)**, this was one of the first large-scale horizontal strip window buildings reflecting European Modernism. Incorporating an earlier 1910 hospital, it is now difficult to distinguish where the earlier and later buildings merge. The landmark feature is the full-height curved wire-glass stairwell, which produced a strong vertical line when illuminated at night. The design included a library, museum and wards.

443 Thai Airways International Limited
Former Royal Exchange Assurance Co House
75–77 Pitt Street, Sydney
1936–37 Norman Seabrook & Alan Fildes
BC, V, A

The first minimalist International Style high-rise building in Sydney designed to be 'ultra-modern' with the object of 'giving Sydney something new'. It was described as 'unique and striking', the only Sydney work of the influential Melbourne firm of Seabrook and Fildes. The three-storey high ground-floor treatment consisted of a concrete trellis with thick glass squares called 'luxcrete' over the entire width of the facade, which has since been removed. The rest of the building face was entirely glass — windows were divided by horizontal bands of coloured and tinted 'vitrolite' glass concealing the edge of concrete slabs. The colour scheme was primrose and green and *Decoration and Glass* magazine referred to it in 1937 as the 'tallest known building to be faced in structural glass'. Unfortunately, this has since been replaced by travertine.

444 Zink & Sons Shop
56 Oxford Street, Darlinghurst
1937 (shop fitout only)
Designed and built by H & E Sidgreaves Shopfitters
GC, V, A

One of Sydney's rare surviving and virtually unchanged Art Deco shopfronts similar to those at the Cremorne Orpheum **(433)**. It has a timber-lined mezzanine gallery and was featured in several 1938 architecture journals. Its original Art Nouveau(ish) shop name is just discernible on the facade below the parapet in coloured tiles.

445 'Mont Clair' Apartments
347 Liverpool Street, Darlinghurst
1938 Esmond B Wilshire & Hodges
GC, V, A

Art Deco apartments (42) with voluptuous entry.

446 Former ACI House
Cnr William and Boomerang Streets, Woolloomooloo
1937–38 Stephenson & Turner with Arthur Baldwinson
GC, V, A

Originally a showcase building for the glass manufacturer Australian Consolidated Industries, it had three levels of showrooms and offices. The exterior was tiled with glass mosaics with glass block infill panels and the entry doors to the foyer featured 'bullet proof' glass. The display windows at street level were of curved convex and concave glass to eliminate reflections. They are similar to Heals department store windows in London. Mutilated in two renovations, the interiors and the ground floor are lost, and the glass blocks replaced.

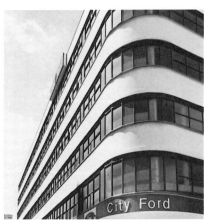

447

449

26 M 20

447 City Ford

Former Hastings Deering Motors
Riley, Kennedy, Crown and Suttor Streets, Woolloomooloo
1938 Samuel Lipson and Peter Kaad
GC,V,A

An inner-city showroom for Ford cars, with workshops since demolished to make way for the Crown Gardens residential development. Streamlined Modern, after Eric Mendelssohn, with double-spiral car ramp and five-storey open cantilever stair above car entry. The horizontal spandrels were fitted with fine steel framed windows; the vertical panels covering the columns are not original. The waffle slab and mushroom column construction is largely intact, as are parts of the original interior fitout.

26 K 18

448 David Jones Department Store

Cnr Market and Castlereagh Streets, Sydney
1938 McKellar & Partridge
GC, V, A

The elevations and planning were determined by the new streamlined 'International Style'. Half-level access allows development of two main sales floors.

Eric Nicholls Houses in Castlecrag

449 *3 The Bastion, 'Camelot' (1938)*
GC, V, NA

A thematic design whimsically responding to the romantic layout of Castlecrag.

450 *12 The Parapet (1940)*
GC, V, NA

This was Eric Nicholls's own house, which demonstrated his approach to organic forms and striking decorative motifs. It is part of an original house by Walter Burley Griffin.

159 R 18

451 House (Collins)

1170 Barrenjoey Road, Palm Beach
1938 Arthur Baldwinson
BC, V, NA

Having worked overseas for Raymond McGrath, Maxwell Fry and Walter Gropius, Arthur Baldwinson (1908–1969) returned to Australia in 1937 full of Modernist verve. After spending a year with Stephenson and Meldrum, he established his own practice on Sydney's northern peninsula. He designed some residential projects on his own account and others in partnership with the engineer Eric Gibson, as well as lecturing at Sydney University. He was an early exponent of Modernism and was strongly influenced by the Scandinavian design, in particular the work of Aalto and Asplund. This house for W Collins, built on a steep site overlooking Barrenjoey Road, was regarded as one of the most challenging and important houses designed during the 1940s in Australia. In an effort to conform to the post-war house size restrictions, no space is allocated to internal circulation. There is no direct access between any bedrooms and the large living room, while the veranda is treated as an external lounge room. Stone that was excavated on site is used to form the base and chimney of the timber construction house. Walls are stained weatherboard.

Below: Living level plan, 1170 Barrenjoey Road, Palm Beach (1936)

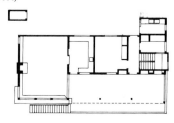

452

454

452 House
4 Springdale Road, Killara
1938 J Aubrey Kerr
GC, V, NA
An interesting blend of Art Deco and abstracted Modernism in the style of apartment buildings of the day.

453 Mario's Restaurant
Former Packard Car Showroom and Workshop
38 Yurong Street, East Sydney
1938 Samuel Lipson and Peter Kaad
1995 Gordon + Valich
GC, V, A
Car showrooms and repair shops became one of the fastest growing developments near main roads around 1920 and 1940, giving much-needed opportunities to architects experimenting with Modernism. Land on either side of William Street, the principal artery to the affluent (car-owning) eastern suburbs, became taken over by automobile centres for brands such as Chevrolet, Packard, Ford and Jaguar. The forgotten Packard centre by Lipson was an important contribution, with its saw-tooth steel-framed roof and two-level access. It sits on the edge of Woolloomooloo Creek, now covered up by Stream Street.

The interior has been successfully converted into Mario's second restaurant by the firm Gordon + Valich, following their earlier design for Mario's in Stanley Street. Much of the original roofing, steel windows and walls is still apparent, while the rear curved window remains untouched.

•••

The new work by Gordon + Valich is highly sensitive to the original Lipson and Kaad building.

454 Metropolitan Water, Sewerage and Drainage Board
339–341 Pitt Street, Sydney
1936–39 HE Budden & Mackey
GC, V, A
Following the success of 'Railway House' **(436)**, architects Budden and Mackey were asked to design offices for the MWSDB, to be built on the site which they then occupied. The seven-storey building is faced with cream coloured faience tiles, set at times on very tight curves running vertically up the service core. The remainder of the building expresses streamlined 'horizontality', featuring bas-relief sculpture, an extensive use of red granite, and a colonnade of curved black granite piers. The upper floors contain offices, a library, lecture hall and lunch room. The sculpture by Melbourne artist Stanley Hammond is said to represent the benefits of water to passers-by.

During 1964 and 1965, when it was decided to enlarge the accommodation, architects McConnel, Smith and Johnson designed an adjoining tower rather than extend the floors, as had been originally anticipated.

455 Minter Ellison Building
Former Mutual Life and Citizens Assurance
Cnr 38–46 Martin Place and Castlereagh Street, Sydney
1936–38 Bates, Smart & McCutcheon
1988 major renovation and conservation works
GC, V, A
This building was the winning design of a 1936 competition. The continuous horizontal lines and high-quality finish presage the International Style, although the eclecticism of the age is revealed in the Egyptian-style tower. Despite appearances, the lobby is not original Art Deco, but the result of the 1988 renovation.

456

456 Art Deco Hotels

The Art Deco pub is an Australian phenomenon, as American liquor licensing laws did not allow the British 'pub' type of hotel and the traditional British pub was not redesigned until after World War II. The acute angle corner was a charged site for many buildings of the 1930s and 1940s.

Duke of Gloucester Hotel
Frenchman's Road, Randwick
1934 Rudder & Grout

Robin Hood Hotel
Bronte Road and Carrington Street, Waverley
1936-38 Copeman Lemont and Keesing

Henson Park Hotel
91 Illawarra Road, Marrickville
1936 Sydney Warden

Golden Barley Hotel (photo)
165-169 Edgeware Road, Marrickville
1939 RM Joy & Pollit

Light Brigade Hotel
2a Oxford Street, Woollahra
1939-40 Sydney Warden

457 Transport House

Part of the Intercontinental Hotel
99-113 Macquarie Street, Sydney
1938 HE Budden & Mackey
GC, V, A

Of the three inter-war Art Deco office buildings designed by Budden and Mackey for New South Wales government departments, Transport House was by far the most contextually sensitive in its style and choice of materials. Designed to accommodate offices of the Department of Road Transport and Tramways, it is sympathetic to the adjoining Treasury Buildings, being built of brick with red granite and sandstone facing and bronze spandrel panels. Reliefs and statues are by the master sculptor Raynor Hoff (see also the Anzac War Memorial **(427)**.

The interior is remarkably intact. The entry vestibule has a chequered marble floor; while the former Registration Hall has red scagliola columns and multicoloured terrazzo floors. The former Board Room features extensive Queensland walnut panelling and joinery, and there is also specially designed joinery and shelving in the Registration Hall.

•••

Compare this design with the same architect's buildings for the Department of Railways **(436)** *and the Water Board* **(454)**, *where compositions of contrasting horizontal and vertical lines are faced with faience tiles.*

•••

In 1985, Lord McAlpine purchased the adjoining Transport House site in order to protect views from the Hotel Intercontinental.

458

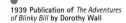

461

25 H 17

458 AWA Building

45–47 York Street, Sydney
1939 Robertson, Marks & McCredie with
DT Morrow & Gordon
GC, V, A

Amalgamated Wireless Australia (AWA) was a household name from the 1930s to the 1950s as a broadcaster and manufacturer of radio receivers, record players and other electronic equipment. The head office building, completed just before World War II, has expressive face brick, with projecting vertical ribs and parapet decoration in the form of a pegasus (the company's logo) in bas-relief, sculpted by Otto Steen. Built to the height limit of the day (150 feet (46 metres)), it became the outstanding Sydney landmark when the lattice steel communications tower was added to the top. It was the tallest structure in Sydney for some decades.

Original detailing to the refurbished ground-floor interiors includes the marble-clad lift foyer and stair, and the timber-panelled foyer with wall decorations in bas-relief and a mosaic 'Pegasus' laid in the floor.

24 J 15

459 Interocean House

Former Feltex House
Cnr George and Jamison Streets, Sydney
1939 Adam Wright & Apperly (first
three storeys)
GC, V, A

One of the best examples of late 1930s use of horizontal line and curved corners in the Streamlined Functionalist idiom. Originally a three-storey building designed to take subsequent floors, it included a roof garden and made extensive use of the then popular glass bricks. The building was later sympathetically extended to nine storeys.

277 Q 19

460 Macleay–Regis Apartments

12 Macleay Street, Potts Point
1939 EC Pitt & CC Phillips
GC, V, A

The last great apartment building completed before World War II and the austerity measures which followed. The freestanding ten-storey building has eighty-seven apartments, including one eastern penthouse with a barrel-vaulted living room and glass-protected roof terrace. With similar planning to the Rockefeller apartments in New York by Harrison, the Macleay-Regis ('King of Macleay Street') contains one- and two-bedroom apartments in a 60:40 ratio. The service kitchen on the eighth floor supplies meals throughout the building. At ground level, there is a large reception area ('enquiry office'), shops and below are common and private garages. Important features are good natural light and room depth. Pitt had previously worked with Bolot on 'Hillside' (**435**) in 1936.

56 Q 19

461 Film Studios

32 Orwell Street, Kings Cross
1939 RJ Magoffin & Associates
PC, V, NA

Built as a dance hall with twin mezzanine levels, this venue has undergone numerous changes of use, but is well known in the area for its strong Art Deco forms. The barrel-vaulted building on the opposite street corner is the former Metro Cafe, now occupied by Kennedy Miller Film Productions.

462

464

28 K 2

462 Motor Traders Association of NSW

Former 20th Century Fox Film Corporation Building
43-51 Brisbane Street, Surry Hills
1939 TW Hodgson & Sons
PC, V, NA

This area of Surry Hills, bounded by Riley, Campbell, Commonwealth and Goulburn Streets, had previously been the subject of a massive slum clearance program by Sydney City Council. With the housing removed, the area was designated light industrial, but very little interest was shown in moving there. The blossoming film industry, marked by the creation of many new cinemas, required fire-proof storage and distribution of celluloid film, which by then was considered an industrial use and risk. Being the closest industrial site to the CBD, two film companies moved there inspiring the erection of the nearby 'Hollywood Hotel'.

Twentieth Century Fox had their New South Wales office on the ground floor and their Australian office on the first floor. Other features include fire proof vaults, and a small theatrette where cinema owners could preview films.

48 J 5

463 House

5 Morella Road, Clifton Gardens
1939 Eric M Nicholls
GC, V, NA

Strong brick forms with Art Deco stylisations in the columns and engaged brick flutes.

•••

Eric Nicholls was apprenticed to Walter Burley Griffin in the early 1920s. A strong friendship developed and, in later years, Nicholls ran Griffin's office in Melbourne, taking on much of the design work as well as the responsibility of running the practice.

25 H 17

464 Red Cross House

Former Hoffnung House
153-159 Clarence Street, Sydney
1937-39 Samuel Lipson with Robertson, Marks & McCredie
1970-72 Lipson, Kaad and Fotherington (remodelling for Red Cross)
GC, V, A

The wholesale and retailing company S Hoffnung and Co. was well established in Sydney before it built its new flagship headquarters building in the Clarence Street warehousing district.

Samuel Lipson (1901-1996) was one of only a handful of architects in Sydney devoted to Modernism, designing car showrooms (Hastings Deering, Packard) and office buildings. This 'between the wars' building was Lipson's largest and most important high-rise commission, in which he was assisted by the well-established firm of Robertson & Marks.

The unbroken line of windows was made possible by setting the heavy mushroom-shaped columns just inside the line of the exterior, as at Hastings Deering **(447)**. A central chevron-shaped window, angled at 45 degrees to the street, gives a strong vertical treatment to the Clarence Street elevation.

•••

The wide business and horseracing interests of Theodore Marks, who was a director of several large corporations including Mercantile Mutual Insurance, brought frequent commissions to the firm of Robertson & Marks. He designed many of the buildings and also undertook alterations at racecourses such as Randwick, Warwick Farm, Canterbury and Moorefield, as well as Moonee Valley and Flemington in Melbourne.

466

465 'Gower Galtees' Apartments
6 Coogee Bay Road, Randwick
1940s Partly attrib. Hennessy and Hennessy
GC, V, A

This substantial modernistic design in face brickwork was built by HA Taylor, who also built St Joseph's College chapel at Hunters Hill. He used the same team of master bricklayers who were accustomed to the detailed work required for church architecture.

The name 'Gower-Galtees' derives from the area of Ireland from whence the original owner's family, the Rowans, originated. The Rowan family ran the nearby Royal Hotel **(234)** and made their fortune from a sweepstake which they ran called 'Rowan's Thousands'.

•••

HA Taylor married the owner/client and lived next door in a house designed by John Hennessy (1853–1924) called 'Gower', which is still occupied by a member of the family. It has been suggested that the 'Gower-Galtees' apartments were not designed by an architect, but rather were the result of client consultation with the builder.

•••

The current owners purchased the building from the original owners and have taken pride in its maintenance. Award-winning restoration work took place in 1993.

466 ACI Factory
Former Australian Glass Manufacturers (AGM)
Cnr Lachlan and South Dowling Streets, Waterloo
c. 1940 attrib. in part to Stephenson & Turner and AGM staff
BC, V, NA

The largest and most important factory complex of its day, Australian Glass Manufacturers promoted the modern spirit in building design (European Modernism), which used far greater glass areas than traditional buildings. The design would sit well in 1930s Berlin, with its highly composed corner elements and dramatic horizontal window lines. Although Sir Arthur Stephenson was AGM's architect, designing AGM House (1936–38) in William Street, it is more likely that this factory was designed and built over a number of years by AGM themselves, following sketches by Stephenson & Turner.

•••

The extensive ACI site has been purchased by a residential development company. Despite the building's obvious architectural significance, it seems likely that it will be demolished in the near future.

1940 20 000 Australian troops embark for service abroad

467

469

467 AFT House

Former Delfin House (Bank of New South Wales)
16–18 O'Connell Street, Sydney
1938–40 C Bruce Dellit
GC, V, A

After the impact of the Anzac Memorial **(427)** and Kyle House **(421)** nine years earlier, this was Bruce Dellit's best Art Deco office building. In the impressive skyscraper form, he has utilised stepped pinnacles at the summit, offset by a giant polished red granite arch infilled with an allegory of modern life at the base. The Australian 'land of plenty' theme is shown in carved bas-relief in the bronze doors executed by HT Worrall. The granite bas-relief over the doors was known as 'Sunrise over the Pacific'. The ground floor, originally a banking chamber, had speculative offices above. The foyer is detailed with decorative pressed metal fittings and the former banking chamber has a vaulted ceiling of neo-Egyptian character.

Alterations and additions were made to the banking chamber by Robertson and Marks in 1964, and to the second floor by McConnel, Smith and Johnson. In 1986–87, architects Jackson, Teece, Chesterman & Willis created new walls, suspended ceilings and introduced new lift mechanics for the finest extant Art Deco lift cars in Sydney.

468 FGS Building

48 Euston Road and Maddox Street, Alexandria
1940
GC, V, A

One of the few surviving Dudok-inspired factory complexes which, like the ACI Factory in Waterloo, command the street corner with a built-up vertical element, offset by the long horizontal lines of the factory behind.

469 Holy Cross Church

Adelaide Street, Bondi Junction
1940 Austin Mackay
GC, V, A

A rare and unusual brick Art Deco church influenced by Dutch architecture.

470 Beyond Pictures

Former Paramount Pictures Studios
53–55 Brisbane Street, Sydney
1940 Herbert, Wilson & Pynor
GC, V, NA

Like the 20th Century Fox Film Corporation before it **(462)**, Paramount Pictures moved to Brisbane Street with exactly the same building requirements as its neighbour. These included state offices on the ground floor, national offices on the first floor, a theaterette and a fireproof vault and loading dock for celluloid. Both buildings are faced with glazed terracotta tiles and have terrazzo floors and vitrolite panels. This building is in much better condition internally than its neighbour.

471 Queensland Insurance Co. Building

Former Bryant House
80–82 Pitt Street, Sydney
1936–40 Emil Sodersten with
TW Hodgson & Sons
GC, V, A

A development of the new architectural expression of the late 1930s on a less demanding site than that of City Mutual Life **(434)**, yet it shows a similar fenestration. The zig-zag window pattern grows out of the flat facade at second floor level by means of inverted pyramidal brick corbelling.

The Contemporary City
1940–1996

1940–1996

World War II brought an international outlook to Sydney.

In the first few years after World War II, as families were reunited, Australia began to develop a new set of values. The loss of human life due to the war had been evenly spread across the nation. Surprisingly, however, there were few memorials or monuments to World War II, as had followed the 1914–1918 war.

By 1947, greater Sydney had a population of 1,700,000, accounting for 22.5% of the national population. With 270,000 factory workers — nearly one-third of Australia's population — Sydney was able to sustain its three economic strengths. It was the major port for Australia (which laid the basis for the national economy); it had become an important finance, business and government centre (after Melbourne's early lead); and it was a powerful manufacturing centre attracting many migrant workers, who initially arrived in Sydney.

Planning for the future took on a new priority, and the first regional planning instrument for Sydney was published in 1948. This scheme for the County of Cumberland was the first legal masterplan for greater Sydney. Gazetted in 1951, it was to operate for the period 1951–1975 and it proposed satellite towns (St Marys, Blacktown, Riverstone, Campbelltown) with decentralised work centres located on road and rail routes radiating from the city centre. It also set aside a web of green belts which entirely surrounded Sydney from the north (Ku-ring-gai National Park) through the west to the south (Royal National Park). This ensured a substantial provision of open space per head of population. Envisaged as **'Sydney's Great Experiment'**, it was considered the epitome of green belt planning. However, by the mid-1960s, the population projections on which the plan was based had been vastly exceeded and the green belts were being eroded by ad hoc local council amendments and the State government's inability to curtail growth.

To counter this, the *Sydney Region Outline Plan 1970–2000* was drafted. This much amended strategy plan — which technically expires in the year of the Sydney Olympics — is now in the last phases of its implementation. It recognised and encouraged the higher than expected population growth by dismantling the green belt concept and reformulating it into the more flexible 'regional open space strategy'. The satellite centre concept was effectively replaced by the 'principle of linear extension along communications corridors', namely ribbon development along transport routes, which the 1951 County Plan had tried to arrest.

Rather than confining urban consolidation to inner parts of the city where there was ample infrastructure, the *Sydney Region Outline Plan 1970–2000* provided a relief valve for growth by encouraging development beyond the well-serviced inner zone and thereby consumed further land and created additional problems of environmental degradation.

FJ Holden Special Sedan, General Motors-Holden, Sydney 1955

Powerhouse Museum, Sydney

The plan also accelerated the measures for providing regional motorways and a non-radial highway grid, which was partly aimed at giving the growing western areas better access to the coast for recreation. However, the plan's most substantial legacy has been to promote the conurbation of Newcastle, Sydney and Wollongong into a megalopolis (served by the highway grid) by encouraging new commercial centres and discouraging employment in the central business district (CBD). This intention is also reflected in the Department of Planning's subsequent document, *Sydney's Future*. This was fuelled by a political objective: the Sydney region must absorb as much of Australia's growth as possible if it is to maintain its pre-eminent status as the nation's most powerful capital city.

The only major buildings commenced and completed during the early 1940s were directly related to the military or the injured. Hospitals, bringing with them a new architectural code – clean lines, clean interiors and no decoration – ushered in the rationalist imperative of functionalist high-rise buildings. 'Sanitary architecture' had arrived with zeal and large brick hospitals rose above the skyline in suburbs such as Camperdown, Concord, Paddington, Surry Hills, Manly, Randwick and Balmain. The Australian architect Sir Arthur Stephenson became a leading international authority on hospital design, influencing hospitals in Europe and receiving the RIBA Gold Medal in 1953. His most important design in Sydney was the **King George V Memorial Hospital** (1938–41) of equal significance to his later design for the Royal Melbourne Hospital.

The hospitals were unparalleled Cartesian monoliths built of bricks at a time of widespread shortages of building materials. Meanwhile, austerity measures had been introduced by the government, limiting both the size and cost of private housing.

Despite the shortages, a new but sparse architectural avant-garde emerged, with a vigour and a more controversial/ethical approach than the residential architects that went before them. In the efficient post-war spirit, many architects now saw their clients as the 'have-nots', as opposed to the 'haves' such as the wealthy retailing and brewing families who had been the patrons of residential architecture in Sydney since 1900. The spirit of change — a robust minimalism — pervaded business, design, transportation and the activities of government.

During the 1950s, Australian scholarship students and others who later migrated to Australia had been taught at American universities such as Yale, Pennsylvania, MIT and Harvard. There they were exposed to the new thinking of modern architects such as Gropius, Breuer, Mies van de Rohe and the organic American architect Frank Lloyd Wright. They trained a new generation to throw out conservative values and to think again about the image of architecture as understood through space, technology and engineering imperatives. Engineering expertise quickly became the key to the expression of the 'new' architecture, which proved difficult to realise in an environment of material shortages and low-technology practices. Sydney Ancher, Harry Seidler and Peter Muller introduced large areas of plate glass, domestic steel frames and lightweight cladding in projects such as the **Mervyn Farley House**, the **Rose Seidler House** and the **Audette House**.

Popular journals and homemaker magazines were fascinated by the sweeping domestic changes which began to appear in architectural designs and the political controversies which occasionally sprang up around them. A few architects demanded their artistic freedom and resorted to the courts to assert that freedom against the conservatism of some local councils. The inner-city councils and, in particular, the State Government welcomed new design and saw the city centre as a place of competing dynamic growth. Some areas such as Paddington, Woolloomooloo and The Rocks were slated for wholesale urban redevelopment, while North Sydney Council attempted to rezone much of its waterfront as industrial and the ridge areas as commercial high-rise.

The first American style high-rise office building was built in North Sydney in 1956. The **MLC Building** brought the glass and thin-panel walling system to Sydney which made steel frame buildings more profitable and easier to erect than ever before. It was closely followed by the ICI Building (now demolished) at Bennelong Point, **Qantas House** at Chifley Square and the **AMP Building** at Circular Quay, all of which signalled a new era of corporations reinventing their image with high-rise architecture. The names of companies were blazoned across building tops with few of the first high-rise buildings being built for property speculation. Many had mechanical teething problems; their low thermal mass, lack of sunshading and inability to accommodate opening windows because of wind effects made air conditioning systems a must. The early installations were inevitably troublesome.

While the corporate changes during the post-war economic boom were considerable, the arts community was not without its day in the sun. In January 1957, a committee of the New South Wales Government announced the winner of an international competition to build the new **Sydney Opera House**. Danish architect Jørn Utzon was selected out of a field of 233 entries, many of which showed innovative approaches. Second place went to American architects Marzella, Loschetter, Cunningham, Weissman, Brecher, Geddes and Qualls, and third to English architects Boissevain and Osmond. Judged by Eero Saarinen, Cobden Parkes, JL Martin and Henry Ashworth, the winning design had some similarities with Saarinen's own design for the TWA building at Kennedy International Airport (1956–62). With the majesty of a Gothic cathedral and the timeless imagery of harbour sails, the building suggested possibilities about modern architecture — the dissolving of walls and roof into one fluid composition — which few buildings could emulate.

The 1960s came and went while the Opera House was under construction. This period brought an unprecedented rebuilding of the low-scale urban fabric of the Sydney CBD as modern high-rise towers consumed the masonry Victorian city below. Various planning commissions, the State Planning Authority and private architects envisaged vast reconstructions of the city centre which involved the demolition of multiple city blocks and entire precincts. However, very few of these proposals went ahead because of delays caused by planning refusals and the short economic cycle in Sydney. The CBD planning experience was reduced to calculations, graphs and charts about pedestrian movements, employment sectors and use

Jumpsuit designed by Prue Acton, Melbourne, c. 1967.

Powerhouse Museum, Sydney

hierarchy. Traditional retailers and small business began losing footholds as site amalgamations enabling large commercial projects to proceed brought previously unheard of land prices. Famous institutions such as the Royal Exchange, The Australia Hotel, the Royal Arcade, the Imperial Arcade and the T & G Building were levelled and their sites excavated. The **Queen Victoria Markets Building** only barely escaped demolition by the Labor City Council for a raised public square with car parking below.

Beyond the city centre, the radial motorway system was consolidated and planned in earnest as the motor car reigned supreme, supported by generally affordable petrol prices. Most suburban growth occurred at the fringes, with commuter trips being pushed up to 90 minutes one way by car. The greater Sydney area extended to Berowra in the north, Bundeena in the south, Cambelltown in the southwest and St Marys in the west, covering about 250 square miles. Much of the fringe sprawl was directly related to the release of Crown land by the State government, which held site auctions for first home buyers. Decentralisation of employment affected vehicle movements, as traffic moved on the circumference from one centre to another. Despite this, the suburbs became not only the setting for life, but also the subject of life during the 1970s in the work of film-makers, authors and artists. Films such as *The Adventures of Barry Mackenzie* (1972), *Alvin Purple* (1973) and *Don's Party* (1976) parodied ordinary life in the suburbs.

In the social and cultural life of Sydney, seemingly led by a revolution in the literary and dramatic world, architects played a relatively meagre part. With the majority of architects in small practices, they continued to work on the individual house often located on bush blocks and steep sites — a process of infilling the unbuildable sites around the inner-city suburbs. Their best work is found around the waterways of Georges River, Middle Harbour and Pittwater.

The **Fombertaux House** (1972) in East Lindfield, **Short House** (1973) at Terrey Hills and the Carlstrom House, **'Nioka'** (1978) illustrated the relatively rare use of expressed steel framing in Sydney. The more common Sydney School approach was defined by brick and timber framing which blended into the bush with dark colours. This later evolved into the houses of project builders like Pettit and Sevitt, employing architects such as Ken Woolley and Terry Dorrough. Exhibition villages of low-set and skillion roof homes can still be found at suburbs like Carlingford and Pennant Hills in the northwest.

Women's leather sandals, made by Merivale, Australia 1970-78

Powerhouse Museum, Sydney

While European cities were being architecturally redefined by their new museums, and Philadelphia and New York were known for their office buildings, Sydney's architectural identity appears to have been defined through the private house. Architects such as Glenn Murcutt, Peter Stronach, Alex Tzannes, James Grose, Richard Le Plastrier, Neil Durbach and Alex Popov concentrated on the natural progression of the modern house, with a consistent design rhetoric seen in the use of interior furnishings, furniture, colours and materials. From similar style directions, the Sydney house was worked over and over again, producing one of the most consistent bodies of residential design to be found anywhere today.

Through the 1980s, the push towards the outer reaches of the city slowed down, and inner areas of the city were revitalised as traffic congestion to and from the city centre, coupled with rising petrol prices, took its toll. Paddington was almost wholly renovated as a white-collar suburb from its earlier workers' housing. Newtown was revived, as were Glebe and Annandale. With the approach of the bicentenary of first European settlement in 1988, major public works projects were also begun. These included: the revitalisation of Macquarie Street and Circular Quay, the reconstruction of Darling Harbour, the **Powerhouse Museum** by the Government Architect (Principal Architect Lionel Glendenning), the **Sydney Football Stadium** at Moore Park by Philip Cox and Partners, the **Sydney Exhibition Centre** by Philip Cox and Partners, the Sydney Aquarium by Philip Cox, Richardson, Taylor and Partners, the Convention Centre by John Andrews International and the **National Maritime Museum** by Philip Cox, Richardson Taylor and Partners. With the old railway yards at Darling Harbour redeveloped, the State Government has set its sights on a series of other large redevelopment projects near the city centre. They include redevelopment of the Finger Wharves at Walsh Bay, redevelopment of Eveleigh Goods Yards into the **Australian Technology Park**, redevelopment of the **Finger Wharf** at Woolloomooloo Bay, and the redevelopment of Pyrmont as a peninsula of six- to ten-storey apartment buildings. Further west, the Australian Defence Industries site at St Marys is under consideration as a new residential suburb; and harbourside facilities at Goat Island, Cockatoo Island and Balmoral held by the Federal government are also under review.

GRAHAM JAHN

'Embryo' chair (polyurethane, steel and neoprene) designed by Marc Newson, made by DeDeCe, Sydney, 1988.

Powerhouse Museum, Sydney

501

64 R 7

501 King George V Memorial Hospital
Missenden Road, Camperdown
1938–41 Stephenson & Turner
Terracotta plaques by Otto Steen
GC, V, A

An international sea change occurred in hospital
design during the 1930s, pioneered in Europe by
hospitals such as the Paimio Sanatorium near
Turku, Finland (1929–33), by Alvar Aalto. In
Australia, Sir Arthur Stephenson (1890–1967)
introduced modern hospital design in 1936 with
the Mercy Hospital in Melbourne. It was
followed by a number of major hospital projects,
including the King George V Memorial Hospital
near Sydney University. While the entry canopy
and circular skylights may be reminiscent of
Paimio, the overall design was considered an
Australian icon in its day, with powerful
expression and well-considered details such as
the staircases, entry, wrap around balconies and
forecourt. Much of the detailed entry design is
attributed to Arthur Baldwinson (1908–69), who

was a senior designer in the practice for a brief
period after he returned from London in 1937.
Baldwinson's hand can also be seen in the
former ACI House in William Street **(446)**.

Today, the King George V Memorial Hospital
remains an elegant interpretation of modern
functionalism and health care: clean lines equal
a clean environment.

●●●

Sir Arthur Stephenson was one of Australia's
most internationally respected architects, being
the first Australian recipient of the RIBA Gold
Medal. At one time, the firm of Stephenson and
Turner was Australia's largest design practice.
Stephenson professed a team approach (despite
being a gifted designer himself), sponsoring
study tours for employees to Europe and forging
powerful loyalty from his staff over many years.

502

236 J 8

502 Sydney Ancher Houses

2 Maytone Avenue, Killara 1951
'Poyntzfield', 3 Maytone Avenue, Killara 1945
(RAIA Sulman Medal 1945)
6 Maytone Avenue, Killara 1950
4 Maytone Avenue, Killara 1948
Sydney Ancher
GC, V, NA

The Maytone Avenue houses are in effect an enclave of modern case-study houses which reflect the linear open plan and grid frame first developed by European architects such as Mies van de Rohe. Sydney Ancher (1904–78), who had travelled widely, attracted attention as a young architect in the years 1930–39 with the Prevost House **(441)**. However, he broke practice to serve in the army in 1940 and returned to Australia with a renewed enthusiasm for the white, simple, flat-roofed modern house.

No. 3 Maytone Avenue, built for the architect himself, has a relatively open plan, good-sized kitchen and a fully glazed eastern side wall. Windows facing west were reduced to a minimum; the study and veranda acting as an extension to the living room. While the remaining blocks were sold on condition that Ancher be the architect, he experienced his first problems with a conservative local council opposing his flat-roof aesthetics.

Below: Plan of 'Poyntzfield', 3 Maytone Avenue, Killara (1945) by Sydney Ancher

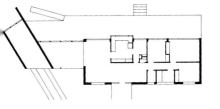

Post-War Reconstruction

The emphasis on post-war reconstruction resulted in a series of texts promoting better houses and better cities. In 1945, Sydney architect Walter Bunning wrote an influential book about the past, present and future of Australian housing which he called Homes in the Sun. *In 1948, under the banner of modern architecture, architect George Beiers included American Colonial, English and American Georgian, Venetian, Chinese, Spanish Californian, Queen Anne and a few others in his book* Houses of Australia.

During the period from 1943–49, Building and Engineering *showed more foreign architectural work than Australian owing to the lack of commissions and the slow post-war recovery.*

Australian architecture had gone into limbo during World War II. The war years, with the limitations on materials and costs, were followed by a period of reconstruction in which low-cost housing predominated. The functional aspects of avant-garde modern style came before aesthetics. As a result, the immediate post-war architecture of Sydney was restrained and disciplined.

Modernism introduced new interest in sun control, with pergolas and screens playing a greater role than the simple awning, in conjunction with large expanses of glass and lightweight walls. This treatment, although derived from international modernist examples, achieved a certain degree of recognition for its distinctive Australian character.   JH

236 J 8

503 House
55 Illeroy Avenue, Killara
1947–48 AHA Hanson
GC, V, NA
Sulman Medal winner in 1948.

504

239 L 11

504 'Windy Dropdown'
1 Molong Street, North Curl Curl
1946–48 Sydney Ancher
(later enlarged with upper storey and lower level additions)
GC, V, NA

Sydney Ancher's (1904–78) return to architecture following army service during World War II was vigorous and committed to the virtues of the modern house. His first commission for an old army friend and engineer, Mervyn Farley, brought Ancher to public notice. He won a test court case against Warringah Council which had declared his flat roof design both a 'startling innovation of the design' and 'an affront to decency'. The council suggested a form of modesty panel – a 600-mm high parapet to conceal the roof – which Ancher and Farley refused to include; they later won their case in the Land and Valuation Court.

Farley had served with Ancher in the Middle East as a surveyor and engineer. He purchased 9 acres of superb headland at North Curl Curl and planned two houses for the site.

Below: Ground floor plan, 1 Molong Street, North Curl Curl (1948)

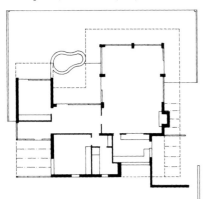

However, the post-war austerity measures limited each dwelling to 1,250 square feet and only one single-bedroom house, which could be added to later, was built. The introduction of the open plan seen here, which appropriated outdoor space as an extension of interior space, understandably flourished under the austerity rules which limited internal area. One of the most significant aspects of the design is the thin profiled cantilevered concrete roof. Formed in situ, it is only 100 mm thick and extends one and a half metres beyond the walls, which have a bagged cement finish.

The Farley court case was a milestone in the 'battle' to introduce the flat roof as an element of modern residential architecture. It was a significant precedent for court cases against local councils, especially those mounted later by Harry Seidler.

66 K 10

505 Wormald Bros Buildings
198-208 Young Street, Waterloo
1946 Stafford, Moor & Farrington
GC, V, NA

This early International Style factory of regular facade elements and concrete slab/lightweight infill construction won the RAIA Sulman Medal in 1947.

The Australian Dream
By 1945, Australia was one of the most suburban countries in the world, and much of its culture centred on the 'Australian Dream' – ownership of a freestanding house set in a garden. In 1948, the Cumberland County Council presented its planning scheme, which was adopted in 1951. John Tate, architect, member of the Mars Group and an activist for a successfully designed low-cost housing project at Ryde, helped spearhead the ideal. JH

●
1947 Australia agrees to resettle
displaced Europeans

●
1948 The first Australian-made
car (the Holden) is launched

●
1948 Don Bradman retires
from first-class cricket

506

215 P 10

506 Rose Seidler House
71 Clissold Road, Wahroonga
1948–50 Harry Seidler
Builder: Bret Lake
(Historic Houses Trust Property)
Open: Sun 10am–5pm
Closed: Christmas Day
GC, V, A

A pupil of Marcel Breuer and Walter Gropius, Harry Seidler (b. 1923) came to Australia after his parents' decision to emigrate and settle in Sydney in 1946. This house for his parents is one of three built for the Seidler family on a 6.5-hectare virgin bushland site overlooking the Ku-ring-gai Chase National Park. The parents' house, perhaps more than the other two, brought the rough/smooth 'modernistic style' reflected in Breuer's residential methodology: romantic spatial aesthetics (vertical voids, random stone walls and hearth), with the most direct approach to planning and structural 'problems' (no external expression of rooms, walls arranged on a grid). Breuer's influence in Seidler's design of small houses is attested to by the almost identical house designed by RD Thompson, another pupil of Breuer, in Foxborough, Massachusetts, built in 1947 and published in 1948. Seidler's house, in turn, received international recognition after 1952 when it was awarded the RAIA Sulman Medal.

The concrete floor is supported by expressed random sandstone walls and contrasting steel pipe columns. The external walls use American-style timber framing, with two layers of exterior boarding, and glass walls fitted with timber frames and steel opening casements. The house is a 'U' plan surrounding an outdoor terrace, marked by the compositionally important ramp which enables secondary access to the site below. No emphasis is placed on the front door, accessed by the original gravel driveway.

As with Breuer's North American houses, there is less exploration in this building of the extended flow between exterior and interior space, which suits the Sydney climate. However, this soon became an important feature in Seidler's house designs. The house is contemplative rather than interactive. Each internal 'space' and the three bedrooms have been carefully considered and furnished with a lyrical interplay between natural stone and the planar and extruded surfaces of walls, ceilings and window furnishings. The kitchen and laundry still contain the original modern conveniences and appliances, and original furniture by Saarinen, Hardoy and Eames.

•••

Recently arrived, the young Seidler was befriended by local modern architects Arthur Baldwinson, Sydney Ancher and Douglas B Snelling, who provided advice on local builders and sourcing materials.

•••

'When completed the house caused quite a stir; sightseers and press reports abounded. On weekends, people swarmed around the house…. looking through the glass walls!'   HS

Below: Living level plan, 'Rose Seidler House' (1948)

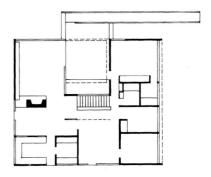

508

`215 P 10` `215 P 10`

507 Rose House

Clissold Road, Wahroonga
1949–50 Harry Seidler
BC, NV, NA

The second house built on the Seidler parents'
estate was for guests. This striking design
possessed the visual power and structural
expression which marked Seidler (even more
than the Rose Seidler House) as an important
architect during his first years in practice. The
design was a foretaste of what was to come,
that primary engineering solutions would
provide Seidler's most compelling means of
abstract expression.

With one elevated bedroom, the retreat was
built using a minimal structural steel frame of
four columns set 10 metres x 10 metres apart.
The floor frame of steel beams is suspended by
diagonal hangers which give support to the
20 metres x 8 metres joisted floor projecting
5 metres symmetrically at each end.

The conception of the three-house estate,
and the internationalism of the designs (equivalent to the work of Paul Rudolph in the USA at
the time) was a powerful statement by the
recently arrived young architect. The building
awaits an opportunity for future restoration.

508 House (Marcus Seidler)

Clissold Road, Wahroonga
1949–51 Harry Seidler
GC, NV, NA

This is the third house in the Turramurra trilogy,
along with Rose Seidler House built 1948–50
(506) and the Rose House of 1949–50 **(507)**.
The ground-floor blade wall features the second
(and last) mural to be painted by Seidler himself.
It was directly influenced by forms and shapes
of Brazilian architects Portinari and Burle Marx,
whom he had met while working with Oscar
Niemeyer in 1948.

●●●

Harry Seidler arrived in Sydney in 1948 and in
the next four years he completed ten buildings
and designed a number of others. Without
exception the completed buildings and some of
the projects had a lasting influence on Australian
architecture, particularly because of Seidler's
effective promotion of modern ideals through
his book, Houses, Interiors and Projects.

Below: Living level plan, Marcus Seidler House (1951)

Below: Living level plan, Rose House (1950)

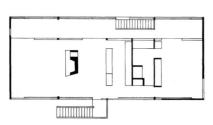

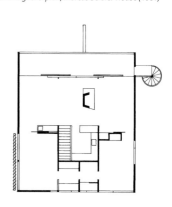

510

509 Former Top Dog Men's Wear Production Centre (Chesty Bond)

Cnr Pittwater and Harbord Road, Dee Why
1950 Spencer, Spencer and Blomfield
BC, V, NA

Built as a manufacturing plant, the various components – offices, factory floor, landmark tower – are subject to skilful massing first used by Dudok and the Scandinavians. A well-known precedent in Sydney is the Australian Glass Manufacturers (AGM) Factory **(466)** by Stephenson and Turner.

Dudok massing continued to influence large commercial building design and some technical schools for a short period. It even appears in Mediterranean guise in the work of crematoria during the 1940s.

Following a campaign by local residents to save the Top Dog Men's Wear factory from demolition, it is currently undergoing substantial adaptation for a new use.

•••

Functional Expressionism

A survey of the comments made by the professional journal Cross-Section *throughout the period reflects the extent to which the honest expression of function was implicitly accepted as a criterion of good architecture. Modernity was closely linked with rationality, which was expressed through clarity and consistency of detailing, and an honest use of materials consistent with their character and properties. In domestic design, there were two principal streams of thought. The rationality and machine ethics of the Bauhaus were represented by the work of the modernists, and a regionalist approach was influenced by Frank Lloyd Wright's organic theories and Scandinavian architecture. Many architects such as Baldwinson, Ancher and Snelling oscillated between the two positions.* JH

510 Apartments

17 Wylde Street, Potts Point
1948–51 Aaron Bolot
GC, V, NA

The complex of thirty-eight 'urban co-operative multi-home units' at 17 Wylde Street on the Potts Point ridge was one of Sydney's earliest circular-shaped apartment buildings. It is one of the most innovative designs of its day, employing the most up-to-date construction methods, planning and materials. It is not typical of Bolot's other more traditional apartment building designs. He produced an excellent and economical plan both at ground floor and on typical floors. The sweeping lines of glass and spandrel consist of stepped external walls of rendered brick infill, with pivot and fixed steel window frames resting on reinforced concrete slabs. Twin means of access are via a pair of lift/fire stairs and open stair cores which serve only two apartments each per floor. Every apartment has an open balcony cleverly centred between the living rooms and both bedrooms, although virtually all have since been sympathetically glazed over. All wet areas have been neatly arranged to the rear of the plan.

Below: Typical floor plan,
17 Wylde Street, Potts Point (1951)

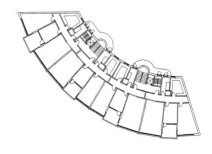

1950 Australia enters the
Korean War

1951 ANZUS security alliance is formed
(Australia, New Zealand and United States)

1952 The first bikini swimsuit causes
a sensation on a Queensland beach

512

24 J 14

511 Museum of Contemporary Art

Formerly The Maritime Services Board Building
Circular Quay West, The Rocks
1940–44 (design)   1947–52 (construction)
WH Withers & D Baxter (MSB Design Office)
Carved panels by Lyndon Dadswell
*1991 Peddle Thorp & Walker (alterations and
additions as an art museum)*
GC, V, A

This monumental 'H' plan office building was
designed to complement the functionalist
appearance of Circular Quay Railway Station,
which itself was the subject of considerable
public controversy during the 1930s. The
concrete-encased steel-framed building, which
is relatively narrow in cross-section, later
required additional area on the George Street
frontage to create sufficient gallery floor space.
The exterior brick walls are faced with Maroubra
yellowrock sandstone and detailed with polished
Rob Roy granite. The foyer is clad with polished
Wombeyan marble and edged with green marble
quarried near Mudgee in New South Wales.
Internally, the mezzanine balcony is decorated
with a wave design balustrade in aluminium.
Windows are bronze framed and, on the whole,
materials have been carefully specified to suit
the harbourside location.

Much of the building's decoration is contained
in bas-relief panels on the central tower and
over entrances, similar to the Rockefeller Centre
in New York. Commencement of construction
was interrupted by World War II; by the time the
building was completed, fashion had changed,
and it was considered an Art Deco dinosaur.

In 1984, after extensive negotiations, it was
offered to Sydney University as a museum for the
largest bequest of cash and modern art in the
university's history, known as the Power Bequest.

257 P 7

512 House (Audette)

265–267 Edinburgh Road, Castlecrag
1953 Peter Muller
GC, V, NA

Peter Muller (b. 1927) returned to Australia after
studying at the University of Pennsylvania, with
a strong direction towards the organic approach
of Frank Lloyd Wright – in marked contrast to
Seidler's elevated, flat-roofed houses influenced
by Harvard and Marcel Breuer.

His first commission was for a 'colonial house'
from an American, RB Audette, yet it emerged in
the dark-stained, site-hugging language of
Wright, with a subtle affinity to traditional
Japanese architecture. Varied interaction with
the site, strong landscaping, accentuated
massing and open planning (consistent Muller
principles) were established with this project.

*Below: Living level plan,
265–267 Edinburgh Road, Castlecrag (1953)*

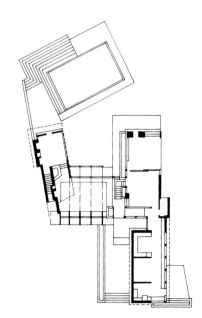

513

58 K 18

513 'The Chilterns'
593 New South Head Road, Rose Bay
1953–54 Douglas Forsyth Evans
GC, V, NA

Soon after the publication of the Unité
d'Habitation apartments by Le Corbusier,
Douglas Forsyth Evans designed the speculative
apartment building 'The Chilterns'. He applied
the same cantilevered structural system based
on the expression of oval-shaped tapered pilotis
elevating the building above the ground. Each
apartment is divided down the centre by the
structural wall resting on the pilotis, producing
oddly proportioned rooms. Two terraces at roof
level have since been wind protected by glass
panels; one is common to the building, the
other belongs to the top floor apartment.

Forysth Evans was an 'entrepreneurial', some
say bohemian, architect (mixing with writers and
artists such as Norman Lindsay). He designed
some unusual Modernist projects, including
apartments and hotels during the 1950s and
1960s. The engineer was Peter Miller.

•••

Although a fully chartered architect, Forsyth
Evans refused to join the RAIA because of its
code on fees. He acted as part architect and
part developer.

199 R 6

514 House (Currie)
Cnr Barrenjoey Road and The Avenue, Newport
1951–52 Harry Seidler
GC, V, NA

An early house by Harry Seidler which has been
recently restored by the architect. The design
included a wall of brightly coloured panels,
similar to the intense use of colour found in
'Treetops' **(612)** at Palm Beach, which was
designed in 1952. His later residential work is
invariably white with shades of grey.

58 Q 13

515 House, (Kelly)
22d Vaucluse Road, Vaucluse
1954–55 Douglas B Snelling
GC, V, NA

Built for Sir Theo Kelly, Chairman of the
Woolworths supermarket chain, this is perhaps
the last significant design in Sydney by the
architect Douglas Snelling (1917–85), who
moved to Hawaii after his marriage to an
American woman. The vast 'L' shaped plan is
extended by a floating roof structure which
completes the square and surrounds an internal
atrium water garden. The folded roof design,
with high-pitched rooflights and expressed
framing, suggests a buré (traditional south
Pacific hut), and has been loosely described as
'Hawaiian Style'. The thirty-room complex, which
includes six main bedrooms, separate guest
quarters, three bars, a heated pool and an
internal atrium water garden, is perhaps closer
to a resort than a single residence. For many
years, the house was owned by a slot machine
manufacturer who undertook some remodelling.
In 1996, it was purchased by a well-known
advertising personality.

Below: Living level plan,
22d Vaucluse Road, Vaucluse (1955)

517

58 J 19

516 Houses

24a, 24b, 22b Victoria Road, Bellevue Hill
1954 (24a) 1960 (24b) Douglas B Snelling
GC, NV, NA

This small group of houses by the Modernist architect Douglas Snelling (1917–85) showed a maturity of style which compared favourably with the elevated houses of his contemporary, Harry Seidler. Snelling's sculpted rectangular rooms with cantilevered flat roofs, full-height glazed walls, overlapping wall planes and artistic stonework are almost timeless in the Modern vein, and anticipate work by younger architects today. Although the 600 square metre house at 24a Victoria Road was at the time the largest new residence built in Sydney after World War II, it is now barely visible to the public.

The horizontal design of three stepped and interlocking wings is built on an acre site which is gently sloping and north-facing. The large ground floor area consists of open living, formal dining and lounge room, and small master bedroom opening on to its own terrace. A tennis court is attached along one side. Floating above the formal lounge are the study and sundeck, wrapped around the central stone fireplace.

The four-bedroom children's wing, which forms a courtyard, is reached by an internal ramp. Massive boulders were brought to the site from the south coast to build the 50 metres of stone retaining walls. This is one of the very few examples in Sydney of a large International Style house that combines abstract European rigour with the textural and overlapping roof language of Frank Lloyd Wright. There is clearly a link between this work and similar Californian case study houses of the period.

160 D 19

517 House (Muller)

42 Bynya Road, Whale Beach
1955 Peter Muller
GC, V, NA

An organic plan resolved by an organic design process which does not incorporate organic shapes. Peter Muller (b. 1927) built this house for his family in one of the most remote locations in Sydney during the 1950s. It was designed on site, incorporates part of the bush rocks and is based on the principle of massive Wrightian piers with cantilevered roof trusses.

•••

See also 36 Bynya Road, a weekender built for Mrs Tony Walcott (1955), based on the prismatic geometry of diamonds and the gridded square.

Below: Living level plan,
24b Victoria Road, Bellevue Hill (1960)

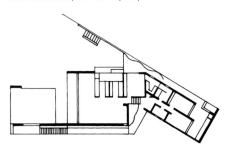

Below: Living level plan,
42 Bynya Road, Whale Beach (1955)

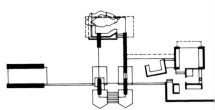

180 B 1

518 **'Kumale'**
949 Barrenjoey Road, Palm Beach
1955–56 Peter Muller
GC, V, NA

Built for the lawn mower magnate Arnold Victor Richardson, 'Kumale' occupies a narrow slice of bushland between Barrenjoey Road and Pittwater, with extensive water views from its cliff edge position. The Adelaide born architect Peter Muller (b. 1927), who had previously completed a Masters of Architecture at the University of Pennsylvania, designed this vast futuristic weekender, free from any direct con-nection with the European Modern Movement and the International Style. It directly borrows the circular geometric vocabulary of Frank Lloyd Wright found in buildings such as the David Wright house (1950), the Guggenheim Museum (1943–59) in New York and Marin County Offices (1954–57) in California. The house consists of a series of intersecting wings with circular appendages which hinge on the circular

foyer and radiating staircases. The recurring concentric circle motif appears in the bronze front door and the rooflight oculus.

The main wing rests on the edge of a cliff-face, approximately 7 metres below the road and 15 metres above the water level. A dynamic vertical element, only visible from the water, was a lift shaft projecting from the pool edge, intended to give access to a sea plane hangar so that Richardson could fly to his factory and home in Concord (the lift was never fitted because of conditions imposed by council). Throughout the interior, the circle is the primary motif, which some suggest sprang from an existing stone well on site. Twenty-nine cylindrical piers made of grey-green cast concrete blocks form the principal internal structure.

With Muller's emerging Buddhism, the circle may have possessed mystical and religious symbolism; however, it rarely appears in his later work. Declaring its separation from all references to the past, the building incorporates 'new' materials such as marine plywood, mastics and polyester fibreglass, and specially cast concrete elements.

●●●

'Kumale' is now hemmed in by houses on either side, even though its original setting was remote. The building is only visible from Pittwater, as it sits below road level.

Left: Living level plan, 'Kumale' (1955)

519

519 House (Goodman)

17 North Arm Road, Middle Cove
1956 Neville Gruzman
GC, V, NA

Neville Gruzman (b. 1928) was one of the first Australian architects to re-examine traditional Japanese architecture at a time when negative attitudes to Japanese culture were still current after World War II. Inspired by the book *The Architectural Beauty of Japan*, Gruzman took the unusual step of travelling to Japan in 1955 for four months, visiting and recording the post-and-beam architecture of traditional Japanese temples.

This house for physician Ben Goodman was Gruzman's first commission after his return. The large 300 x 300 square timber columns, stained black timberwork, copper panels and concave surfaces were a direct result of Gruzman's Japanese sojourn.

520 Commonwealth Bank

46–48 Market Street, Sydney
1956 Commonwealth Dept of Works
1988 Major street level alterations
Sculptors: Gerald Lewers, Lyndon Dadswell
AC, V, A

After plans for a new nine-storey branch of the Commonwealth Bank were shelved in 1941 because of the war, the scheme was redesigned during the 1950s as a narrower 12-storey building following Sydney City Council's widening of Market Street, which sliced 2.4 metres from the site. Below-ground works, involving three basement levels, were complicated, and the structure punctured the underground railway tunnels.

Sydney School

The term 'Sydney School' often refers to a group of university graduates who reacted against international Modernism during the 1960s. They preferred a regionalist approach and were drawn to rustic materials, clinker brick, low gutter lines, and raked roof lines rather than flat roofs — producing an architecture of walls rather than windows, which was contextual and blended into the landscape. In many ways, this group might be more accurately described as the 'Sydney University School'. A more appropriate use of the term 'Sydney School' would start with Peter Muller and Bill Lucas, who adopted the motto 'the best architecture is no architecture'. It is a school of thought which regards communing with nature as the primary role of the dwelling. Virtually confined to the house typology (except for some Murcutt buildings), and generally but not solely to Sydney's northern peninsula area (Pittwater), it has survived for more than forty years, longer than any equivalent vernacular approach in Melbourne or any other Australian capital city.

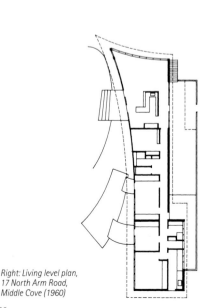

Right: Living level plan,
17 North Arm Road,
Middle Cove (1960)

522

521 House (Jack)

62 Boundary Road, Wahroonga
1956–57 John Allen and Russell Jack
GC, V, NA

By 1957, architects in Sydney with an interest in contemporary design, but who were disappointed with modern European architecture, turned to Frank Lloyd Wright and Japan. Those in the group who visited Japan photographed buildings and collected books, and brought their findings back to informal gatherings in architects' homes.

This war loan house (controlled in both budget and size), designed by architect Russell Jack for himself, is one of many that hesitantly reflects this change in direction. Influenced by the approach of Wright and founded on the assumed 'nature' philosophy of pre-war Japan, these houses had common themes: exposed construction (believed to be cheaper); natural materials (brick, stone, timber); modular plans with a primary structure and infill walls.

•••

Russell Jack was a graduate of Sydney Technical College. He believed that 'none of us [is] totally pure, and we tend to become uncomfortable in environments that do not accommodate our weaknesses'.

Below: Living level plan, 62 Boundary Road, Wahroonga (1957)

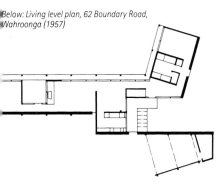

522 MLC Building

105 Miller Street, North Sydney
1956 Bates Smart & McCutcheon
GC, V, A

Sydney's most important early office building is in good condition and still occupied by the original client corporation. It heralded the coming to Sydney of the steel-framed and lightly clad machine pre-formed office buildings developed in the United States of America.

It was for a time the largest office building in Australia, limited only by the New South Wales State government's 150-foot height limit imposed in 1912, and was the penultimate major building required to comply with the code before the restriction was lifted for the AMP Building at Circular Quay built by the AMP Society **(532)**.

The slick design by Melbourne architects Bates Smart & McCutcheon was based on the construction principles and technology of Skidmore, Owings and Merrill's Lever House (1952) in New York, and was carefully detailed for ease and speed of construction. The same design was reproduced in a number of capital cities, with the first trial in Perth and the larger version being built in Sydney. So large was the impact that it transformed North Sydney into an alternative commercial business district.

The long, open-planned floors are rigidly connected steel-framed modules, with fire stairs at either end; the centre stiffened by a wind-resisting service core behind the building. The curtain wall, so called because it is literally hung from the frame, consists of heat-resistant glass with heavily anodised aluminium spandrel panels which cover the slab edges and provide the necessary fire protection between floors.

523

523 Qantas House

Cnr Chifley Square and Hunter Street, Sydney
1955–57 Rudder, Littlemore and Rudder
GC, V, A

Built for Qantas Airways, this was an expensive and very progressive building of the 1950s, which finally generated the semicircular form of Chifley Square (as it was intended in 1908). It also terminated the vista of Elizabeth Street looking north, which joins the twisted street grid of early settlement. Opened by Prime Minister Robert Menzies with great fanfare, it symbolised the aeronautic future of Qantas Airways and implied self-reliance and national pride in an Australian enterprise through the advertised use of locally sourced materials.

The curved 46-metre high facade (150 feet was still the height limit in Sydney) consists of a double-glazed curtain wall of green glass with enamelled steel spandrel panels, which conceals eleven steel-framed floors above a double volume glazed foyer. The northern end features a full height sandstone-faced wall which returns around the curvaceous plan at the top of the building. Above the sandstone banding is a recessed roof line containing company staff facilities and a rooftop recreation area.

Although much of the office interior has been modernised, the exterior closely resembles the original design including the use of Australian stone. It was the first to use Australian black granite from Adelong and Bookham green granite from the Yass area. Marble was sourced in the country town of Mudgee (green coloured) and the Wombeyan Caves area.

The interior features Australian timbers such as sycamore, mahogany and walnut. It was judged the best new building in the British Commonwealth by the Royal Institute of British Architects in 1959, and was awarded the Bronze Medal.

524 House (Lucas)

80 The Bulwark, Castlecrag
1957 Bill and Ruth Lucas
GC, NV, NA

Architects working with little or no budget, designing minimalist shelters for their own occupation during the 1950s, were the beginning of the natural, minimalist approach. The saying 'the best architecture is no architecture at all' reflects their attitude.

This tree house by Bill and Ruth Lucas reveals 'site thinking' with an inventive approach. The use of 'off-the-shelf' materials in its construction is reminiscent of Peter Muller's own house and office at Whale Beach, built two years earlier. From these tentative shelters by Lucas and Muller, a continuous minimalist shelter-in-nature movement grew up in northern Sydney, with the architect Richard Le Plastrier later becoming its spiritual leader. The 'glasshouse', as it is known, consists of a square, steel-framed, timber-joisted platform supported on four steel columns with extensive steel rod cross-bracing. Interconnected rooms are laid out around the perimeter of the square, with narrow balconies along the full length of two sides. The centre of the square consists of an open deck facing a square void, which looks through to the steep, tree covered site below.

Below: Living level plan, 'The Glasshouse' (1957)

527

528

`58 J 16`

525 House (Hauslaib)
22 Wyuna Road, Point Piper
1957 Arthur Baldwinson
GC, NV, NA

Arthur Baldwinson (1908-1969) was an important architect responsible for designing many modern movement buildings in Sydney. He returned from London in 1937, having worked for Maxwell Fry and Walter Gropius. The Hauslaib House is arguably Baldwinson's most prestigious residential commission, supported by a budget which allowed the architect to introduce textural refinements only tentatively suggested in previous works.

Horizontal lines, sheer walls of glazing, a strong parapet line and a textured stone base contribute to the external form. The upper and lower levels are connected by internal stairs and striking external stairs (a signature of early International Style houses) not unlike the designs of Harry Seidler. Organic timber details are introduced internally, including sculptured handrails and veneered wall panelling.

•••

Baldwinson was for many years an influential teacher of architecture at Sydney University, with an extensive first-hand knowledge of modern European buildings recorded in his notes, slide collection, drawings and lectures.

Below: Living level plan, 22 Wyuna Road, Point Piper (1957)

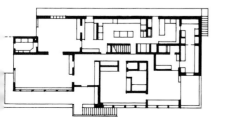

`26 L 17`

526 William Bland Centre
229-231 Macquarie Street, Sydney
1958 HP Oser
AC, V, A

The minimalist curtain wall reduces architecture to a grid of lines.

`28 K 4`

527 Office Building
72-84 Mary Street, Surry Hills
1960-61 HP Oser, Fombertaux and Associates
GC, V, NA

Relatively little is known of Oser and Fombertaux, although during the 1950s and 1960s they were highly regarded niche Modernists within architectural circles. This office building was commissioned by Tooheys Limited as showrooms and offices, with specific accommodation for the share registry.

`58 L 19`

528 House (Auswild)
609 New South Head Road, Rose Bay
1960-61 Ken Willoughby
GC, V, NA

The little known 'artist–architect' Ken Willoughby was commissioned to prepare sketches for a house to be sited on a parcel of land carved off the front of the original house. The actual building documents were prepared by a draftsman. The carefully detailed main entrance is located in the side street and survives in pristine condition. The first owners still live in the house, which has been impeccably maintained with its original 1960s interior, including custom-made furniture.

When first built it was the sensation of Sydney's fashion-conscious eastern suburbs. The family has recently split the house into a duplex. The original house of the estate is behind, divided into eight flats.

● 1956 Melbourne hosts
the Olympic Games

● 1957 Ballerina Margot Fonteyn
tours Australia

● 1958 Slim Dusty has No.1
hit 'The Pub with no Beer'

529

45 G 9

529 Blues Point Tower

14 Blues Point Road, McMahons Point
1961–62 Harry Seidler & Associates
GC, V, NA

In 1957, a vast area of McMahons Point and
North Sydney was to be rezoned as 'waterfront
industrial' by North Sydney Council, but a
resistance group was formed by local residents
and vocal architects, led by Harry Seidler (b. 1923).
They argued for an alternative residential vision
for the peninsula: in Seidler's version, a Corbusian
scheme of twenty-nine apartment blocks set in
gardens. A huge model was built, which was
driven around on the back of a truck, and the
proposal turned into a media event which
attracted political attention. In 1958, the New
South Wales government overturned the
council's proposal and the campaign for
residential zoning succeeded. At this point
Seidler's grand vision disintegrated; property
sale prices escalated, people started renovating
their own houses and the council made no
effort to enforce the scheme. Seidler's own
office today looks out over land which was part
of the massive plan.

Of the scheme, which consisted of a landmark
hotel, seven high-rise towers, twelve mid-rise
blocks and nine low-rise blocks, only the hotel
site on Blues Point was developed as apartments
by Lend Lease Corp founder, GJ Dusseldorp.
Seidler compared the density of the scheme to
that of Potts Point, and aimed at accommodating
150 people per acre (330 people per hectare). At
first there were difficulties selling the units and
many were rented. The mix includes studio, two-
and three-bedroom units. Alternating window
arrangements on the facade directly reflect the
fire separation codes of the day, while art
aficionados may make some visual association
with Josef Albers painting *The City* (1928). The
structure consists of concrete shear walls,

which penetrate the building like an egg slicer,
restricting the future enlargement of the small
apartments. As an orphan tower, it became,
perhaps unfairly, an easy target for critics of
modern architecture, and was featured in
cartoons and articles, which ultimately drew
defamation suits from the architect.

● ● ●

Sometimes called Sydney's most unloved
building, Blues Point Tower has often been the
butt of criticism: Ted Mack, a former mayor of
North Sydney, was quoted in the Sydney
Morning Herald *as saying: 'It represents the full*
flowering of the ideals of the Bauhaus
movement of the 1920s, and as such deserves
to be listed by the National Trust — not our
National Trust, the German National Trust'.

Below: Plan of tower at ground level clearly shows the
blade wall construction called 'shear wall' used to stiffen
the building against swaying.

530

531

24 J 15

257 L 4

530 Liner House
13–15 Bridge Street, Sydney
1959–61 Bunning & Madden
Artists: Douglas Annand, Z Vesley
GC, V, A

A dignified interpretation of the International Style commissioned by the Wilh Wilhelmsen Agency, Norway's largest shipping company. Ignoring the opportunity to build a modern tower following the removal of height controls, the company decided to respect the historic street height and build to the same height as the adjoining Burns Philp Building. The curtain wall design, with its transparency and functional presentation is said to be influenced by Casa del Fascio, Como, Italy (1936), by the architect Guiseppe Terragni.

Maritime carvings decorate the flanking walls, and a mural screen was designed by Douglas Annand, a noted designer at the time. The glass wall is tempered with projecting awnings of shading louvres, while the transparent foyer features a mezzanine floor with a spiral staircase.

In 1997, the building was purchased by the Moran Health Care Group as its administrative headquarters.

531 House (Holland)
31 Rembrandt Drive, Middle Cove
1960–62 Neville Gruzman
Engineer: Miller, Milston & Ferris
GC, V, NA

This house designed for Douglas Holland occupies what was considered an 'unsaleable' site because of its poor access and sheer drop. Part of the land was 3 metres below the roadway, while the remainder of the bushland site was 15 metres further down, bisected by a rock ledge. There are two structural systems: vertically stacked masonry blocks where the rise is minimal, and steel and timber where there is the massive drop. Two large 'I' beams were drilled into the rock face itself to act as primary support arms for a pavilion sitting on a timber deck. The exterior consists of self-bracing structural 'T' section steel windows, with water-proof plywood decks and a built-up roof.

The floating, unhandrailed decks, cantilevered into space, were said to remind Mrs Holland of a 'stage' which, being a professional actress herself, she found very appealing.

•••

This large house attracted considerable public attention when completed, and was well received by architectural critics.

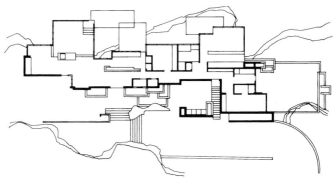

Right: Living level plan,
31 Rembrandt Drive,
Middle Cove (1962)

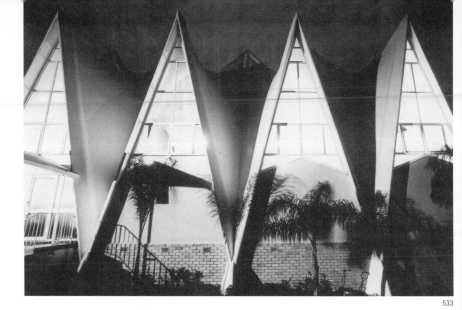

533

24 K 14	239 E 6

532 Australian Mutual Provident (AMP) Building

Alfred, Young and Phillip Streets, Sydney
1962 Peddle Thorp & Walker
Sculptor: Tom Bass
GC, V, A

As early as 1956, the AMP Society began discussions with Sydney Council for an office tower considerably larger than planning controls would permit. In 1957, a Bill was passed by the NSW Parliament enabling the application to proceed and plans were finally submitted in 1959. The proposed tower covered 55% of the site and the remainder was public area. This generated considerable public debate for more than a year, as it was more than twice as high as any other city building (excluding the AWA Tower).

The consultant team was directly influenced by the new Gordon Bunshaft-designed curtain wall office towers in New York, which used a rigid frame of concrete-encased steel, supporting steel cellular floors. The design brought with it many technical problems. Early air-conditioning problems during hot summers, facing a reflective harbour, were significant.

•••

The AMP building was Sydney's first skyscraper to challenge and remove the 150-foot height limit which had been a uniform restriction over central Sydney since 1912.

•••

Floor space ratios in the city emerged from an earlier 150-foot height control. Older buildings achieved twelve floors, newer buildings with air-conditioning thirteen floors. A maximum figure of 12 and later 12.5 to 1 was agreed on purely pragmatic grounds, ignoring traffic, width of streets and aesthetic issues. Only cities in the USA and Hong Kong exceeded Sydney's FSRs, with most European cities having floor space ratios of about half of those in Sydney.

533 St Kevin's Catholic Church

50 Oaks Avenue, Dee Why
1959–62 Gibbons and Gibbons
GC, V, A

St Kevin's is a rare organic/structuralist design of the late 1950s using moulded precast and in situ shell construction. The building replaces an earlier church destroyed by fire in 1958. Sydney architects Gibbons & Gibbons, incorporating the thin curvilinear concrete principles advanced by Felix Candela, commenced construction in 1960 by initially tracing the outline of the proposed structure in steel pipe scaffolding. Precast concrete elements forming the basic shape of the structure were then placed in position. High-tensile steel wire was drawn through and the whole structure was post-tensioned, after which concrete infill panels were added.

Under this method of construction, formwork for only one section at a time was required to build the bays. Concrete casting was done at the workshop and brought to the site.

The artists John Coburn and his wife Barbara designed the stained-glass windows and made the fourteen stations of the cross located around the walls of the church. Ordinary bathroom tiles were broken into small pieces and glued into place to form the stations. The bell tower on the eastern side rises 17 metres above ground. The bell was a gift to the church (which is run by the Scalabrinian Fathers) by the NSW Board of Fire Commissioners to commemorate its rebuilding after the tragedy.

•••

This little-known church reflected design developments in concrete shell technology found worldwide. Other churches employing the same techniques are found in San Francisco, Mexico, Canada and France.

1960 First production of Alan
Seymour's play *The One Day of the Year*

1961 Current affairs program
'Four Corners' begins on ABC

1962 Australian Ballet
Company established

536

26 L 17

534 Reserve Bank of Australia

65 Martin Place and Macquarie Street, Sydney
1962–64 Special Projects Division,
Commonwealth Department of Works
Sculptors: Bim Hilder, Margel Hinder
1994 Peddle Thorp & Walker (refurbishment)
GC, V, A

The Reserve Bank was created in 1959 after
Federal Parliament legislated to separate the
Central Bank's regulatory functions from the
retail and commercial functions of the
Commonwealth Bank. The design, which is
decidedly Miesian, is executed in marble, bronze
and glass, with a reinforced concrete column
and beam frame rather than rigid steelwork. As
a tower/podium ensemble, the design is sharp
and striking, and with its north-facing position
on Martin Place, it clearly demonstrates the
width of street frontage required to support
buildings of this height (264 feet) and scale.

375 H 7

535 House (Muller)

67a Lilli Pilli Point Road, Lilli Pilli
1963 Harry Seidler & Associates
GC, NV, NA

A forerunner of Seidler's developing approach
to a more refined heavy masonry house, as
exemplified in his own house at Killara **(544)**.

Below: 67a Lilli Pilli Point Road, Lilli Pilli (1963)

213 B 16

536 'Mirrabooka'

372 Old Northern Road, Castle Hill
1961–64 Bruce Rickard
GC, NV, NA

Nestled in a hillside, facing west with sweeping
views, this house designed by Bruce Rickard
(b. 1929) represents an important period of
1960s design in Sydney. Rickard was the most
skilful proponent of Frank Lloyd Wright's middle
period architecture: intersecting volumes,
floating roof planes, timber detailing and
interlocking planning. 'Mirrabooka' is one of
Rickard's most interesting houses, despite early
design revisions. The original clients still live
there, having purchased the site to pursue their
horticultural interests. Visitors enter via stepping
stones across a fish pond and arrive at an
interior of concrete floor pavers finished in a
China red topping. All of the interior furnishings
and joinery remain in excellent condition.

•••

The interior sandstone walls of random coursing
and projecting pieces were directly influenced
by the Van Damme residence in Alfred
Hitchcock's North by North-West. Photographs
of the set from MGM in Hollywood were used
by the stone masons as reference on site.

Below: Living level plan, 372 Old Northern Road,
Castle Hill (1964)

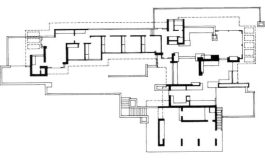

26 K 17

537 'The Cullinan'
Former La Salle Building
70 Castlereagh Street (Cnr King Street), Sydney
1964 Ian McKay
GC, V, NA

The La Salle Building was a rare attempt at designing a high-rise retail building like a 'vertical shopping arcade' – a concept which at the time was thought to be a high-rise answer to the horizontal shopping arcade of the 19th century. Unfortunately, the scheme was a commercial failure, and the floors have since been converted to offices with a Chanel boutique on the ground floor. It has a refined and well-designed facade treatment of wide vertical bands and closely spaced vertical mullions, both in bronze.

26 J 20

538 New Metropolitan Water, Sewerage & Drainage Board Building (MWS&DB)
Cnr Pitt and Bathurst Streets, Sydney
1965 McConnel, Smith & Johnson
GC, V, A

Designed by McConnel Smith and Johnson, the MWS&DB's 27-storey tower represented an early reaction against the lightweight imported glass office tower. The deeply shaded facade, with smaller window areas and sandstone-toned precast concrete tried to establish a visual link with the sandstone buildings of Sydney's Victorian past.

Each facade is designed according to its orientation, dictating the size or absence of openings. Precast concrete hoods give protection against sun penetration, reduce glare and serve as window cleaners' balconies, and eschew decoration. This 27-storey structure was the first major office tower outside the central business district, bringing high-rise to the southern part of the city.

49 B 9

539 Wentworth Memorial Church
Fitzwilliam Street, Vaucluse
1964–65 Clarke Gazzard and Yeomans
Design Architect: Donald Gazzard
GC, V, A

After the rediscovery of traditional Japanese architecture in the 1950s by post-war architects, several international critics (such as Bernard Rudofsky and Norberg Schultz) began to promote southern Italy and Greece as sources of vernacular architecture. A few Sydney architects (Glenn Murcutt and Don Gazzard included) viewed their designs from a more poetic and vernacular perspective, drawing on simplistic forms which might not reveal the hand of an architect.

The Wentworth Memorial Church, designed by Donald Gazzard (assisted by Richard Le Plastrier) is prominently located on a rocky outcrop and can be approached from below (next to the Wentworth Mausoleum) by a winding path that provides a sequence of vistas of the building. The process of gradual revelation has a Greek sense of three-dimensional form and sequential progression.

278 A 19

540 Apartment Building
Elizabeth Bay Road, Elizabeth Bay
1967 Ancher Mortlock Murray & Woolley
GC, V, NA

This lavish five-storey scheme has two double-storey apartments of 280 square metres each and a single-level penthouse of 110 square metres. The unusual organic plan responds to building setbacks and is built of thick precast concrete loadbearing wall panels and prestressed concrete T-beam floor panels.

541

543

541 House (Lyons)
733 Port Hacking Road, Dolans Bay
1967 Robin Boyd, Romberg & Boyd
GC, NV, NA

This is the only Sydney house designed by Melbourne architect Robin Boyd (1919–72). It was supervised in Sydney by Boyd's university friend Stan Smith from McConnel Smith & Johnson. The house is unusually built around an inground swimming pool located in an internal courtyard, and is clad in timber.

542 Wentworth Hotel
Former Qantas Wentworth Hotel
61 Phillip Street, Sydney
1962–66 Skidmore Owings and Merrill
(San Francisco) with Laurie and Heath
GC, V, A

In 1962, Qantas Airways, buoyed by their expanding business and the sophisticated office building on Chifley Square **(523)**, announced their intention to demolish the Wentworth Hotel on Church Hill, erect an office tower **(573)** on the site, and build a new 'Wentworth Hotel' at Chifley Square. When it opened its doors, it was Australia's largest hotel, with 452 rooms incorporating a number of early technological feats such as being the largest high-rise brick building and having the largest air-conditioning system in the Southern Hemisphere.

In co-operation with the relatively conservative Sydney firm of WR Laurie and EF Heath, international architects Skidmore Owings and Merrill created a landmark structure based on a horseshoe form with a sinuous prefabricated copper awning. The original interiors were considered the best example of 1960s modern (design by Audrey Borgenhagen), but have sadly been replaced with a more anonymous, sanitised gilt and glitter look.

543 Australia Square Plaza and Tower Building
Cnr George, Bond and Pitt Streets, Sydney
1961–67 Harry Seidler & Associates
GC, V, A

With the claim of being the world's tallest lightweight concrete office building (183 metres), Australia Square was built by Civil and Civic, and designed by Harry Seidler (b. 1923) following the amalgamation of thirty smaller inner-city sites. The developer was GJ Dusseldorp, the founder of Lend Lease Corporation which still owns and occupies the building. The scheme contains an integrated development of office space, small retail shops, car parking and a public plaza, and features ribbed floor structures by the Italian engineer PL Nervi.

In his proposal, Seidler suggested that the circular tower 'would eliminate the dark canyon effect of rectangular buildings' after an earlier rectangular scheme had been proposed by his Harvard classmate IM Pei. Together with the State Office Block, finished in the same year, Australia Square dispensed with the podium which retained street definition. According to Seidler, 'both from a rational and aesthetic viewpoint, modern architecture can only begin to express itself in the free-standing building'. Despite the recent reaction against setback and freestanding buildings, the urban space between the tower and the Pitt Street building is one of the more successful and frequented privately owned public spaces in the city.

Tapestries by Le Corbusier and Vasarely are hung in the foyer and a Calder stabile is located near the George Street entrance.

•••

In 1969, the artist Christo proposed to wrap up the tower but, after encountering considerable difficulties, decided to wrap Little Bay near La Perouse instead.

544 House (Seidler)

13 Kalang Avenue, Killara
1966–67 Harry and Penelope Seidler
GC, NV, NA

Set in a leafy valley surrounded by a bushland reserve, Harry and Penelope Seidler built their own substantial house.

The plan consists of four suspended concrete bridges arranged as split-levels supported by transverse reinforced concrete block piers. The cross-pier grid generally divides the interior into a central circulation zone, 'active' or day-time rooms facing north, and 'passive' or bedrooms facing south. The split-level plan is organised around a central open well with a fireplace, through which the stairs pass, but the well, surprisingly, is not skylit. As with the earlier houses, external access — in this instance a concrete stair to the lawn area — and the concrete entry bridge animate the external elevations as tensional compositions.

545 House (Schuchard)

29 Battle Boulevarde, Seaforth
1967 Stan Symonds
Engineer: Max Newman
GC, V, NA

Known in Sydney as 'the spaceship', this large 450 square metre, eight-bedroom house designed by architect Stan Symonds relies on curved reinforced concrete forms to conquer the very steep site. Without stable access for machinery, all the work had to be done by hand, including the concrete for the columns which was poured in sections. Infill walls were made from bricks salvaged from demolished terrace houses in North Sydney, called 'North Sydney whites'. The original design included a courtyard with trees growing in the centre of the house.

●●●

Further variations on the 'spaceship' design by Stan Symonds are located at: 2 Amaroo Crescent, Mosman; 2 West Crescent, McMahons Point; 5 Sandra Place, Seaforth; Ilya Avenue, Bayview; and McCarrs Creek Road, Church Point. One of Symond's most prominent designs is the octagonal 'concrete bunker' house in Northview Road, Palm Beach.

Below: Living level plan, 13 Kalang Avenue, Killara (1967)

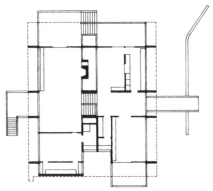

Below: Living level plan, 29 Battle Boulevarde, Seaforth (1967)

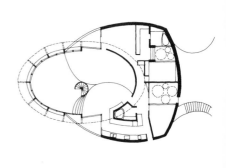

547

546 State Office Block

74–80 Phillip Street (Cnr Phillip, Bent and
Macquarie Streets), Sydney
1967 EH Farmer (NSWGA)
Design Architect: Ken Woolley
AC, V, NA

Using land which was part of the original
Domain, the New South Wales government
consolidated their administrative functions into
three buildings: a 35-storey office tower, a nine-
storey north wing, and a ten-storey Premier's
wing. In addition to housing six government
departments, the brief called for a theatrette,
post office, library, cafeteria, information centre,
conference rooms, cabinet room and state
reception area.

The corner of the site has a helical spiral
fountain made of copper and unpolished
granite. The site was recently sold to Lend Lease
Corporation, which intends to demolish the
structure and replace it with two towers
designed by Italian architect Renzo Piano.

547 Reader's Digest

Cooper, Waterloo and Adelaide Streets,
Surry Hills
1968 John James
GC, V, NA

A distinctive building housing offices and
printing facilities for the Reader's Digest
company by John James, a noted scholar and
architect. James, who had returned to Australia
in 1957, was philosophically opposed to
Brutalism. Avoiding grey off-form concrete, the
sculptured, almost organic appearance of the
major elements of the building are proportioned
in a 2:1 ratio of the Fibonacci series. This
required precise formwork and exacting setout.
Principally concerned with craft and assembly,
the architect's curvilinear shapes are based on
humanist considerations, including view framing
and the behaviour of rain on surfaces.

548 'The Penthouses'

57–61 New Beach Road, Darling Point
1968 Ancher Mortlock Murray & Woolley
GC, V, NA

During the 1960s, there was a boom in apartment building with considerable development in
the inner-city suburbs of Elizabeth Bay, Potts
Point and Rushcutters Bay. In this project, a
balance was sought between the accommodation
of a suburban house and the convenience of
high-rise apartment living.

The building stands on a sloping harbourside
site providing fine views to the north and west.
The units terrace back from the street frontage,
affording each level a generous, planted patio at
the front. Privacy is ensured by the design of the
balustrades and the placement of planting
boxes. To the rear, a well-planned system of
vehicular and pedestrian entries affords identity
and protection to each apartment.

● 1965 Opera singer Joan
Sutherland returns to Australia

● 1966 Australia converts to
decimal currency

● 1967 Murderer Robert Ryan last
person to be executed in Australia

549

550

47 B 4

549 House (Collins)

2b Mosman Street, Mosman
1970s Rourke and Collins
GC, V, NA

This fibreglass house designed and built by architect Ian Collins for his own home sits neatly within the confines of the steeply sloping triangular site overlooking Mosman Bay. The pavilion plan, with a repetitive structural grid of steel columns, tightly organised service areas and matter-of-fact cladding material, seems to anticipate the elevated bush houses designed by Glenn Murcutt a decade later. The relatively solid wall surfaces provide privacy from surrounding buildings and the pedestrian access to Mosman Wharf. The use of dry-jointed prefabricated fibreglass panels was not intended as a prototype for further houses. Floor and roof are both made of concrete. The structure, which has been carefully inserted under a mature tree canopy, creates minimal site disturbance, although it sits in stark contrast to nearby Federation style housing.

●●●

The building was passed without a hiccup by Mosman Council in 1974, the only request being for minimal information about the fibreglass construction.

233 F 2

550 House (Smith)

25–27 Glenhope Road, West Pennant Hills
1969–70 Enrico Taglietti
GC, V, NA

Enrico Taglietti (b. 1926), an Italian-born architect, has been based in Canberra since 1954. He has completed a small number of projects in Sydney in his angular concrete sculpturist style. This Pennant Hills house, commissioned and constructed by a builder and civil engineer (for whom the architect has designed two other projects), demonstrates Taglietti's chamfered compositional techniques, particularly in the pavilion roof forms. It has sculptured concrete elements in the garden walls, and exaggerated gutter projection which cuts across the middle of the two flattened-pyramid shingled roofs.

●●●

Other projects by Taglietti include St Anthony's church at Marsfield (1968) and a three-storey apartment building (1971) in Herring Road, Marsfield.

Below: Living level plan,
25–27 Glenhope Road, West Pennant Hills (1970s)

Below: Living level plan,
2b Mosman Street, Mosman (1970s)

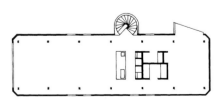

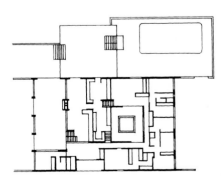

551

258 A 5

551 House (Buhrich)
375 Edinburgh Road, Castlecrag
1968–72 Hugh Buhrich
GC, V, NA

Literally perched on a cliff edge in Castlecrag — the suburb which was once Walter Burley Griffin's vision for a new society — this small house designed for his family by the Austrian immigrant architect Hugh Buhrich (b. 1911) is theoretically (and partially) an addition to a former Griffin 'Knitlock' home.

The single-storey pavilion contains an open living/dining room and kitchen, bright red moulded fibreglass bathroom, and two bedrooms. The ceilings are lined with extra thin timber boards, which were soaked in water and applied to the ceiling framing in the shape of an organic wave. The exterior is a mixture of materials. In the kitchen/dining area, clear toughened glass appears to support a concrete spandrel beam and a wall of perforated timber louvres (to ventilate the kitchen units), all supported on a small tube steel column. The form and plan is almost entirely decided by the site shape and planning controls. An intriguing and important project this, the second Buhrich house, is elegant, experimental, slightly rough, highly original and built by the architect himself.

The Buhrich house is a visual reminder that the history of interesting post-war houses in Sydney is told through architects' designs for difficult, steep sites. 'Unbuildable' sites were often left pockets of land which could not be built on without the input of an architect and engineer. Many Sydney architects have built their own homes on such sites.

58 R 11

552 House (McFarland)
40 Wentworth Road, Vaucluse
1970s Guilford Bell
GC, V, NA

This house was one of the largest residential projects designed by Guilford Bell. Largely an eastern suburbs society architect, Bell had a contemplative and humanist view and was often drawn to the exotic and symmetrical grandeur of temples and palaces. Many of Bell's designs resemble Moorish, Spanish or Roman villas, with arcaded courtyards and reflecting pools.

Below: Living level plan,
40 Wentworth Road,
Vaucluse (1970s)

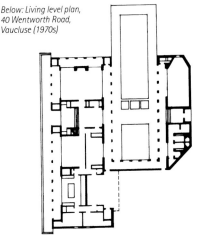

Below: Living level plan,
375 Edinburgh Road, Castlecrag (1972)

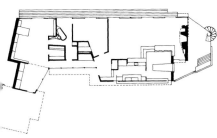

553

24 M 12

553 Sydney Opera House
Bennelong Point, Sydney
1957–63 Jørn Utzon (Stage 1)
1963–73 (NSWGA), Hall Todd & Littlemore
(Stage 2 – interiors and glass walls)
Engineers: Ove Arup & Partners
GC, V, A

An extraordinary site on Sydney Harbour at Bennelong Point, an ambitious state Premier (Joseph J Cahill), a visiting American architect (Eero Saarinen) and a young Dane's billowy sketches (Jørn Utzon) were the key factors which generated one of the world's most important modern buildings. Designed at the vast scale of the harbour itself, its low edges contain enough visual appeal for human interest. More remarkable is that the scheme makes no reference to history or to classical architectural forms. The roof is more important than the walls, consequently the language of walls – columns, divisions, windows and pediments – has been effectively dispensed with. As a public building, it conceals its usage in its lack of historical associations, and restores the concept of the 'monument' as being acceptable in social terms.

The Sydney Opera House also embodies timeless popular metaphors. The building's organic shape and lack of surface decoration have made it both timeless and ageless. Moreover, it demonstrates how buildings can add to environmental experience rather than

detract from it – something of spiritual value independent of function. The building and the setting look orchestrated, and the synergy between the setting and the building make it appear that the scheme actually involved flooding the harbour valley to set the building off to best advantage.

Despite so much richness, the building has had virtually no influence on the shape and form of Australian buildings which followed. It remains something of an enigma which crowns the silent collapse of Western Classical architecture from being the one language for great public buildings.

Jørn Utzon's historic resignation caused a furore and divided the Sydney architecture profession. There were rallies and marches to Sydney Town Hall led by architects such as Peter Kollar and Harry Seidler; other architects resigned their profession and became teachers, chefs, film makers and artists in protest, and the Victorian Chapter of the RAIA (but not NSW) black-banned the replacement of Utzon by an Australian architect. However, as with Governor Macquarie, Greenway, Light, Barnet and Griffin before him, Utzon's vision had exceeded the norm. The immense difficulties of achievement were seen as a waste and the importance of controlling the state's expenditure won the day. On 19 April 1966, the new architectural team (Lionel Todd, David Littlemore, and Peter Hall) was appointed in a whirlpool of debate.

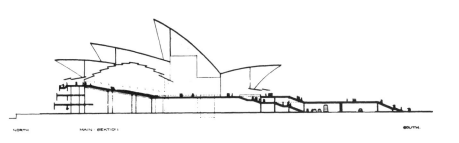

NORTH   MAIN · SEKTION   SOUTH.

Top: Model photos from the Red Book
Above: Design section by Jørn Utzon before the final roof solution was found (State Library of NSW)

•••

The location of Bennelong Point, which was formerly the site of the 'Fort Macquarie' tram shed as well as a fort and earlier Bennelong's hut (1790), was identified by Eugene Goossens, conductor of the Sydney Symphony Orchestra, as a splendid location for a performing arts centre in the 1950s when trams were being phased out.

•••

In 1956, the government announced an international competition for the design of an opera house. Judging took place in January 1957 and the winning design (according to legend) was selected from a pile of rejects by the late-arriving judge Eero Saarinen.

On 3 March 1966, more than 1000 protesters marched on Parliament House demanding the reinstatement of Jørn Utzon to complete the Sydney Opera House. The crowd was addressed by architects Harry Seidler, Peter Kollar and Michael Nicholson. They insisted that 'the Royal Australian Institute of Architects tell the Government that no Australian architect should take over the job'.

A competing demonstration by the Builders Labourers Federation actually arrived at Parliament House first, and counterdemanded of the government that 'Australian architects be invited to finish the job, and that labourers be given higher pay'.

554

237 B 13

198 A 12

554 House (Fombertaux)

23 Karoo Avenue, East Lindfield
1970–72 Jean G Fombertaux
GC, V, NA

A striking, elevated, steel-framed house
designed by the architect for his own
occupation. This project is an experiment in
vertically linked internal space, with the external
expression of infill walls and frame reduced to a
simplified system of assembly. Belgian glass is
extensively used throughout, together with 70-
mm thick reinforced concrete panels, cast on
site and tilted into place.

This is perhaps the first steel-framed building
with vertically stacked rooms, a construction
principle which only occasionally appeared in
Sydney over the next decade.

•••

Note: Last-minute research revealed the design
date of this house as being 1963, the present
owner (the son of JG Fomberteaux) having lived
there since 1966.

•••

Jean Fomberteaux (1920–75) came to Australia
at 16 years of age. After graduating from the
Sydney Technical College in 1948, he spent a year
in New Caledonia and a year in Paris, where he
was offered a position with Le Corbusier (never
taken up due to the ill health of his father).

Below: Living level plan,
23 Karoo Avenue, East Lindfield (1972)

555 House (Short)

307 McCarrs Creek Road, Terrey Hills
1973 Glenn Murcutt
GC, NV, NA

A black steel-framed house reminiscent of Mies
van de Rohe's work as later interpreted by Craig
Ellwood in America during the 1960s.

The action of sliding screens and sun louvres
has been described in romantic terms by some
critics – a sliding louvre becomes a 'veil' and
a louvred roof a 'transparent barrier'. These
descriptions go towards the argument of Man
against (and working with) Nature, and Man
against the Sky. While the concepts ultimately
revitalised the 'Sydney School' thinking, the
heroic and smooth-skinned form is particularly
non-Sydney School and very masculine. An
interesting original feature is a fire sprinkler
system, which is a water pond on the roof,
activated during a bush fire.

Below: Ground floor plan,
307 McCarrs Creek Road, Terrey Hills (1973)

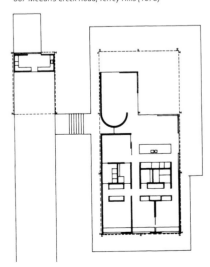

556

558

46 K 8

556 Offices

2 Glen Street, Milsons Point
1971–73 Harry Seidler & Associates
1986–88 Harry Seidler & Associates
1992–93 Harry Seidler & Associates
GC, V, A

Fascinated by the logic of construction methods, Seidler explored the total integration of structure, lighting, and air-conditioning into a single design concept. A concrete lift and services core provided the shear walls necessary for the building's stiffness, while the remaining three elevations are a simple concrete frame. Precast 'T' beams, made in expensive polished steel forms, simply span 11.3 metres from the core to the outer frame, their organic shape reflecting the changing engineering require-ments to deal with the loads. Exposed air-conditioning ducts with integral up-lighting produce a dramatic and controlled effect, which was as sophisticated as any open plan system in the world at the time.

The building's external expression is direct. East and west elevations are shielded by precast vertical sunblades which, owing to their proportion and careful design, are almost timeless. The open-plan system only supports partitions in one direction (along the 'T' beam rib), which makes it less suitable as a generic office model than originally thought.

•••

The Jury report on Sir John Sulman Award 1981: 'The office building standing on a cliff is strong, aloof and exclusive ... turning its back on the street to exploit a magnificent outlook for the benefit of its occupants'.

23 E 13

557 House (Cullen)

23 Edward Street, Balmain East
1972–74   Glenn Murcutt
AC, NV, NA

This was the first non-Miesian design by Glenn Murcutt (b. 1936) to receive popular attention after he left the firm Ancher, Mortlock, Murray & Woolley. The first scheme designed in 1972 showed a spartan Corbusian influence, which was reworked into a less referential design after an overseas trip taken in September 1973.

The building has an expressive vaulted corrugated roof, rectangular plan and screen skylight which suggest the direction to be taken by Murcutt in future years. The building is enveloped in vegetation.

•••

On the adjoining site to the north of the Cullen house is the Glenn Murcutt-designed Hetherton house, completed in 1982.

25 H 19

558 Offices

263–273 Clarence Street, Sydney
1975–76 Mario Arnaboldi
GC, V, A

An unusual 'facade' treatment by a well-known Italian architect. It is built entirely from Italian materials consisting of machined stainless steel frames and tinted glass panels set in a geometric pattern. The car park has bright red ductwork which, at the time of completion, was reminiscent of the pipework at the Centre Pompidou in Paris.

559

559 **Former King George Tower**
Also known as the **American Express Building**
King and George Streets, Sydney
1976 John Andrews International (principal architects: Barry Beck and Michael Jenkin)
PC, V, A

A brutal intrusion into the neo-Classical fabric of George Street and Martin Place, the King George Tower was hailed an exemplar of modern commercial architecture. Not least among its 'successes' was that the client (Hooker Corporation) ultimately agreed to compromise its position rather than the architect. Like a latter-day reworking of Emil Sodersten's 1936 City Mutual Life Building **(434)**, the design addresses the corner of the site on the diagonal, and animates the windows with a triangulated system of stainless steel-framed polycarbonate sun screens (coined 'sunglasses') which justified a large amount of partially sunshaded glass.

Internally, the building offers open-plan office space, although the architectural jury which examined the building after its completion discovered that 'interruption of the areas by the large interior columns and the triangular plan necessitates the placement of some partitions on the diagonal, thus creating layout problems'. Due to undergo a massive facelift by the Rice Daubney Group, the building will soon have five 4-storey tall aerial gardens built into the new southwestern facade which will be lit up at night, making it Sydney's first 'bio-climatic' tower. Completion is scheduled for early 1998.

•••

Newspaper items popularised the toilets as 'loos with a view' as they, along with other services, are located in the corner towers.

560 **Berowra Waters Inn**
Berowra Waters
1977 Glenn Murcutt
GC, V, A

This was one of the most famous eating establishments in Australia during the 1980s, and is still well patronised even after the departure of its famous chef and owner, Gay Bilson. The project is a major reworking of a 1920s teahouse cum hotel which had overnight rooms, moorings for visiting Halvorsen and Owens Cruisers, and petrol and ice supplies for day trippers from Cottage Point or Bobbin Head. The Glenn Murcutt design for the fifty-seat restaurant was simple and direct — a louvred wall to the water, a steel tube frame, and a skylit kitchen to the hillside. The rest was made magic by the food and the setting.

561 **House (Babet)**
41 The Scarpe, Castlecrag
1977 Kloots and Morgan
GC, V, NA

This is another extremely difficult site of stacked levels connected by an open stair. It presents a naturalistic palette of materials with a sparing use of colour.

Below: Living level plan,
41 The Scarpe, Castlecrag (1977)

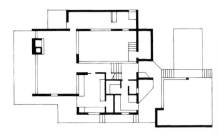

1978 New Federal Parliament House commissioned

1979 A bomb kills three people at the Hilton Hotel in Sydney during the Commonwealth Heads of Government Regional Meeting

562

34 Q 20

180 D 18

562 House, 'Nioka'
40a Upper Cliff Road, Northwood
1978 Furio Valich
GC, NV, NA

'Nioka' was designed by the architect Furio Valich (b. 1948) for the photographer owner Kraig Carlstrom. This semicircular house resting on nine steel columns is centred on a steep bushland battleaxe block which is hidden from the street. Accessed via a steep drive, the building is entered at the uppermost of four levels which contain five bedrooms, two living rooms and two large balconies.

Coined the 'Star Wars House' by real estate agents, 'Nioka' is built from square steel column sections, welded rectangular beams, louvred windows and lightweight infill walls. Pipe and expanded mesh balustrades wrap around the inset terraces and across the face of the living areas where there are full-height doors. Despite changing owners in September 1987 and April 1996, it still retains the Valich trademark jacaranda-mauve colour scheme.

•••

This design follows on from an earlier Modernist experiment by Valich, the Andrews house (1975) in Peronne Avenue, Clontarf.

Below: Living level plan,
40a Upper Cliff Road, Northwood (1978)

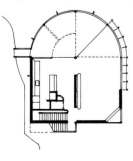

563 House
3 Bilgola Avenue, Bilgola
1973–78 Richard Le Plastrier
GC, V, NA

This very private house is enveloped by a tropical garden in a small palm-filled valley behind Bilgola Beach. Built for a bachelor, it consists of two vaulted pavilion rooms connected by a partly open corridor with a long attached service zone containing bathroom and kitchen. The steel-framed rooms have links which are carefully threaded over the ground, with considerable allowances for existing vegetation and landscape. The atmosphere of the natural surrounds is akin to that of an aboriginal bark hut, with only partial protection from bad weather.

Quality materials have been employed throughout; the roofs are sheeted in copper and the interiors use fine timbers crafted by shipwrights, driven by the architect's interest in shipbuilding. An ochre rammed earth wall forms an enclosure within which the dwelling sits, isolated from its neighbours.

•••

Richard Le Plastrier (b. 1939) graduated from Sydney University in 1964 and spent a short period working for Clarke Gazzard (Wentworth Memorial Church). He worked for Jørn Utzon on the Opera House (as did a number of young graduates) and the Utzon House at Bayview. In Japan, he worked with Kenzo Tange and, in England, with Howard Lobb. After returning to Australia, Le Plastrier entered private practice, with a strong interest in all things maritime. Boatbuilding techniques and craftsmanship are employed in his houses, while his planning approach appears to have been considerably influenced by Utzon.

565

256 G 2

564 University of Technology, Ku-ring-gai

Formerly William Balmain Teachers College
Eaton Road, Lindfield
1978 NSWGA Design Architect: David Turner
Landscape architect: Bruce Mackenzie
GC, V, A

An institutional college which revels in its plateau bushland setting. This was a very different approach to the college campus after the clearfell site approach of the 1960s. The off-form concrete buildings are strewn along a circulation path like a pedestrian street through a linear village. To reduce bulk, the buildings are stepped and staggered over a number of levels like a naturally occurring craggy rock outcrop, with terraces interspersed to break down the mass. Concepts were ruggedness, extendibility, and a commitment to the native landscape.

26 K 17

565 MLC Centre

Cnr King and Castlereagh Streets and Martin Place, Sydney
1975–78 Harry Seidler & Associates
GC, V, A

The MLC Centre consists of a 65-storey office tower, two-level shopping arcade and a below-ground proscenium theatre replacing the Theatre Royal, which was demolished to make way for the project. Much of the ground space has been utilised for north-facing plazas linked by ramped steps which ascend to the tower lobby. The design uses an engineering and construction-based strategy where the spandrel panel is structural and the tapering outer columns stiffen the tower in a simple action against the core to control wind pressure. The structural consultant was the Italian engineer PL Nervi, who played a major part in the foyer ceiling design. The scheme includes artworks by Calder, Albers and Perry.

179 G 15

566 House (Shaw)

Eastside, Scotland Island
1979 Morrice Shaw
GC, V, NA

This building develops the interconnected pavilion theme first discussed with the Bilgola House by Richard Le Plastrier **(563)**, and possesses even greater similarity in the use of barrel-vault roof construction. During the 1970s, an increasing number of architects were reducing building programs into smaller parts, and the generic house was easily divided into active and passive or daytime and night-time zones. From these zones, some designs are broken down into smaller constituent free-standing rooms.

Architect Morrice Shaw designed this house as a series of stepped pavilions connected by a circulation 'spine', to which he added a poetic image of a cloud or wave in the rolling roof forms of the pavilion plan. These were said to evoke images of waves hitting a beach, although Scotland Island itself is not subject to the wave forms of the Pacific Ocean. The four barrel-vaulted pavilions provide a floor area of 150 square metres, made of 90-mm steel tube, curved in a shipwright's yard and fabricated in a sprinkler systems workshop.

Below: Living level plan,
Wave House, Scotland Island (1979)

567

567 House (Curry)

5 Pindari Place, Bayview
1980 Bruce Rickard & Associates.
GC, V, NA

The architectural work of Bruce Rickard is
distinctive in Sydney. Over a thirty-year period,
he has developed an open-plan design approach
which originated in the middle period work of
Frank Lloyd Wright. This is the second house
(ten years on) designed by Rickard for this
family. The steep site challenged the use of
elongated plans with interconnected volumes,
and given the size of the house, Rickard
resorted to a substantial concrete frame which
is unusual in his domestic portfolio. Despite this,
the interior has a flowing spatial expression
between mezzanine floors and raised interior
spaces connected by bridges enabling a
continuous view of the water outside. Other
than the exposed concrete made with Nepean
River aggregate, the materials are familiar to
Rickard. Timber is used extensively throughout
the interior and is allowed to weather externally,
floors are slate and sandstone is used discreetly.

568 University of NSW, St George Campus

Former Alexander Mackie College of
Advanced Education
Cnr Oatley Avenue and Hurstville Road, Oatley
1976–80 NSWGA Principal Architect: Les
Reedman; Design Architect: Colin Still with Rice
and Daubney (consultant architects)
GC, V, A

Australian Brutalism at its most mannered,
the former Alexander Mackie College is an
heroic contrast between the ruggedness of the
site (brickpit) and the boldness of the structure.

Following on from Ku-ring-gai College **(564)**,
the New South Wales Higher Education Board
chose a disused brickpit site at Oatley for a
1500-student campus of 9570 square metres for
teacher training. The building is both sculptural
and geometric, showing the characteristic
preoccupation with the 45-degree composition
exemplified in the Former King George Tower
Building **(559)**.

Further institutional designs of this period
were concerned with 'spines' and 'voids', formal
massing, and a belief that concrete and
formwork could achieve an entire building
expression. The circulation-driven planning
appears to be influenced by Canadian colleges,
including the work of John Andrews at
Scarborough and the Simon Fraser Campus near
Vancouver. The exposed air-conditioning,
simplified 'T' beams and off-form concrete work
are also reminiscent of Harry Seidler's work,
without the same approach to detail. According
to Colin Still, the planning was also influenced
by the Berlin Free University, in relation to the
circulation networks and the location of service
units. As with Ku-ring-gai College, the landscaping was by Bruce Mackenzie.

Left: Living level plan,
5 Pindari Place, Bayview (1980)

569

569 Mt Druitt Hospital

Railway Street, Mt Druitt
1976–81 Lawrence Nield & Partners
GC, V, A

This is a sophisticated reinterpretation of hospital planning and design embedded in the 1970s planning principles of the internal 'circulation street'. The exterior avoids the blocky, stepped and angular form of structural grid units, and introduces a sinuous and horizontal line through external sunshades.

570 House (Merson)

7 Pacific Place, Palm Beach
1981 Harry Seidler & Associates
GC, NV, NA

Echoing the same principles and materials first used in the 1950 Bowden house in Canberra (unpainted rough masonry walls, sculptured fireplace, skillion roof, full-height glass walls), the Merson house and its sister house for Dr Basser in Castle Cove are quadrant-shaped with a continuous array of uses from kitchen to bedroom in one sweep.

Below: Living level plan,
7 Pacific Place, Palm Beach (1981)

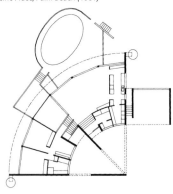

571 House (Ball)

Lot 1 Halcrows Road, Glenorie
1982 Glenn Murcutt
GC, NV, NA

An extruded 'shed house' for artists Sydney Ball and Lyn Eastaway near Glenorie, northwest of Sydney, which shows Glenn Murcutt's (b. 1936) approach to promoting a responsive and delicate dialogue between new buildings and precious non-urban sites. The building sits above a rock shelf in virgin bushland almost floating and making only one connection to the ground via an entry platform.

The Ball house explores the refinement and abstraction of the house's outer shell, which escalates the difference between the natural site and the man-made object. This facilitated Murcutt's pursuit of absolute precision and refinement in the detail of his work. The client originally approached Murcutt with a sensitive appreciation of the site's qualities and sought to preserve it relatively undisturbed. The 'transportable' pavilion frame, now familiar to Murcutt, was adapted to suit the 102-mm steel tube frame, a structural system commonly incorporated in his other projects.

•••

There is an interesting contrast that developed between the open connected pavilions of Shaw and Le Plastrier during the 1970s, and Murcutt's interest in the power of enclosed space.

Below: Ground floor plan,
Lot 1 Halcrows Road, Glenorie (1982)

572

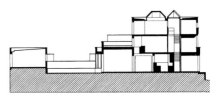

1981 Three brothers — Mark, Glen and Gary
Ella — all members of winning Australian
Rugby union team

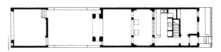

159 Windsor Street, Paddington
Top: Section
Above: Living level plan

572 House (Henwood)
159 Windsor Street, Paddington
1982–85 Lewin Tzannes
GC, V, NA

The Henwood house was one of Alexander
Tzannes' first private commissions when he
commenced practice in 1982. The design,
notable for its careful proportional relationships
and reliance on shadow for surface rendering,
visually diminishes in apparent floor height as
the building rises. With the exception of the
raked 'stone coursing' to the rendered brickwork
facade, there is a surprising shortage of
traditional detail, yet the overall effect appears
classically mannered in its composure. The
upper floor, fitted between the maximum
parapet line and the floor immediately below,
visually functions as an attic storey without the
limitations of a reducing pitched roof. In this
way, the usable floor area is increased without
altering the building's bulk or footprint area.

This idea produced three floor levels, each
with distinct uses. The ground floor combines
living and potential work areas which relate
to outdoor landscaped areas. The middle floor
contains children's bedrooms with a large,
secure outdoor terrace over the ground floor
living room. Above this, the upper floor
contains adult sleeping quarters, a bathroom
and a small terrace.

Sectionally, the house is divided front to rear
by a single-flight staircase topped with a glass
skylight. This allows daylight to enter the centre
of the building, particularly at the upper levels.
Despite the concessions to the context of the
neighbourhood, the Henwood house was
rejected by council on aesthetic and technical
grounds for its lack of conformity. Having won
building permission by appeal, it is now used as
a council model development, eventually
contributing to a review of planning controls.

573 Former Qantas Centre
9 Lang Street, Sydney
1970 (Design)
1973–82 (Built) Joseland and Gilling
Structural Engineer: Miller Milston and Ferris
GC, V, A

The site became available when Qantas Airways
decided to relocate and rebuild the Wentworth
Hotel near Chifley Square. Originally intended to
be part of a massive three-stage development,
only the first two stages were able to be built
in what was one of the most protracted
constructions in Sydney's history. The first stage,
a 5000 square metre underground computer
centre, especially designed for a Qantas main-
frame computer system, was already redundant
by the time it was completed.

Drawing on the integrated service innovations
of Harry Seidler, found in his own office
building **(556)**, the 50-storey second-stage
tower was designed to provide integrated
structure and services. Precast concrete T-beam
floor elements span from core to perimeter, and
service distribution units provide air-
conditioning, sprinklers and lighting below the
precast concrete ceiling. Power and
communications are distributed beneath an
infinite access floor throughout the building.

•••

The Qantas site was subject to the infamous
black bans by building unions, delaying
construction by years. Unions claimed that the
experimental nature of the building should be
reflected in special provisions and payments for
workers. The well-established architects,
Joseland and Gilling, barely survived the drawn-
out construction and legal challenges.

574

575

255 P 6

574 Australian Film and Television School
Epping Road (Cnr Balaclava Road), North Ryde
1982 Daryl Jackson Basil Carter
GC, V, A
This is one of the last higher educational
schools to be planned on the graphic of the
diagonal line. It just barely shakes off the
Brutalist ingredients of in situ off-form concrete
and piercing circulation pathways.

23 H 12

575 Wharf Theatre
Pier 4, Hickson Road, Walsh Bay
1984 Vivian Fraser
GC, V, A
The massive hardwood piers at Walsh Bay
were built by the Sydney Harbour Trust between
1907 and 1922 in a government-led resumption
and reconstruction of what had been a maze of
privately owned wharves. The buildings were
principally used to store bales of wool for export
and were fitted with hydraulic pressing, hoisting
and handling equipment. The Wran Labor
government found sufficient funds to repair and
replace broken piles, and to fit out the Sydney
Theatre Company and restaurant. The 1984
conversion by architect Vivian Fraser is generally
considered to be a most sympathetic treatment,
leaving as much of the original woodwork as
possible, including the lanolin-soaked floors.

Accommodation includes two theatres and a
restaurant with two balconies. There is rehearsal
and performance space for the Sydney Dance
Company on the lower level. The apron is
retained at water level and is still used by locals
for fishing. The entire Walsh Bay precinct is still
under consideration for redevelopment, with
the state government considering a proposal
by the consortium of Transfield and Mirvac.

Sydney's Steep Sites
*The architectural movement of the 1950s and
1960s known as the 'Sydney School' was
characterised by the appreciation of native
landscape and the honest use of natural
materials. It developed into an informal, clinker
brick and tiled roof architecture of the bush
suburbs around Sydney, which avoided
conventional form and historical language.*

*The vacant pockets of land around Sydney's
foreshores began to be filled during this period
by architects in command of strong engineering
principles, such as the steel cage, the steel
portal, the concrete tube and the cascading
split level. Innovation came from two areas:
architects who purchased unbuildable blocks
for their own occupation; and clients who could
not proceed on a steep site without an able
architect. Often engineering solutions would
dismiss consideration of conventional house
forms; or the architect's planning solutions
would dictate a particular type of stepped,
cantilevered or split level floor plan.*

179 C 17

576 House (Hoffman)
Bilgola slopes
1985 Ed Duc
GC, NV, NA
A systems building concept providing an
industrial kit home, of which few were built.

Below: Living level plan, Hoffman house (1985)

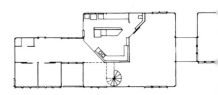

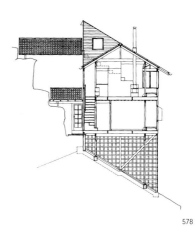

577

578

257 K 3

160 B 18

577 House (Frischknecht)
1a North Arm Road, Middle Cove
1985 Paul Frischknecht
GC, NV, NA

On another of Sydney's 'unbuildable' sites, Swiss-born architect Paul Frischknecht designed and built for himself a symmetrically planned steel-framed house with the precision of Swiss watch detailing. Perhaps unconsciously, the design appears to embrace and rework the concepts found in the pioneering Fombertaux House **(554)** designed in 1963. The plan is divided into three bays, with the stair in the centre bay and rooms on either side. The steel framework is externally expressed and contrasts with the lightweight sandwich infill panels, giving the house the definite feel of modular construction. Entry is via a bridge at the uppermost level, with the building surrounded by dense bushland looking over Middle Cove. The external sandwich panel cladding is tautly arranged with the minimal steel frame, set back to enable outdoor terraces. In these instances, and at roof level, the frame continues to outline the external spaces creating outdoor rooms rather than projecting balconies.

•••

The first houses in Sydney which articulated (rather than concealed) their steel frames were the Fombertaux House (554) by JG Fombertaux, the Short House by Glenn Murcutt (555) and the Carlstrom House (562) by Furio Valich.

Below: Living level plan, Frischknecht house (1985)

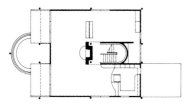

578 House (Woolley)
21 Florida Road, Palm Beach
1984–85 Ken Woolley
GC, V, NA

This is another quintessential architect's home on a difficult and steep site, requiring foundations to be rock-bolted to the sandstone escarpment.

This design for an all-timber weekend cottage by Ken Woolley is an unusual blend of pictorial themes. It shows little concern for the alleged aspirations of Modernism – lightness, transparency, spatial flow and visual extension. The idea for the building revolves around the architect's personal and cultural recognition of form, the creation of private and intimate spaces, and the loose and almost ad hoc use of relaxation space usually associated with a holiday cottage. The wide eaves sitting on a ring of windows make the roof appear to float like a hat above the building, ultimately cementing the notion that the building is a tower, and the principal occupancy must be at the top under that roof. The 'tower' solution of stacking rooms is divided into functional groups: three bedrooms on the lower level; living and kitchen at entry level; and sleeping loft over the kitchen. The timber panelled lower level with small openings, conceals any sense of structure; reinforced by enclosing the underside with trellis.

Below: Living level plan, Woolley house, 21 Florida Road, Palm Beach (1985)

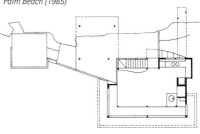

579

579 House (Littlemore)
5 Kilminster Lane, Woollahra
1983–86 Glenn Murcutt
GC, V, NA

An extremely rigorous design on a 5.8-metre wide terrace house site which exploits the opportunity of one elevation facing a public park. The house is effectively split into two pavilions, separated by an internal garden courtyard, which are connected along the blind party wall by the linear service spine containing kitchen, bathrooms, storage, staircases and laundry. The main features of the house are the three-storey high glass walls to the park, glass blockwork at ground level, and external venetian-screened windows to the two upper levels. This provides significant daylight throughout the building.

The three children's bedrooms have their own internal lofts which take advantage of the curving roof form. The kitchen and dining area has gardens at either end, with a continuous brick-paved floor surface combining the outdoor areas.

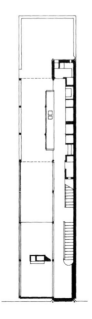

*Right: Ground floor plan,
5 Kilminster Lane,
Woollahra (1986)*

580 House (Barrett)
29 Cynthea Road, Palm Beach
1985-87 Jim Koopman
GC, NV, NA

The Barrett holiday house is derivative of the work of architects of the Sydney School with particular reference to the 1963 Lochhead house at Avalon by Keith Cottier and the work of Bill Lucas.

It was built as a photographer's escape, sitting against a hillside below the road which climbs the southwestern face of the Palm Beach headland. The gable roof has a traditional European farmhouse pitch of 40 degrees. The roof (and its construction) is the principal point of order to this building; the planning, substructure and enclosing skin are dictated by its enveloping form.

All framing elements are forward, near the edge of the roof, providing an initial structural reading before the glass planes are encountered. Unlike most contemporary Australian houses, the Barrett house at Palm Beach displays scant nostalgia for the Australian shed. It appears to have its own cross-cultural image – part Asian, part Dutch and part Australian.

*Below: Living level plan,
29 Cynthea Road, Palm Beach (1987)*

581

581 Sydney Football Stadium
Moore Park Road, Moore Park
1985–88 Philip Cox Richardson
Taylor & Partners
Engineers: Ove Arup and Partners
GC, V, A

Seen from the air, this is one of Sydney's most dramatic sports buildings, and is regarded by many to be one of the best atmosphere stadiums in the world. Designed by Philip Cox Richardson Taylor & Partners, construction commenced in April 1986 and the stadium opened in January 1988 to coincide with Australia's Bicentennial celebrations. It seats 40,000 spectators, with 25,000 under cover, and is the premier venue for rugby league, while also hosting rugby union and soccer matches.

The swooping shape of the 'Mexican hat' is based on the desire to amass the maximum number of spectators about the halfway line on both sides of the 143 metres x 69 metres pitch, a well-established device to harness the best sight lines. This produces a swelling in the stand at the centre of the long sides which, when incorporated into an enclosing plan around the field, produces an oval seating band of varying width. As columns are unacceptable in a modern stadium, the dynamic roof shape is a three-dimensional cantilever. The tension and compression struts supporting the roof transfer forces to a braced truss anchored to the ring of concrete columns and walls which connect to the grandstand raking beams. This transfer from light steel to massive concrete base has some difficult visual moments as the connections are seen from outside the stadium. Seen from inside, however, the hovering roof edge, with wind pressure reducing slots and continuous recessed lighting, is spectacularly enveloping.

582 Apple Computer National Headquarters
16 Rodborough Road, Frenchs Forest
1986–87 Allen Jack & Cottier
GC, V, A

The offices, training centre, and warehousing for Apple Computer. The reinforced concrete frame with tilt-up wall construction, displays an unusual collision between late modern and post-modern forms.

583

583 Overseas Passenger Terminal
Circular Quay West, Sydney
1985–87 Lawrence Nield & Partners
GC, V, A

During the 1980s, attention was sharply focused on the planning and public use of Circular Quay as the city's most dynamic urban place. An isolated building was the Sydney Cove terminal designed in the 1950s and opened in 1960 to handle cruise ship passengers. The SS *Oriana*, on her maiden voyage, was the first ship to use the original terminal.

Within ten years, the predominance of air over sea travel made the terminal too large for its function and it began to deteriorate through lack of use. An RAIA 'ideas' competition considered the building's use in relation to reduction of building mass, improvement of public space and transformation of its architectural appearance. Among the joint winners was a submission by architect Peter Tonkin for shortening the building and making a small plaza.

The southern third of the building was removed to make way for Rocks Place, and structure was salvaged to use in other parts of the building. The ground floor was entirely glazed on the eastern side and screened with mesh on the west, which allows views through to the harbour.

Essential elements in the language of the remodelled terminal were derived from the existing structure, e.g. great portals and floating butterfly roof. The tower at the northern end is considered to be an urban pivot and a reference to the nearby towers at the Australian Steam Navigation building and the Mining Museum. The overall form of the building includes non-functional shapes for aesthetic effect.

584 House
9 Forbes Street, Paddington
1984–88 Allen Jack & Cottier
GC, V, NA

In normally conservative Paddington, this design by Peter Stronach for an advertising executive sits in dramatic contrast to its neighbours through its brightly coloured tiled walls and interjecting forms. The house gained planning approval in 1980 and the local council accidentally omitted from its conditions of approval that the colours and materials were to be approved. Consequently, the architects relished the opportunity to be outrageous in colour. Blue marks the main facade, mauve the side walls, tan the primary steel elements and yellow for secondary steel.

Below: Living level plan,
9 Forbes Street, Paddington (1988)

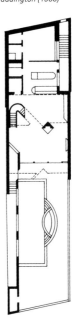

585

585 Darling Harbour Exhibition Centre
Darling Harbour
1988 Philip Cox Richardson Taylor and Partners
GC, V, A

The rapid development of Darling Harbour transformed a derelict 54 acres of track, railway goods sheds and cargo wharves near the central business district core into a recreational public playground. In addition to gardens and a retail complex, the master plan provided for five pavilion-type buildings. These included a large convention centre, a casino, the Sydney Exhibition Centre, the Sydney Aquarium and the National Maritime Museum. The last three projects were all awarded to Philip Cox Richardson Taylor and Partners.

The rationale for the building's appearance, according to the architect, was based on three considerations: extending the 'grand tradition' of steel and glass exhibition buildings; adopting a structural system with maritime imagery; and accepting an urban role through a 'linear configuration' and 'distinguished form.'

The upright mast system, with its horizontal spreader arm, belongs to a structural system refined by the engineers Ove Arup & Partners. The 25,000 square metres of floor area were divided into five equal halls or units which are interconnected. Each 87 metre x 60 metre bay is structurally and mechanically autonomous and can be sectioned off from the adjoining space using mechanically operated panels suspended from overhead gantries.

The elevated 'mezzanine' concourse provides pedestrian access between all five halls along the eastern side. There is a mixture of loadbearing construction which comes up underneath a tension roof structure. The external walls consist of tinted glass, glass blockwork or insulated sandwich panels.

586 Powerhouse Museum
500 Harris Street, Ultimo
1988 NSWGA, Principal Architect: Lionel
Glendenning
Denton Corker Marshall (entry area)
Open: 10am–5pm every day except
Christmas Day
GC, V, A

The Powerhouse Museum is a major part of the Museum of Applied Arts and Sciences established in the 19th century to hold and display technological achievements. It was founded in the derelict buildings of the old power station used to generate electricity for Sydney's tram system, which has since been removed.

The existing buildings, which include the former turbine, switch and boiler houses, have been stripped back to the bare essential structure. Exhibits, including airplanes, motor vehicles and helicopters, are hung in space. The new work was largely confined to the Wran Wing, a barrel-vaulted room, partially glazed with an external colonnade along Harris Street. From the entry, ramps, escalators and lifts lead the visitor to the various parts of the museum and the interactive displays.

587 Office Building
59 Buckingham Street, Surry Hills
1985–88 Allen Jack & Cottier
GC, V, A

This project resulted from a joint venture between the firm of architects, which designed this building, and Ausminco, a firm of mineral traders. The roof has tennis courts and a lunch area, while the ground floor level cleverly conceals car parking behind a perforated brick wall design.

● 1983 Perth Millionaire Alan
Bond wins America's Cup

● 1984 At 14, Fiona Coote becomes the youngest
person to undergo a heart transplant

● 1985 Australia's first all-female surf
lifesaving carnival held in Sydney

588

67 D 8   **24 J 15**

588 Federation Pavilion

Centennial Park, Sydney
1986–88 Alexander Tzannes
Landscape architect: Wally Barda
Artist: Imants Tiller
GC, V, A

The Federation Pavilion was the result of a
bicentennial architectural competition, won
by Alexander Tzannes, who had recently
returned to Australia after studying for a
masters degree at Columbia University. The
competition called for a suitable replacement
for the original Federation Pavilion which had
been removed some years after it was built in
1901. Tzannes' neo-Classical design was
controversial in a number of ways: its direct
reference to classical European architecture,
its use of heavy masonry and its simplistic
symmetry. Few, if any, architects in Sydney
were capable of considering such distorted or
abstracted neo-Classical designs at this time
and, to answer its critics, it made many other
entries seem like temporary bus shelters.

It has been observed by the historian Jennifer
Taylor that the design is in fact 'unclassical',
perhaps because it is out of scale with its
context, has a two-part elevation, a slight
convexity of the internal column, and a floating
copper-clad cupola, which reinterprets this type
of European monument. The interior has
inscribed texts and a painting inside the dome
by Imants Tiller.

589 Grosvenor Place Offices

225 George Street, Sydney
1982–88 Harry Seidler & Associates
GC, V, A

Built during Seidler's most productive period
(mid-1980s), the steel-framed and concrete-
cored Grosvenor Tower, with its permanent
formwork facing of granite and reinforced
glass, is one of the city's most elegant towers.

The system of projecting sunshade units
on a curving facade was initially conceived in
conjunction with Marcel Breuer for the
Australian Embassy, and further developed for
high-rise use on an unbuilt 1980 scheme in
Kuala Lumpur which had twin curving floors
with segmented floor units. This simple
geometry is based on 15-metre wide column-
free construction using identical steel floor
beams and repetitive facade elements, despite
the curvature created by the segmented units.
Seidler excels in creating variety and movement
in forms consisting entirely of repetitive units.
The parapet has a large recess fitted with solar
collectors which are used to produce ice at
night for the air-conditioning system. The lobby
artworks are brightly coloured three dimensional
works by Frank Stella, specially commissioned
for the project.

589

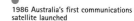

591

590 House (Cherry)
8 Rockley Street, Castlecrag
1986–89 Alex Popov
GC, NV, NA

This house commissioned by the Cherry family sits within an enclave of Walter Burley Griffin houses overlooking Middle Harbour. It is composed of three pavilions – living, dining, bedroom – stepped across the site and connected by column corridors articulated around the pool and terraces. The construction is generally of deeply corbelled brickwork, with copper and glass skylights, and features areas of Rockhampton sandstone set into the formal walls as a reference to Griffin. The house rests on deep floor beams, producing suspended floors to allow the natural water course to run under the building.

'The architecture of Castlecrag must be subordinate to the landscape' according to Walter Burley Griffin. There is an aim to retain the degree of textured surface, to allow it to weather as intended by Griffin. The feeling for materials and geometry, and the process of design from the interior out, puts Popov in company with his mentors: Alvar Aalto, Frank Lloyd Wright and Jørn Utzon.

591 Rockpool Restaurant
107 George Street, Sydney
1988–89 D4 Design
GC, V, A

The Rockpool became one of Sydney's most famous 'new' restaurants of the 1980s and a decade later its decor has still managed to survive the credibility gap. To the brief of chef Neil Perry, the firm of D4 – consisting of three designers, Bill MacMahon, Stephen Roberts and Michael Scott-Mitchell – designed everything from the champagne stands and chairs through to the structural apparatus which holds up the roof. All components are treated as an ensemble.

The layout threads together a collection of 19th-century shops and rooms which have been opened up to form a continuous space. Skill is evident in the careful knitting together of the different rooms so that the spaces connect fluently. The upstairs bar, reached by a steel staircase with spaghetti handrail, provides a more literal interpretation of a rockpool.

A glass-roofed room at the rear was originally designed with walls saturated in a deep yellow hue.

Below: Living level plan,
8 Rockley Street, Castlecrag (1989)

Below: Section, Rockpool Restaurant (1989)

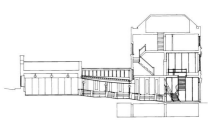

592

49 E 7   **67 C 4**

592 House (Lloyd Jones)

294 Old South Head Road, Watsons Bay
1988–90 Graham Jahn
GC, V, NA

A one-bedroom house originally designed by the author as part of a compound with the adjoining 'guest' building separated by a water garden filled with water lilies. The 24-metre long living room is a grand space opening on to a harbour view, while the upper living level and bedroom are connected by a glass lift.

•••

The basement gallery was originally designed to hang a collection of paintings by William Dobell.

Below: Living level plan,
294 Old South Head Road, Watsons Bay (1990)

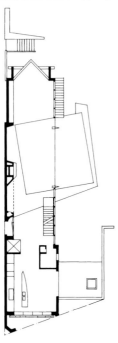

593 House

88 Sutherland Street, Paddington
1986–90 Glenn Murcutt
GC, NV, NA

Barely hinted at from the street, the rear and interior of this typical terrace house were considerably transformed by the architect Glenn Murcutt (b. 1936) for the same clients of the much publicised Bingi Point House on the NSW South Coast. While internally remodelled Victorian terraces are commonplace in Sydney, two aspects of this design are noteworthy.

Beyond a generous skylit entry space, the internal floors are partially split level, providing a sense of internal light and space. One floor appears to float between the solid party walls, allowing a view to the living spaces beyond. This transforms the enclosed nature of the terrace into interconnected floor planes. With strategically placed skylights, the interior has natural light in winter and is shaded from direct sun in summer.

The second aspect is the provision of a roofed balcony which produces a striking two-storey rear garden elevation, complete with sailcloth awning. A water feature is provided for the full length of one garden wall.

Below: Ground floor plan,
88 Sutherland Street, Paddington (1990)

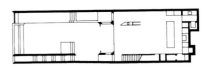

1989 Earthquake in Newcastle
kills 12 people

1990 Worst economic recession
in Australia in 40 years

1991 Reforms introduced for
Aboriginals held in custody

594

596

26 K 16

24 J 12

594 Capita Centre
Castlereagh Street, Sydney
1988–90 Harry Seidler & Associates
Porcelain mural by Lin Utzon
GC, V, A

On a restricted site and unable to achieve a freestanding tower, Harry Seidler (b. 1923) proposed an entirely different approach for the 30 metre x 42 metre site of the Capita building. Parts of the tower form are hollowed out, creating an external atrium effect, with smaller floor plates (700 square metres), which in turn enabled the building to be twice as high, at 31 storeys, as the planning code permitted for a full-site coverage.

The building is made stable by the externally braced truss which is stitched to the side shear walls and the intermediate floors. Although the original perspective envisaged large palm trees at ground, mid- and high-rise levels, other more resilient species have been introduced to survive the taxing urban conditions.

26 M 16

595 Glasshouse Complex
Royal Botanic Gardens, Sydney
1985–90 Ancher Mortlock & Woolley and NSWGA
GC, V, A

Glasshouses in Sydney are designed to protect tropical plants from heat, rather than cold, and to provide humidity. Following the dramatic form, but not the functional shortcomings, of the Botanic Gardens existing pyramid, the new barrel-vaulted glasshouses were designed to accommodate a greater variety of taller trees through the extruded form. The stainless steel structure is essentially a number of radiating wedge-shaped trusses separated by tubular purlins which support the main glass sections without traditional glazing bars.

596 Park Hyatt Hotel
7 Hickson Road, The Rocks
1986–90 Ancher Mortlock & Woolley
GC, V, A

In 1986, this, the last undeveloped industrial marine site near Circular Quay, was offered as a design and construct tender by the NSW government by way of a staged competition. The aim was to maintain visibility of the parkland by the Harbour Bridge pylons when viewed across Circular Quay from the Opera House promenade. This, coupled with the narrow and curvaceous site, predicated the ribbon form of the building.

There is a clear intention to reinforce conventional architectural order at two distinct levels. At one level, the almost impersonal resolution of detail and the absence of eccentricity suggest that the building is not a set-piece, but rather a completely contextualised work. The choice of materials and colour, and the consciously generated weighty appearance are derived from the historic masonry character of The Rocks area in which the building is located. The base and entrance are sandstone and the upper walls are sandstone-coloured precast concrete with ochre-coloured render. This is one of the most intimate and public foreshore promenades on Sydney Harbour.

Facing the harbour, the hotel is fronted by a generous timber boardwalk, below which slipways, ramps and the remains of earlier structures can still be viewed.

•••

The Park Hyatt Hotel provides a compelling example of how the controversial East Circular Quay site might have been developed providing a reduced and more intimate scale.

193

597

599

23 H 14

597 ANA Hotel
Harrington and Essex Streets, Sydney
1987–91 Mitchell/Giurgola & Thorp
GC, V, A

This project resulted from a design and
construct tender by the New South Wales state
government, originally called the Lilyvale site
after Lily Cottage **(146)**. It was designed by the
architects who won the National Parliament
House competition. It consists of a sinuous
tower with a podium base, which relates well to
the adjoining buildings in the block. Part of the
tower sits over the underground railway tunnel,
with the large hotel ballroom located under
Cumberland Street.

258 K 10

598 House (Arnold)
35 Beatrice Street, Clontarf
1990–91 Andrew Metcalf
GC, NV, NA

A curvilinear steel-framed house designed by
the academic and theoretician Andrew Metcalf.
The post-modern design incorporates De Stijl
primary colours to the steelwork and roofline.

258 H 14

599 House
28 Hopetoun Avenue, Balmoral
1992 Glenn Murcutt
GC, V, NA

Because of the restricted site and steep fall,
this house, designed for a well-known Sydney
artist, is in three units: an upper unit containing
the garage with its secluded sunbaking terrace;
a long east gallery beside the lane which links
the upper south unit with the lower north unit;
and a third two-storeyed block that contains
the main day living areas which open onto an
austere courtyard dominated by a frangipani
tree and a complementary swimming pool. The
main bedroom, which is tucked under the
garage, opens directly onto the courtyard from
the south side.

The gallery space dominates the interior.
The 'V' profiled glazed roof has a system of
electrically operated louvres which filter and
direct the light. The external colour proposal
submitted by the owner became a contentious
issue with the local council.

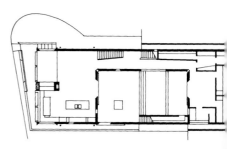

Right: Ground floor plan,
28 Hopetoun Avenue, Balmoral (1992)

600

601

600 House

7 Ginahgulla Road, Bellevue Hill
1992 Dawson-Brown+Ackert
GC, V, NA

American-born Kimberly Ackert and Sydney architect Robert Brown collaborated on a small number of projects in Australia before Ackert returned to New York. This multi-level open-plan design was chosen in a limited architectural competition by the commissioning owners. Perhaps unintentionally, this house appears to continue the architectural language and form from where the Douglas Snelling-designed houses of the mid-1950s left off **(516)**. The design explodes the modern pavilion house plan internally, mixes it with abstract prismatic geometry, and adopts daylighting as the principal sectional device. It takes the typical modern Sydney house plan (linear living space with back-up service space) and moulds it into an architectural sculpture.

The building sits on its site like an early Frank Lloyd Wright house, with overlapping planes, terraced elevation, setback planes and a somewhat distant engagement with the street. The main elevation faces the city to the west, necessitating devices for sunlight control.

601 ABC Ultimo Centre

700 Harris Street, Ultimo
1990–92 Ancher Mortlock & Woolley
GC, V, A

The Australian Broadcasting Corporation, like its British counterpart, is an important organisation which has traditionally competed with the commercial broadcasting industry without the strictures of political or commercial directives. Sometimes critical of the government that funds it, and generally at the forefront of investigative journalism, parody and satire, it is coming under increasing pressure to be privatised, and therefore controlled. Besides its network of national radio and television stations, the ABC also funds and services an orchestra and a variety of live entertainment.

This building complex, designed in 1990 by Ken Woolley, attempts to collect and socialise what were previously disparately located parts of the organisation. The main space is a shaded glass-roofed atrium through which most of the circulation passes and in which the 550-seat rehearsal hall is located. While the atrium and the interior are both architecturally underplayed, the rear of the office wing facing north has one of the most interesting glazed wall designs in Sydney.

Below: Ground floor plan,
7 Ginahgulla Road, Bellevue Hill (1992)

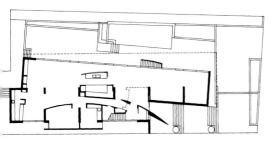

602

604

602 Shop and Offices (Blanket)
163 Edgecliff Road, Edgecliff
1992 Alex Popov
GC, V, NA
The street facade was required to be rebuilt
to the late 19th-century appearance. The rear
elevation, however, shows a clean and simple
expression which reinterprets the terrace
elevation with direct symmetry.

603 House (Friend)
End Northview Road, Palm Beach
1987–92 Gordon & Valich
GC, V, NA
A crisp two-pavilion design which would be as
easily at home on the hills of Los Angeles as in
Sydney. The manipulation of modular rectangular
volumes on a lightweight subframe is reminiscent of the Californian case study house of the
1950s and 1960s.

604 Loyola College
North Parade, Mt Druitt
1992 Denton Corker Marshall
GC, V, A
Loyola College, built for the Jesuits by Denton
Corker Marshall, imparts an atmosphere of
tranquility in its various courtyards and spaces.

605 House
237a Whale Beach Road, Whale Beach
1992 Mitchell/Giurgola & Thorp
Project Architect: Richard Francis-Jones
GC, V, NA
The centre of this house has a formal, almost
Corbusian main space, heroically scaled to
the ocean with a two-storey porch, yet highly
controlled in its detail on the inside. There is
an affinity here, rarely found in Sydney houses,
with the early houses of the American group
known as the New York 5. Corbusian frames
which outline geometric volumes and axial
planning with a twist were the group's hallmark.
The twist in Francis-Jones' design is clearly
evident in the basement room arrangement
which forms a balcony to the lower floor.

Below: Ground floor plan,
Northview Road, Palm Beach (1992)

Below: Ground floor plan,
237a Whale Beach Road, Whale Beach (1992)

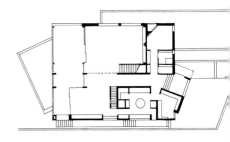

607

609

---

56 F 18

606 National Maritime Museum
13a Union Street, Pyrmont (Darling Harbour)
1986–92 Philip Cox Richardson Taylor &
Partners; Exhibition – Denton Corker Marshall
GC, V, A
The high braced walls and diving roof forms
have been designed to accommodate the masts
of boats contained within the museum.

177 F 6

607 House (Farris)
20 Cowan Drive, Cottage Point
1989–92 Luigi Rosselli
GC, V, NA
Having worked in Mario Botta's office in Lugarno,
Switzerland, Luigi Roselli has created a residential
language which incorporates much of Botta's
concrete block banding and use of materials,
with his own reinvention of the Classical villa.
The work is quite outside the Modernist Sydney
milieu of spartan pavilion spaces furnished with
Finnish furniture. In this house, the plan often
incorporates duality of form or symmetry in
composition. The plan consists of two distinct
copper-roofed boat shapes which thrust
forward towards Cowan Creek.

Below: Ground floor plan,
20 Cowan Drive, Cottage Point (1992)

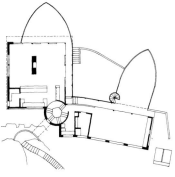

57 H 16

608 House (Green)
110 Wolseley Road, Point Piper
1993 Richard Christianson, landscape by
Stephen Yates
GC, V, NA
This lavish residence built for a US mining
tycoon contains a wide range of imported
elements such as Tuscan fireplaces and antique
French doors.

57 20 C

609 House (Podles)
21 New Beach Road, Darling Point
1990–93 Neil Durbach
GC, NV, NA
On a bench against the hillside, hidden from
view, Neil Durbach designed a tiny house
consisting of two pavilions joined at the navel.
The larger building consisting of kitchen and
dining/living, has an upstairs space accessed
by an internal gallery while the smaller, skewed
pavilion has two bedrooms with an external
stair from the first floor leading to an upper
roof area wrapped in pink bougainvillea. There
is an intricacy in the circulation, via internal
and external stairs, bridges and terrace inspired
by the original pedestrian link to the street.

Below: Ground floor plan,
21 New Beach Road, Darling Point (1993)

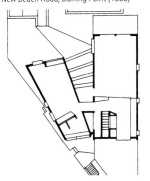

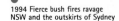
611

612

26 K 16

160 C 20

611 Chifley Tower

Cnr Hunter, Phillip and Loftus Streets, Sydney
1988–93 Kohn Pedersen Fox (USA) and
Travis Partners
GC, V, A

The international commercial city is based on
the premise that it is more profitable to develop
air space than it is to develop land space. For
Sydney, Chifley Tower is one of the most
expensive projects to date, with an overall cost
approaching $1 billion. Incorporating
technology seen in their East Wacker Drive
project in Chicago, the American firm of Kohn
Pedersen Fox grafted on the picturesque
romantic skyscraper stylism found in early 20th-
century American office towers.

The lift cores, microwave technology and
rooftop mechanical plant are contained in a
turret feature topped by a flag pole creating a
dramatic outline on the skyline, a feature
avoided by earlier modernist towers.

With 4-metre high floor-to-floor heights, the
building has been designed to accommodate
high-technology communications and services.
Three electrical substations, with provision for
another two, power the building with
uninterrupted electrical supply suitable for
computers. To counteract building sway in high
winds, a steel block weighing 400 tonnes is
suspended from eight 75-mm diameter steel
wires, suspended from the top of the building.
This giant pendulum is connected to a hydraulic
dampened gravity system which in turn
restrains the building's movement in high winds.

612 Seidler Houses

21 Cynthea Road, Palm Beach
1991–93
'Treetops' (Waterman)
23 Cynthea Road, Palm Beach
1952
GC, V, NA

Side-by-side, these two houses literally
demonstrate Harry Seidler's approach to
residential design forty years on. 'Treetops' was
a small £1000 house built just after the post-
war austerity period as a weekender for an
executive of Philips Electronics. Painted out
now, the original design was a composition of
coloured planes including a deep blue wall
facing east. The primary colour approach is
similar to Seidler's Currie house **(514)** in
Newport, which was restored in 1992.

The more recent house built of split blockwork
with a 'wave-shaped' corrugated steel roof
illustrates the move away from colour to shades
of grey and white. The planning is far more
horizontal and the roof is used to develop a light-
filled cross-section. There is only the faintest
attempt at external landscaping, a common
thread through all of Seidler's residential work.

613

616

24 K 15

613 & 614 Museum of Sydney and First Government House Place

Cnr Phillip and Bridge Streets, Sydney
1993–95 Denton Corker Marshall
Artists: Janet Laurence and Fiona Foley
[Historic Houses Trust]
Open: Daily 10am–5pm
Closed: Good Friday and Christmas Day
GC, V, A

This development incorporates the site of the First Government House in Sydney. Architects Denton Corker Marshall designed a five-part redevelopment of the entire city block bounded by Bridge, Phillip, Bent and Young Streets. When finished, it comprised the Museum of Sydney, First Government House Place, Governor Phillip Tower, Governor Macquarie Tower and two rows of historic terrace houses.

The design followed a major architectural competition which was abandoned. Subsequently, DCM were selected by the developers after an informal second-stage competition.

The Museum of Sydney

The north-facing museum contains the collection brought to the surface after the archaeological dig on the remains of First Government House, once erected on part of the site. The museum is interpretive; much is made of imagining the original building — an elevated viewing area allows visitors to comprehend the original outline of the First Government House depicted in the pavement outside — while principal rooms of the now demolished building are re-created in the galleries. The collection contains governors' records, possessions, works of art, furniture and artifacts which came directly from the First Government House. Glass panels in the floor of the museum allow the footings and part of the dig to be viewed from above. The museum includes a 125-seat theatrette and a cafe.

First Government House Place

The plaza, which faces north, is paved on a 2-metre grid. For future archaeological digs, the grid enables individual paving sections to be lifted without disturbing the quality of the plaza. Sections can also be replaced with glass panels or glass pyramids.

Dominating the space is a major stylised stone wall construction with the steel frame and glass element of the museum projecting through it. The wall is symbolic of Sydney's architectural history; the different stone dressings represent different layers of Sydney building history.

Glass viewing windows and paving design depict the remains of the First Government House. At the western end of the square, the *Edge of the Trees* sculptural installation by Janet Laurence and Fiona Foley tells of how the indigenous people nearly came to an end at the hands of the colonisers. The totem sculptures are fitted with shells, ash and bones representing the vanished middens of the Eora people's encampments, with references to flora, fauna and the torching of the land. If you listen close to the 'tree', recordings of Aboriginal voices may be heard. It has been observed that the calm mini-malism contrasts dramatically with the excesses of the surrounding corporate architecture.

615

615

615 & 616 Governor Phillip Tower and Governor Macquarie Tower

Cnr Phillip and Bridge Streets, Sydney
1993–95 Denton Corker Marshall
Project Architect: Richard Johnson
GC, V, A

The 40-storey Governor Phillip Tower commences ten stories above the ground and rises to a height of 223 metres above Young Street. There are thirty-eight lettable floors, although when the building was completed it was described as a 64-storey tower (if you include ten storeys below ground and the void of the foyer). A second, shorter building was designed after the competition for the first tower was over. This building, called Governor Macquarie Tower, rises thirty storeys with approximately twenty-five lettable floors and both are interconnected at ground level with sumptuous foyers.

The skylit ground floor foyer of Governor Phillip Tower has grand proportions; it features a space-frame glass ceiling set 16 metres above the floor. Sandstone and granite inlaid with stainless steel and bronze are used throughout. Both foyers include substantial pieces of modern art.

•••

The building has made a significant contribution to the Sydney skyline, its crown being referred to as the 'gridiron' or the 'egg-slicer'.

617 Crown Street Housing Project

Crown Street, Surry Hills
1991–94 Travis McEwen Group
Project Architect: Frank Stanisic
GC, V, A

Sometimes referred to as the 'Euro-block', this large project of mixed uses contains 236 apartments and townhouses, offices, shops, cafes, meeting rooms and recreational facilities such as courtyard swimming pools, rooftop tennis court and basement car parking for 286 cars. Built on the site of the former Crown Street Women's Hospital, it covers two inner-city blocks measuring 1 hectare in area.

The larger building, approximately 24 metres high, is dedicated to 'private housing' and the lower building, approximately 13 metres high is dedicated to 'public housing' with 92 pensioner units for public housing tenants.

The project's fragmented perimeter organisation is a direct response to the sloping topography of Surry Hills, with its temperate and windy climate. A strong design intention was to 'define the street walls', that is, to build to the street alignments without major setbacks which erode the containment of the street. This enabled a large courtyard to be created in the centre of the 'private housing' block, with the highest part of the development at the southern corner, avoiding unnecessary overshadowing.

The projecting and receding planes, semi-enclosed balconies and tri-coloured face brickwork are reminiscent of the interwar inner city apartment buildings found in Sydney's eastern suburbs such as Potts Point, Elizabeth Bay and Randwick.

619

| 24 J 13 | 298 J 2 |

618 The Rocks Square

Argyle Street, The Rocks
1994 Tonkin Zulaika Harford
Project Architects: Peter Tonkin, Andrew Nimmo
GC, V, A

Small enclosed public squares are surprisingly rare in Sydney. The Rocks Square, which opens into Playfair Street, is one of the few urban spaces which is nicely elevated and has appropriately scaled buildings on either side. The square connects with passages and stairs, which in turn link with other streets and lanes. The square has been repaved in sandstone, with careful attention to access for the disabled.

The project also involved new construction, which included the refacing of the poorly designed Scarborough House, which previously addressed the space. The new section provides a skylit loggia in solid brickwork which has robust civic proportions and timber-framed verandas on stepped terraces.

619 House

9 Bulkara Road, Bellevue Hill
1994 Alexander Tzannes
GC, V, NA

A large mansion, designed by Alexander Tzannes, appears to recapture the heavier masonry feeling once associated with the Mediterranean School of Sydney in the 1930s. Sliding screens, strong roof lines, unpainted but tinted render, loggias and terraces combine to provide a contemporary formality and large scale. The house is spread over four levels, with garaging on the lowest level, a self-contained apartment with a garden terrace on the next level. The living level overlooks a private swimming pool and a north-facing winter lawn. A tennis court at the rear has its own private viewing terrace. The scale of the building is emphasised by the slope of the site and its elevated setting.

Below: Living level plan,
9 Bulkara Road, Bellevue Hill (1994)

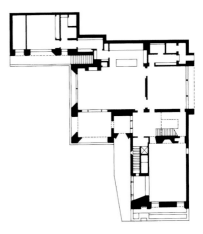

620

621

620 House (Israel)

107 Riverview Road, Avalon
1995 Stutchbury & Pape
Builder: Ken Israel
GC, V, NA

Continuing evidence of the vitality of the
Sydney School, particularly in the Pittwater area,
is found in a number of projects such as this
small retreat. The vocabulary is simple. Roof
forms (either skillion or gentle curve), post and
beam timber framing, compressed cement,
plywood or timber board external cladding,
timber decking and the diagonal 'plank' for
access are all hallmarks of this school. Many of
the initial concepts and compositional graphics
present in this type of Pittwater house extend
concepts which were worked out in the mid-
1960s in classrooms at Sydney University where
Richard Le Plastrier was teaching.

While not quite subscribing to the motto 'the
best architecture is no architecture at all' (*see*
page 160, 'Sydney School'), the timber interior
has the usual yacht-like details and maritime
associations of this 'cold water' fraternity.

621 House (Krempff)

465 Liverpool Street, Darlinghurst
1995 Margaret and Jean-Marc Krempff
GC, V, NA

An oddly shaped corner terrace house bought
(sight unseen) at auction was the first project
designed by Margaret Krempff, a recent
architecture graduate, and built by her husband
Jean-Marc. Only the crenellated facades to both
streets were retained, creating the opportunity
for an internal courtyard which would be
present at all levels throughout the new house.

Spread over three floors, the bedrooms are
stacked at the southern end with the living and
family rooms and rooftop sundeck at the
northern end. A great deal of attention was paid
to the use of materials including laminated
timbers and metalwork to the staircase and
courtyard glazing.

Small details abound. For example, the
courtyard walls are clad with compressed
cement panels without the horizontal joints cut
at angles thereby encouraging good drainage of
the joint and preventing staining.

Below: Ground floor plan,
465 Liverpool Street, Darlinghurst (1995)

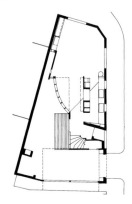

Below: Ground floor plan,
107 Riverview Road, Avalon (1995)

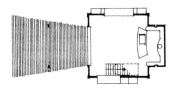

622

622 'Affordable' Housing

63–80 Mary Ann Street, Ultimo
1995 Allen Jack & Cottier + Design 5
Design Architect: Peter Stronach
GC, V, NA

New urban infill using traditional forms to heal the wounds in the broken terrace landscape of Ultimo. 'Affordable' housing, the new term for low-cost public housing, provides a range of different sized accommodation for long-term residents of the area. The project, designed by Peter Stronach of Allen Jack & Cottier, consists of two north-facing buildings lying parallel to each other, but separated by a communal space. The design has strong visual elements, nice compositional qualities and a directness which is well regarded in professional circles for not overselling precious detail or fussy finishes. For many, this is an ideal model urban-infill project, providing very attractive public housing at a relatively low cost.

623 House

12 Bulkara Road, Bellevue Hill
1994–95 Architectural Projects
Project Architect: Jennifer Hill
GC, V, NA

An extensive renovation of an existing house which is both decorative and playful, while still belonging to the Modernist tradition. The design, by Jennifer Hill, uses strong colours and floating planes. Reconstruction of the plan brought about the notion of two wings separated by a double height corridor.

The corridor 'zone' is part of the architect's game, which establishes markers throughout the house including an orange plywood screen wall, three storeys high, which is perforated by openings. A play is also made of the ambiguity between the corridor and the movable wall planes which double up as sliding screens. The new upper floor deceptively adds 110 square metres of area in a very compact shape.

Below: Ground floor plan,
12 Bulkara Road, Bellevue Hill (1995)

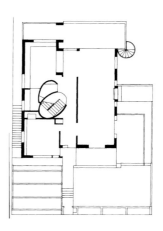

625

57 D 5	65 G 7

624 House (Inwald Thorburn)
73 Holdsworth Street, Woollahra
1992–94 Sam Marshall
GC, NV, NA

Old terrace house conversions are frequent projects for young Sydney architects who thoroughly understand the typology and its possibilities. Although hidden entirely from view, this visually stunning conversion by Sam Marshall has a remarkably conventional terrace house plan, yet makes the rear garden an extension of the interior. A strong feature is the exaggerated storage wall unit along the side of the kitchen and dining room with the complexity and curiosity of an adult's doll house.

625 House (Price/O'Reilly)
44 George Street, Redfern
1995 Engelen Moore
GC, V, NA

Built on what was once a pair of terraces house sites each only 8 metres wide by 28 metres long, this studio with full-height doors opening on to a pool at the rear was created by Tina Engelen and Ian Moore. Council controls established the height, depth of the parapet and the division of the building elevation to represent the original two allotments on which it now stands. Using industrial materials such as a steel portal frame with concrete blockwork, aluminium panels and louvre windows, a large amount of space was created on a slim budget. The desired spartan effect is perfectly achieved.

Below: Ground floor plan,
73 Holdsworth Street, Woollahra (1994)

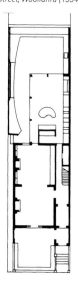

Below: Ground floor plan,
44 George Street, Redfern (1992)

626

36 K 13

626 Pair of Houses
85–87 Cliff Road, Northbridge
1994 Hill Thalis and Peter John Cantrill in
association
GC, V, NA

As is often the case, this was one of Sydney's unbuildable sites – steep, damp, weed-infested, south-facing with limited vehicular access, awkwardly subdivided and adjacent to a bushland park. It was regarded by the local council as not fit for development.

Around a shared entry stair and court, the house plans are inflected to accord with the property boundary, cliff line and a magnificent native tree. The slope generated a different stepped section for each building, with the roof terraces set just below the cliff top.

Loft living rooms occupy an entire floor placed on top of bedrooms and service areas to gain the best view. In the 'square' house, a uniform ceiling plane unites a regular plan, and a tiered section conceals a bisecting stairway that gives entry in the middle of the room. In the 'long' house, a series of centrifugal stair-cases provide a promenade around a complex interlocking section of the plan.

Below: Ground floor plan,
85–87 Cliff Street, Northbridge (1994)

160 C 18

627 House
16 Florida Road, Palm Beach
1995 Alex Popov
GC, V, NA

This project represents a major addition to a 1960s Palm Beach house on a remarkably steep site by building right under the existing house. The roof of the new building becomes a deck, a virtual indoor room to the existing house, which is in turn punctured by a pyramid bringing light down through the bedroom level and deep into the centre of the living room. Twin balconies, split by the two-storey galvanised steelwork which 'frames' the view, provide an unusual composition when seen from below.

274 D 10

628 Sydney International Athletic Centre
Sydney Olympic Park, Homebush
1995 Philip Cox Richardson Taylor & Partners/
Peddle Thorp
GC, V, A

The Sydney International Athletic Centre captures much of the spirit of the successful Athletic Stadium in Canberra designed by Philip Cox and Partners which was one of the firm's first large projects. The track (which will be the warm-up track during the Olympics), has a slender roof line with an external truss supported by cables from two tall masts. The cable-braced masts, similar to masts of a yacht, support the baffled lighting arrays which illuminate the field at night.

629

629 Converted Warehouse

24 Taylor Street, Darlinghurst
1995 Kerridge & Wallace Design Partnership
GC, V, NA

For many years a landmark in its dilapidated
state, this former coach and carriage repair shop
was converted by the then husband and wife
team into their own home and studio. Entry is
through a large rusted door set into the
underplayed exterior, marked only by the lead
mansard roof treatment. The ground floor which
opens directly onto the common courtyard was
used as a design studio, with the living area
raised one level above the courtyard.

The detailing of the kitchen and living room
has the feeling of a New York loft, with plywood
furniture and brightly coloured highlighted
surfaces. The bedrooms are reached by a
seemingly perilous staircase, with variable width
treads more suited to alpinists.

●●●

The firm Kerridge Wallace has since been
dissolved and the property sold.

Below: Ground floor plan,
24 Taylor Street, Darlinghurst (1995)

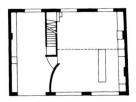

630 House

Wolseley Road, Point Piper
1995-96 Allen Jack & Cottier and Tim Allison
GC, V, NA

To avoid the confines of a relatively built-out
and narrow site with westerly harbour views,
this new residence by Stronach and Allison has
been twisted a few degrees on its axis to bring
both views and daylight deep into the building.
The internal design is rich and refined, while the
detailed exterior elements have a certain crisp-
ness and panache.

Below: Living level plan,
Wolseley Road, Point Piper (1996)

1996 Lone French Yachtsman Thierry Dubois
rescued 2600 km southwest of Perth

631

632

631 Imax Theatre
Darling Harbour
1996 HBO + EMTB
Design Architect: Lionel Glendenning
GC, V, A

'Architecture as billboard' may be an apt
description for the Imax Theatre, jammed as it is
between freeway overpasses and set on a difficult
site half on land and half over water. The form
of the theatre is generated by two curves: one
of the giant screen, the other the curve of the
amphitheatre. The 'eye' is referred to in both the
elevation and the plan of the building. The
design uses an oculus geometry with theatre
foyers, lobbies and terraces overlooking Cockle
Bay. The audience sit in steeply raked seating
(24 degrees), which is in a countercurve to the
screen. The projected image is so large that it
goes beyond the peripheral vision of the
audience. The exterior is treated as a pop art
road sign with alternating courses of different
finishes to the aluminium.

Below: Main plan,
Imax Theatre, Darling Harbour (1996)

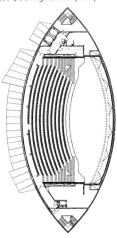

632 The Observatory Tower
Formerly the IBM Building
168-170 Kent Street, Sydney
1994-96
Principal Architects: Crone & Associates, Project
Architect: Nicholas Back
Consulting Design Architect: Thomas Hamel
Interior Architect: Wally Barda
GC, V, A

The former IBM building by Stephenson and
Turner (1964), with its precast concrete external
sunshades, was a notable office tower with a
concern for the problems of heat load. It was
also one of the few office towers ripe for
conversion to residential accommodation with
its small manageable floor plate size, lower floor
to ceiling heights than present office buildings,
and less than standard lift capacity. Its most
significant attraction for easy conversion was
the full steel frame with demountable lift cores
which were not depended upon in the original
building for shear resistance against wind. A
further ten floors were added after some
column amplification, which increased the
capacity of the building to 200 apartments.

Called the 'stealth bomber' by commuters
approaching the Harbour Bridge, the exterior
was cleverly transformed into stylish wrap-
around balconies which are nostalgic of the
1930s, yet also futuristic. The final appearance
was a team effort between consultants and
client. The external colour scheme of dark green
and black was favoured by the client who,
according to one interview, 'wanted it to be like
a car – dark and slick and sexy and mysterious'.

Generally thought to be an unusual addition
to the Sydney skyline, the Observatory Tower is
likely to be one of the last commercial office to
residential conversions because of rising city rents.

GLOSSARY

acanthus

ashlar

baluster

bossaged

capital

castellated

ACANTHUS a plant used in classical ornamentation, particularly capitals.

ARCHITRAVE the moulding around a doorway, window or arch.

ARRIS a sharp edge formed by the meeting of two planes.

ASHLAR precisely cut and squared block of masonry.

ATRIUM large interior space often roofed with a skylight and usually extending the full height of a building.

AWNING a light or temporary roof with at least one open side.

BALUSTER a post helping to support the handrail which together form a balustrade.

BARGE BOARD decorative board attached to the edge of a roof.

BATTLEMENT low wall around the edge of a roof broken by vertical slots.

BOND the method of laying bricks or stone to bind them together in a wall (English, Flemish, Colonial, Stretcher).

BOSSAGED column treatment, alternating between round and square.

BUTTRESS a support against a wall to counteract thrusts – usually from the roof load.

CANTILEVER a horizontal projection supported by a downward force behind a fulcrum.

CAPITAL the top part of a column, often decorated according to its order.

CASEMENT a vertically hinged window which opens like a door.

CASTELLATED decorated with battlements.

CAST IRON iron smelted and shaped in a mould.

CLERESTORY an upper window level of a building rising above adjacent roofs (from clear storey).

COPING a course at the top of a brick or stone wall to keep out water.

CORBEL a projecting block for the purpose of supporting a load.

CORNICE externally: a horizontal projecting moulding crowning the top of a building; internally: a moulding at the junction of a wall and ceiling.

CUPOLA a small dome.

CURTAIN WALL a non load-bearing wall, typically mostly of glass, applied in front of the framed structure of a building.

DADO the finished or faced lower part of an internal wall.

DENTIL one of a series of small separated rectangular blocks forming a part of a cornice.

DORMER a vertical window with its own small roof and side walls projecting from a larger sloping roof.

EAVES the lower edge of a roof, intended to throw rainwater clear of the walls below.

ENTABLATURE in Classical architecture, the part of an order above the column consisting of the architrave, frieze and cornice.

ENTASIS the slight convex curve of the shaft of a column.

FANLIGHT the glazing above a door usually with radiating glazing
   bars in a fan shape.
FASCIA a flat, on-edge member forming the edge of a roof.
FINIAL the ornamental finishing piece at the top of a canopy, buttress,
   roof, gable, corner of a tower, etc.
FORMWORK wood or metal forms into which concrete is poured.
FRIEZE the middle division of a classical entablature, between
   the architrave and the cornice.

cornice

GABLE the upper triangular part of an external wall at the edge
   of a pitched roof.
GALVANIZE strictly to coat a metal by electrical–chemical action.
   When used as 'galvanized iron', it is to coat iron with zinc
   usually by dipping or spraying.

dentil

HEADER a brick laid so that an end of the brick forms part of
   the face of the brickwork.
HIP the external angle formed by the meeting of two sloping
   roof surfaces.
HYPAR a hyperbolic paraboloid shape, usually in the form of a doubly
   curved roof element generated by straight lines.

entablature

JALOUSIE a swinging external window or door shutter with
   louvred slats.
JOIST the immediate supporting member of a floor or ceiling.

keystone

KEYSTONE the central stone or brick of an arch.

LANTERN a small structure on a roof with glass sides to light
   the interior of a building.
LINTEL a structural piece of timber, concrete, stone or metal,
   spanning a flat-headed doorway or window opening.
LOGGIA an open-sided arcade.
LOUVRE overlapping slats of timber, glass or other thin material
   with spaces between to admit air but exclude rain, or light if opaque.

lantern

MANSARD a roof in which each roof plane has two slopes, the lower
   portion being longer and steeper.
MODILLION bracket used to support a cornice.
MOULDING a contoured band used to decorate a wall or
   other surface.
MULLION the vertical part of a frame between the lights of a
   window or other opening.

modillion

NICHE a recess in a wall intended to contain a statue.
NOGGING a piece of non-structural framing between the members of
   a timber wall frame.

niche

pediment

pilaster

portico

ORDER the architectural mode manifest in the style and proportions of a column and entablature. The Classic Orders are either Greek (Doric, Ionic, Corinthian) or Roman (Tuscan, Doric, Ionic, Corinthian, Composite).

ORIEL a polygonal projecting windowed alcove on an upper floor.

PARAPET a low solid protection wall at the edge of a roof, formed by carrying the main wall past the eaves line.

PEDIMENT (a) a gable in a classical building (b) a triangular, partly-circular or other geometrical shaped decoration crowning a window, doorway, archway or other wall opening.

PERGOLA an open trellis-like roof intended for supporting climbing plants

PERISTYLE a colonnade surrounding a building or an open court

PILASTER a column which is engaged with a wall or the slightly projecting base of a column or a building.

PORTICO a porch supported by columns and open on at least one side.

PRESTRESSED a term applied to concrete in which high-strength steel cables are used instead of steel rods as reinforcement. The cables are placed in ducts cast in the concrete and then stressed to induce compression in the concrete before it is loaded.

PURLIN a horizontal roof beam laid parallel with the wall plate and the ridge beam at intervals up the slope of the roof, usually supporting rafters.

QUOINS corner stones at the angles of a building.

roundel

RAFTER a sloping member of the framework of a pitched roof.

REINFORCED CONCRETE concrete strengthened by steel rods put in place before pouring.

REVEAL the side face of a window, doorway or other wall opening.

RISER the vertical part of a step between the treads.

ROUNDEL a round or oval-shaped medallion-like ornament.

RUSTICATE to finish stonework with a very rough surface, but with deeply cut, precise and accurate joints. Various types are used, including diamond-pointed, cyclopean and vermiculated (worm-eaten).

sash

SASH in general, a frame which holds the glass of a window. A sash window is one which consists of two or more vertically sliding sashes, usually counter-weighted.

SKILLION a one-way pitched roof of even fall running from a highest point at one side of a building to the lowest point at the opposite side.

SPACE-FRAME a three-dimensional framework, usually triangulated, for enclosing a space, in which all the members are interconnected and act as a single entity, resisting loads applied in any direction. It is able to cover very large distances without intermediate supports.

SPANDREL the roughly triangular space between the curve of an arch and the rectangular frame enclosing it, or between adjoining arches.

stylobate

STILE a vertical framing member in joinery, particularly in doors and windows.

STRING a course, moulding or projecting band running horizontally across a facade.

STUD an upright supporting member of a timber wall frame to which wall coverings and linings are also fixed.

STYLOBATE the three-stepped base of a Greek building; or the tiered base of any colonnade.

TENON the end piece of wood shaped to fit into a corresponding cavity or mortice.

TENSIONING the application to a structural member of a permanent stress opposite to that to be expected from the working load, often used in reinforced concrete work.

TERRACOTTA red-brown fired clay.

TRANSOM the horizontal part of a frame between the lights of a window or between the top of a doorway and its fanlight.

TREAD the flat horizontal part of a step.

TRUSS a load bearing structural frame built up of comparatively light members.

TUCK POINTING the application of a narrow strip of mortar over the face of the joints in brickwork to give the appearance of precision and regularity.

VALENCE a decorative strip or panel below a roof.

VAULT an arched ceiling or roof, of stone or brick, sometimes imitated in stucco, plaster or timber. A barrel vault is semi-cylindrical in shape.

voussoir

VOUSSOIR a wedge-shaped stone block or brick, making up the curve of an arch.

WATTLE AND DAUB a type of wall construction in which slim pliable pieces of wood (wattles) are fixed to, or between, framing timbers and thickly plastered, usually with mud (daub).

WEATHERBOARD a long thin board fixed horizontally or, occasionally, vertically, with overlapping edges, as an external wall covering.

SYDNEY ARCHITECTS

Only a handful of architects brought architecture to Sydney between the date of first European settlement in 1788 and the dawn of the Victorian period in 1850. Most emigrated from England and Scotland; a few came from Canada and the USA. Except for the Joubert brothers from France, who worked as builders in Hunters Hill, no architects of note from continental Europe practised in Sydney until 1900.

The outstanding early architect, Francis Greenway, was a convict transported to Sydney and it was he who gave form to the urban visions of Governor Lachlan Macquarie. He was followed by Mortimer Lewis, Edmund Blacket and James Barnet, all English-born, who brought a great degree of quality through government buildings as Government Architects. A great schism, and lasting resentment developed between struggling private-practice architects, and the Government Architect of the day, whose job was to deliver all the new public buildings of a brand new city. Private architects were largely left to express themselves in private domain work: the largest area of which was residential design.

That legacy carried through to contemporary times, with domestic design regarded as the identifiable ingredient of Sydney architecture. Architects including John Horbury Hunt, Leslie Wilkinson, Walter Burley Griffin, John Sulman, William Hardy Wilson, Alexander Stewart Jolly, Emil Sodersten, Sydney Ancher, Harry Seidler and Glenn Murcutt, all contributed to the developing interpretation of the Sydney house.

Young architects today explore their ideas largely through the house; a concept and an opportunity which is alien in most parts of the world. The transition to larger buildings often comes through commissions for buildings on university campuses. Public architecture designed and built by the government has almost disappeared.

To date, no tradition of innovative commercial office building design has been established, but there are signs of improvement.

FRANCIS GREENWAY (1777–1837)

Francis Greenway.

Mitchell Library, State Library of New South Wales

Born in the West Country of England in 1777, Francis Greenway came from a family of masons, quarrymen, builders and architects. Having been found guilty of forging an endorsement on a contract, he was sentenced to be transported to New South Wales and arrived in Sydney in 1814 after a harrowing plague-ridden voyage.

Greenway brought with him a personal introduction from a former governor (Phillip) to Governor Lachlan Macquarie and soon after his arrival he was summoned to Government House. Being a forthright man with little regard for the existing architecture in the colony he scoffed at Macquarie's pattern book ideas for a new town hall and court house. Indeed, had it not been for Greenway's skills and Macquarie's urgent need of them, his outspokenness might not have been forgiven.

Greenway's first duties for Macquarie were building inspections, until in 1816 he was appointed Acting Government Architect and Assistant Engineer. His first major project was the lighthouse on the South Head of Port Jackson (1816–18). Pleased with Greenway's work, Macquarie granted him emancipation, which allowed Greenway to travel in the colony without restriction. Later, on completion of Hyde Park Barracks in May 1819, he was granted a full pardon.

Greenway realised that conditions in Australia required a different architectural approach to that which was applied in England. He considered climate, the materials to hand and the availability of good craftsmen when undertaking his designs. Greenway demanded high-quality materials and workmanship and it was he who introduced the system of progress payments to a previously poorly administered building industry. His designs raised the standard of architecture in the colony dramatically.

With Greenway as Government Architect, Governor and Mrs Macquarie set out to build a city with magnificent buildings, but their plans soon received unfavourable attention in Britain. A commission of inquiry was established and JT Bigge was dispatched to the colony. His report was generally favourable towards Greenway, but found Macquarie's taste for ornamentation to be indulgent.

After Macquarie's departure, the difficult relations between Greenway and the new Chief Engineer, Major Ovens, led to his services as Government Architect being dispensed with. He then went into private practice, but with little success.

Greenway died in 1837, a year after moving to a small grant of land in the Hunter Valley.

The Hyde Park Barracks.

Mitchell Library, State Library of New South Wales

JOHN VERGE (1782–1861)

John Verge was born in Christchurch, Hampshire, England, in 1782, the son of a bricklayer. His work in the family trade had given him a practical knowledge of architectural styles and techniques and these were to distinguish him in his later career.

Verge soon moved to London, where he became an established builder. By 1828, he had become a man of means, with a considerable amount of property. However, after his marriage failed, he decided to emigrate to Australia.

His first land grant was 2560 acres of land on the banks of the Williams River, south of what is now the town of Dungog. However, Verge's capital reserves were not enough to enable him to develop the property to a self-sufficient state and he returned to Sydney. Back in the city he soon established himself as an architect and builder, gaining a clientele of influential citizens, including John Macarthur, William Charles Wentworth and Mary Reiby, all of whom desired houses in the English style. John Verge's previous experience in London placed him in an outstanding position in the Sydney of 1830.

While Verge had a sound knowledge of building, his assistant, John Bibb, was a good planner and stylist, and their collaboration produced a number of excellent buildings including Elizabeth Bay House for Colonial Secretary Alexander Macleay. When Verge retired in 1837, Bibb took over the practice.

Verge's retirement was sudden and unexpected after only seven years as the colony's society architect. He moved north to become a farmer on a remote property grant near Kempsey, where he commenced farming.

John Verge died in 1861, aged seventy-nine, and was buried at Port Macquarie.

Elizabeth Bay House.

Edmund Blacket and children.

Mitchell Library, State Library of New South Wales

EDMUND BLACKET (1817–1883)

The son of a cloth merchant, Edmund Blacket arrived in Australia in 1842 with little architectural experience. However he brought with him letters of introduction to important members of Sydney society including Bishop Broughton, the first and only Anglican Bishop of Australia. These introductions were to stand him in good stead as only a few months after his arrival he had designed his first building in Australia: All Saints Church at Singleton.

Blacket's appointment as Diocesan Architect immediately raised his standing in the Sydney building community. His practice thrived and in 1849 he became Government Architect, replacing Mortimer Lewis. He held this position for five years until lured by the great opportunity to design the new Sydney University, he returned to private practice.

Most of his church designs and also that for Sydney University, were Gothic Revival. This style had been promoted in England by Pugin and had become seen as the only style befitting church and school architecture. It was a style in which Blacket shone. He was not an innovative architect, but he used materials sensitively and his buildings were finely proportioned and well-built.

Edmund Blacket was a well-liked man and other architects, Horbury Hunt, James Barnet and William Kemp, all of whom had worked for him, were amongst the pall bearers at his funeral in 1883.

St Mark's, Darling Point.

Dixson Galleries, State Library of New South Wales

WILLIAM WARDELL (1823–1899)

Born in London in 1823, William Wardell emigrated to Melbourne in 1852 having already established his reputation as an architect in England, his formal training having been as an engineer.

In 1859 Wardell became the Inspector-Clerk of Public Works in Victoria and in the following year Inspector-General of the Public Works Department, with the right of private practice. He was also involved in engineering works, but his major contribution was to architecture. The leaders of the Catholic church were members of the colonial gentry and, having converted to Catholicism in 1834, Wardell was perfectly placed to take on their major commissions. The style of the churches and cathedrals which he built was consistently Gothic, as evidenced in St Mary's in Sydney, but none lived up to the standard of St Patrick's in Melbourne, his first Australian commission.

Australian Steam Navigation & Co.

In 1878, after nineteen years of service, Wardell was dismissed as Victorian Government Architect, in the aftermath of corruption allegations against the Governor, Sir George Bowen. A Royal Commission was appointed and there was criticism of construction standards and over-spending on Public Works.

Following an extensive study tour through Europe, Wardell set up practice in Sydney. Here he restricted his work to non-ecclesiastical projects. He also expanded his range of styles to include Italianate, Palladian and Venetian. Amongst his major works were the Union Club, the New South Wales Club and the English, Scottish and Australian Bank.

William Wardell died in 1899 of a heart attack.

JAMES BARNET (1827–1904)

The son of a builder, James Barnet was born in Scotland in 1827. He went to London in 1843 and apprenticed himself to a builder, but his architectural ambitions were frustrated by a lack of patronage, which was so necessary to gain important contracts.

The opportunities in the colonies sounded much better, so Barnet took ship, arriving in Sydney in December 1854. Once again lack of patronage proved to be a problem as his first application for a position with the Colonial Architect's Office was unsuccessful.

He then established himself as a small building contractor, specialising in masonry works and the following year he worked for Edmund Blacket as Clerk of Works on the foundations of the Randwick Asylum. After this job, Blacket offered him the same position during construction of the University of Sydney, during which time he also became involved in design matters.

By now, Barnet had an established reputation and was appointed Second Clerk of Works in the Colonial Architect's Office in 1860. Almost immediately he was requested to prepare plans for major extensions to the Australian Museum. In 1862, Barnet was appointed Acting Colonial Architect and replaced Alexander Dawson as Colonial Architect in 1865. He held this position for the next twenty-five years, producing more than 1,000 new buildings, a result of the demand for public and private buildings after the gold rush.

Barnet was an able administrator who established a pattern of organisation which was to become the prototype for future large architectural offices. He was a promoter of new technology, used concrete and fire-resistant materials, introduced electricity into his buildings and was first to install a telephone in a government office.

After retiring, Barnet remained active in public life, often speaking out on matters which concerned him. He was opposed to many of the radical changes which were taking place in the architectural scene, and did not disguise his aversion to the work of his successor, Vernon.

James Barnet died on 16 December 1904 and was buried at Rookwood cemetery.

The Australian Museum.

Mitchell Library, State Library of New South Wales

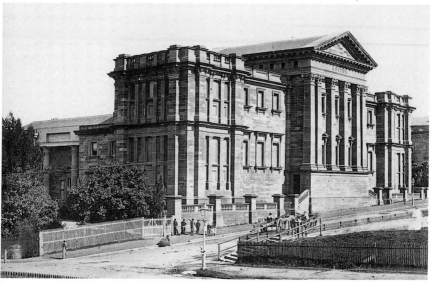

JOHN HORBURY HUNT (1838–1904)

Born in 1838 in New Brunswick, Canada, John Horbury Hunt, the son of a builder, decided at the age of eighteen to become an architect and left home for Boston. He began articled training under EC Cabot, with whom he worked for six years. Then in 1862, at the beginning of the American Civil War, Hunt set off to live in India. During the voyage, his ship put in to Sydney and James Barnet, the Colonial Architect, persuaded him to stay in the colony. Hunt stayed, but joined Edmund Blacket as an assistant rather than Barnet.

In 1869, Horbury Hunt set up his own practice. He was one of the main crusaders for a return to brickwork and, by the 1880s, multi-coloured brickwork came to be seen on stores and office blocks as well as churches and houses.

Hunt cut an extraordinary figure, riding a bicycle to jobs around Sydney fitted with a collapsible drawing board and ink reservoir. He designed his own suits with special pockets to accommodate his architectural implements; papers he kept in his hat. This individuality carried through to Hunt's architecture, he once specified the quality of brickwork to be that which 'when struck shall emit a sound which is music to the ear of the architect'.

His personality was fiery and forthright. His spats with rival John Sulman were notorious, particularly during Hunt's time as President of the Royal Australian Institute of Architects, a position coveted by Sulman.

Hunt's library held Australia's largest collection of books on architecture. He kept abreast of trends in Britain, America and Europe, and his designs began to include modern architectural features such as the functionally expressed parts of houses. In his day, his buildings were criticised by his colleagues, who were still using the elaborate Victorian style, as being too plain and sterile. Hunt preached against stylistic pretence, believing in 'original variations developed within the severe discipline of a personal idiom'.

In 1893, Horbury Hunt's practice virtually ceased due to the economic depression. He died of Bright's disease in 1904.

The Highlands, Waitara.

WALTER LIBERTY VERNON (1846-1914)

Walter Liberty Vernon was born in England in 1846. He was articled in 1862 to the London architect WG Habershon, and during this period he attended lectures at the Royal Academy of Arts and went to the South Kensington School of Art at night.

Vernon ran an office for the London architect Charles Moreing at Hastings and subsequently set up his own practice there in 1872. He also established an office in London.

Due to recurring bouts of asthma, Vernon was advised to leave England, and reached Australia in November 1883. He was soon busy and was commissioned to build a department store for David Jones Ltd., on George and Barrack Streets. He built his own home, 'Penshurst', at Neutral Bay in 1884, and built other villas on adjoining land.

From 1884 to 1889, Vernon was in partnership with William Wardell. Then in 1890 he replaced James Barnet as Government Architect in the new branch of the Department of Public Works, which had been created to allow private architects to compete for the design of all public buildings estimated to cost more than £5000. The government architect was to supervise the construction, with a commission paid to the selected architect. By the end of 1894, Vernon was able to demonstrate that the new system cost twice as much as designs from his own (government) office and competitions were never reinstated during his tenure from 1890–1911.

Vernon's major public buildings were monumental and finely wrought in stone; suburban buildings took on the scale and character of their surroundings; and country buildings were designed with cross-ventilation, shady verandas and sheltered courtyards.

WL Vernon died on 17 January 1914 from septicaemia after the amputation of a leg, and was buried at Gore Hill.

Art Gallery of NSW interior.

Hood Collection, State Library of New South Wales

JOHN SULMAN (1849–1934)

John Sulman was born in London in 1849. Educated at the Architectural Association and the Royal Academy of Arts, he won the Pugin travelling scholarship in 1871. His practical training was gained in the architectural offices of Thomas Allom of Haymarket, Harry R Newton in Regent Street, and Sir Gilbert Scott.

Sulman came to Sydney in 1885, at the age of thirty-six, seeking a warmer climate for his wife Sarah who had developed tuberculosis. Arriving in the midst of the building boom, he was able to begin practice almost immediately having been an established architect in England with over seventy buildings and churches to his credit. He was also acting as president elect of the Architectural Association.

Soon after arrival, Sulman bought into a partnership with well-known Sydney architect CHE Blackmann. Under the terms of their agreement, should anything happen to either partner, the other was to provide for their wife and children. A few weeks after signing the agreement, Blackmann absconded to America with all the firm's money and a notorious Sydney barmaid, leaving Sulman to fulfil the terms of the contract.

In 1886, Sulman set up the Palladian Club in order to give some professional respectability to the Sydney architectural community. The group met once a month to show projects and offer informed criticism of the work of its members, who included William Wardell, George Mansfield, WL Vernon and Arthur Blacket amongst others. Sulman's underlying intention was ultimately to gain power within the Institute of Architects, and in 1887 he led his club members to the annual general meeting during which the incumbent president, Thomas Rowe, was re-elected and Sulman elected vice-president. John Horbury Hunt had similar aims to Sulman, but their contrasting approaches and personalities — Hunt fiery and obtuse and Sulman the reserved Englishman — led to a lifetime of antagonism.

Sulman published many papers on structural and aesthetic aspects of architecture and in 1889 he became a trustee and later, in 1919, president of the National Art Gallery. From 1916 to 1927, he was lecturer in town planning at Sydney University and, from 1921 to 1924, he was chairman of the Federal Capital Advisory Board. He was knighted in 1924 for his public services.

Before his death in 1934, he created a fund to provide the Sir John Sulman Medal for Architecture, which is still competed for by members of the NSW division of the Royal Australian Institue of Architects.

He died in 1934 aged eighty-five.

Thomas Walker Hospital, Concord.

WALTER BURLEY GRIFFIN (1876–1937)

Walter Burley Griffin was born in 1876, near Chicago, and was trained at Nathan Ricker's School of Architecture at the University of Illinois, graduating in 1899.

From 1901–1906, he worked as an associate of Frank Lloyd Wright at Oak Park. Griffin started his own practice in 1906 and within a few years established his reputation as an architect of the Prairie School.

In 1911, Griffin married Marion Mahony, the second woman to graduate in architecture from the Massachusetts Institute of Technology. The Griffins came to Australia in 1912, having won the Federal Capital Competition for the design of Canberra, a project they had worked on together. They were joined in Australia by Walter's sister, Genevieve, and her architect husband Roy Lippincott, who had also worked with Frank Lloyd Wright. By 1919, there were problems with the Canberra project. Griffin had endless struggles with the authorities and, in 1920, he resigned his position as Federal Capital Director of Design and Construction.

Walter Burley Griffin.

Griffin then formed the Greater Sydney Development Association to purchase 263 hectares in Middle Harbour, which became known as Castlecrag. He devoted the next fifteen years to developing and promoting the area, while maintaining an architectural practice.

Griffin believed dwellings should play a subordinate role in the scheme of nature. The houses, including Griffin's own, at 8 The Parapet, were small and intimate. He aimed toward the most natural use of land and the selection of indigenous plants. He also developed an economical construction system of pre-cast interlocking structural tiles, which he called 'Knitlock', and used it widely, as well as stone, in the houses of Castlecrag.

In the early 1930s, Griffin built incinerators, for the destruction of household garbage, in various cities and suburbs in the eastern states of Australia. They provided a canvas for experimentation with form and texture for the architect, but sadly few have survived.

Griffin's work took him to India in 1935 and he died there two years later of peritonitis. Although not considered a success in his lifetime, appreciation of his work came later. In 1963, on the 50th anniversary of the naming of Canberra, a commemorative stamp was issued with his portrait and, in 1964, the Canberra Lake (made to a form which Griffin had strongly opposed) was named after him.

House, Castlecrag.

WILLIAM HARDY WILSON (1881-1955)

William Hardy Wilson was born at Campbelltown, New South Wales, in 1881, into a wealthy, third-generation Australian family. On leaving Newington College in 1898, he attended evening architectural courses at the Sydney Technical College while articled to the firm of Kent and Budden.

In 1903, Wilson travelled to London to study architecture and art where his many Australian friends included established artists of the Heidelberg School, such as Arthur Streeton, Tom Roberts, George Lambert and John Longstaff. With his lifelong friend and partner, Stacey Arthur Neave, Hardy Wilson made the Grand Tour of Europe and later America, where he was particularly impressed by the Colonial Revival architecture. He became an associate of the Institute of Empire Architects in 1905.

Returning to Sydney, Wilson found it architecturally backward and set out to create an architecture which would suit the Australian landscape and continue the colonial heritage. He had a great admiration for colonial architecture and wrote and sketched prolifically on the subject. His book, *Old Colonial Architecture in NSW and Tasmania*, was published in 1924.

Wilson set up in partnership with Neave in the Commercial Bank Chambers in Sydney, and designed his first real house for his friend the artist Lionel Lindsay. A new partner, John L Berry, joined the firm in 1920 and it seems he and Neave kept the practice running while Wilson devoted most of his energy to writing and art. Hardy Wilson was particularly fond of Chinese art, and explored the notion of integrating western ideas with those of the east.

At the age of forty-six, Wilson decided to spend the rest of his life writing and travelling. He died in 1955 aged seventy-four.

Eryldene, Gordon.

LESLIE WILKINSON (1882–1973)

Leslie Wilkinson was already a distinguished architect before he arrived in Sydney. A graduate of the Royal Academy in London, he had won the silver medal in 1903 and the gold two years later and travelling scholarships had allowed him to tour France, Italy and Spain.

In 1900, Wilkinson was articled to James S Gibson, becoming his assistant in 1903. Later he became assistant to Professor FM Simpson at University College, London, and held the position there of assistant professor from 1910–18.

Leslie Wilkinson.

Mitchell Library, SLNSW

Wilkinson came to Australia in 1918 to take up the new chair of architecture, in the faculty of science, at the University of Sydney. Two years later his proposal for a separate faculty of architecture was accepted with himself as dean. He emphasised the intellectual and artistic over the more mundane aspects of architecture, which was to become a source of conflict with other members of the profession. As a result of criticism of the students' level of practical knowledge by the Institute of Architects, Alfred Hook was appointed associate-professor in charge of construction and related sciences, leaving Wilkinson to teach design and history.

As University Architect, Wilkinson's master plan for Sydney University included completing Blacket's Gothic Revival quadrangle; building a new chemistry building and a Mediterranean-style physics building. The first house which he built in Australia was for himself and he called it 'Greenway' in homage to Australia's first great architect Francis Greenway. His houses and flats soon became very fashionable, though he himself believed 'it is not so important to be in style as to have style'.

Wilkinson was Dean of the Faculty of Architecture at Sydney University until 1947. He was made a life fellow of the Royal Australian Institute of Architects, of which he had twice been elected president (1933 and 1934); in 1960, he became the first architect to be awarded its gold medal. In 1961, the Wilkinson Award was established for domestic Australian architecture.

In 1968, when aged eighty-six, Wilkinson built his last house, at Vaucluse. He died on 20 September 1973.

ALEXANDER STEWART JOLLY (1887–1957)

An eccentric and non-conformist architect, AS Jolly led an extraordinary life. From a northern tableland timber family, Jolly moved to Sydney in 1918 where he designed a handful of houses. However, because of bad health he gave up architecture and moved to Palm Beach, about 30 kilometres to the north. There he joined up with a real estate agent and built speculative houses, often camping on site in a tent. During this time, Jolly designed some extraordinary buildings which were totally outside the Sydney architectural scene. Some designs had stonework of craggy natural rocks, walls of tree trunks and logs, and window frames made from intertwined twigs, hand grooved for glazing. A particularly famous example was the Elephant House (1935) at Taylor's Point.

During the Depression, Jolly took to writing children's books. A sufferer from uncontrollable alcoholism, he finally quit by cutting off a finger with an axe. Aged fifty-five at the outbreak of World War II, he lied about his age and joined the army to dig trenches in the Middle East. He was later appointed an intelligence officer with the Australian Army.

ARTHUR GEORGE STEPHENSON (1890–1967)

Born in Melbourne in 1890, Arthur Stephenson studied architecture at the technical colleges of Melbourne and Sydney, and gained practical training at several offices in both cities, most notably that of Alec S Eggleton, for whom he developed a life long admiration and friendship.

Stephenson served with distinction in the AIF in World War I, and was awarded the Military Cross. After the war, he returned to architecture and became a student at the Architectural Association in London and later an associate of the RIBA.

Starting his own practice on his return to Australia, Stephenson became the revered head of Australia's largest architectural firm, with offices throughout the capital cities, as well as in New Zealand and the Middle East. Stephenson was a strong believer in the idea of the team and his staff were generally devoted to him and his methods. He established scholarships at the Universities of Sydney and Melbourne, helped many students to study abroad, and trained apprentices in his offices.

Stephenson became a fellow of the RAIA, RIBA, and the New Zealand Institute of Architects and was made an honorary member of the American Institute of Architects. In 1953 he was awarded the Gold Medal of the RIBA, the first Australian to be so honoured. In 1964, Arthur Stephenson became a knight of the British Empire and was awarded the Gold Medal of the RAIA.

He died on 18 November 1967.

King George V Hospital.

EMIL SODERSTEN (1901–1961)

Emil Sodersten studied architecture at the Sydney Technical College and, in 1919, attended Leslie Wilkinson's first design *atelier* at Sydney University.

In the 1920s, Sodersten worked on Brisbane City Hall, and with Tate and Young on the Manchester Unity Building, from which he gained a thorough command of decorative stylism. He formed a belief that 'traditions are but the foundations from which new creative forms should be developed' and he became one of Australia's first truly modern architects.

Sodersten began private practice in 1925, making him, at age twenty-four, the youngest architect in practice. His first buildings include the Tudor and Wall houses in Sydney, St Bede's Church of England at Drummoyne, Werrington Flats at Potts Point and the remodelling of cinemas around the inner-city suburbs. Much of his inspiration came from American architects of the time such as Raymond Hood and Bertram Grosvenor Goodhue. With Sodersten's City Mutual Building (1936) and the Anzac War Memorial (1934) by a colleague, C Bruce Dellit, Art Deco was established as the popular style of the 1930s.

In 1927, at age twenty-six, Sodersten won the international competition for the National War Memorial in Canberra. This caused an uproar amongst architects and consequently John Crust was awarded the commission jointly with Sodersten.

The popularity of the Art Deco style began to wane in the late 1930s and Sodersten turned towards a more modern form, as the International Style began to manifest itself on the Australian architectural scene. After a tour overseas in 1935, the influence of the Dutch architect Dudok became apparent in his work with the use of striped brick, curved glass and the rejection of embellishment. Sodersten was quick to embrace new materials and methods such as the use of glass, electric light, synthetic materials, structural steel and reinforced concrete. His City Mutual Building of 1936 was the first fully air-conditioned office building in Sydney.

Birtley Towers, Elizabeth Bay.

Mitchell Library, State Library of New South Wales

SAMUEL LIPSON (1901–1995)

Born in Scotland in 1901 to Lithuanian Jewish immigrants, Lipson began architectural training in 1916 at the Glasgow School of Arts. In 1918, he was employed as an articled student and assistant draughtsman by the office of Honeyman & Keppie architects, the same firm Charles Rennie Mackintosh had entered twenty years previously. Lipson was particularly impressed by the Modern School of Dutch Architecture and the work of Dudok.

Arriving in Australia on an assisted passage in 1925, he had with him a letter of introduction to the Chief Architect for the Commonwealth of Australia, Sandy Murdoch, who had also trained in Glasgow.

In the Sydney branch of the Department of Works, Lipson was given the opportunity of working with Leslie Wilkinson in the construction of the School of Tropical Medicine at Sydney University and later the Macmaster School of Veterinary Science.

Lipson's most important work in the early stage of his career was the remodelling of the Head Office of the Commonwealth Bank in Martin Place. During this project he was noticed by the bank's Governor, Sir John Little, who would later recommend him for several private commissions.

Due to the Depression, Lipson was retrenched from the Department of Works and began private practice in 1932. He also took on a teaching position at the Sydney Technical College. The Trust Building of 1933 displayed Lipson's talent and facilitated his path to success.

In the mid-1930s, he joined forces with Peter Kaad and together they established one of the most fashionable practices of the inter-war period, producing such buildings as the Hastings Deering Car Service Station (1937) and the Hoffnung Building (1938). Many of the works of this period were photographed by Max Dupain, a personal friend of Lipson.

During World War II, Lipson was directed by the government to design air raid shelters and hostel buildings in country areas. After the war, Lipson & Kaad designed low cost housing for the Housing Commission and documented new branches of the Commonwealth Bank.

Apartment Block, Lipson & Kaad.

*Private Collection
held in Mitchell Library, State Library
of New South Wales*

SYDNEY ANCHER (1904–1978)

Born at Woollahra in 1904, Sydney Ancher became interested in drawing at an early age, experimenting in watercolours and entering drawing competitions. Ancher's architectural education began at the Sydney Technical High School where he took subjects which focused on architecture in conjunction with general schooling.

While at Sydney Technical College (1924–29), Ancher was an articled pupil with EWS Wakeley and, in 1927, he began as a draughtsman with Prevost, Synot and Ruwald. He produced presentation drawings for many architects and worked as an advertising illustrator to earn extra money.

In 1929, Ancher was awarded the Australian Medallion and Travelling Scholarship from the NSW Chapter Board of Architects. He was overseas for five years working for Verity & Beverley (London), Joseph Emberton (working at the time on Olympia at Earl's Court and Blackpool Pleasure Beach), Textaphote (who designed exhibition stands) and Thompson & Walford.

The turning point in his thinking was seeing the 1931 International Building Exhibition in Berlin, his first contact with the International Style. Ancher was attracted by the simpilicity of the model house by Mies van de Rohe and later believed that 'in designing my houses I think I have had Mies at the back of my mind'.

On his return to Australia in 1935, Ancher worked for Emil Sodersten until he accepted a junior partnership with Prevost, after declining an offer from Stephenson & Turner.

Ancher became a founding member of what was to become one of Sydney's major firms, Ancher, Mortlock, Murray & Woolley. Throughout his career Ancher concentrated on domestic architecture. His houses showed an adaptation of form to the conditions of Australian bushland sites and the Sydney climate. Typical features of his open plan houses were large verandas, sheltered patios and an opening of the interior to the landscape.

Ancher found that his own education had been an inadequate preparation for his career as an architect and consequently devoted much of his time to the education of architects through talks and articles in magazines and architectural journals.

House, Killara.

Private Collection held in Mitchell Library, State Library of New South Wales

HARRY SEIDLER (1923)

Harry Seidler was born in Vienna in 1923, but left for England at the age of fifteen, following Hitler's annexation of Austria. When refugees were interned in England, Seidler found himself moved from one camp to another until he was finally transported to Canada in 1941.

He was allowed out to study architecture at the University of Manitoba, graduating with first-class honours in 1944. From there he won a scholarship to study at Harvard's Graduate School of Design, attending Walter Gropius' Master Class of 1946. Seidler subsequently studied design under Josef Albers at Black Mountain College, North Carolina and became Marcel Breuer's chief assistant in New York (1946–48).

After working with Oscar Niemeyer in Rio de Janeiro, Seidler was asked to design a house for his parents who had recently migrated to Sydney. This was in 1949 and it marked the beginning of his architectural practice in Australia. The house, now known as the Rose Seidler House, won the Sir John Sulman medal of the Royal Australian Institute of Architects in 1951, the first of a number of awards which were to follow, including the RAIA Gold Medal in 1976 and the Royal Institute of British Architects Gold Medal in 1996.

Harry Seidler's work continues to change the Sydney skyline. A major overseas project which will take him through the millenium is a large public housing scheme to accommodate 2,500 people in his native Vienna.

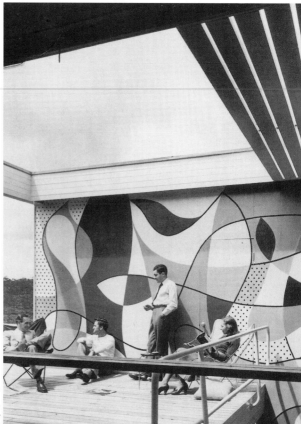

Rose Seidler House.

Private Collection held in Mitchell Library, State Library of New South Wales

GLENN MURCUTT (1936–)

After being born in London in 1936 when his his parents were en route to the XIth Olympiad in Berlin, Glenn Murcutt spent his early childhood in the Upper Watut area of Papua New Guinea. In 1941, at the outset of the war in the Pacific, the family returned to Australia.

Murcutt's father subscribed to several architectural magazines and the young Glenn became acquainted with architects like Mies van de Rohe and Frank Lloyd Wright at a very early age. The teachings of Thoreau with his appreciation of nature and practical husbandry were also a fundamental ingredient of Murcutt's early education.

His architectural education was gained at the Sydney Technical College, from which he graduated in 1961. Some of his early work experience was with Neville Gruzman, Allen & Jack, and Ancher, Mortlock, Murray & Woolley.

Murcutt began his Sydney practice in 1969. He attributes his appreciation of nature, an ever present reference in his architecture, to the lessons of the bush learned from his father in his childhood. His houses, like the bush surrounding them, evidence the action of sun, wind and rain and aim towards harmonious relationships with their sites, at the same time not disguising their synthetic nature. This response to the environment has made Murcutt famous for being able to express a specifically Australian architectural form, focused on light, space, movement, ventilation and sun control.

In 1992, Glenn Murcutt was presented with the prestigious Alvar Aalto Award in Finland, adding to an impressive list of Australian awards which includes the Gold Medal from the Royal Australian Institute of Architects in 1992. He continues to work as a sole practitioner in Sydney, with commissions throughout the country.

PHILIP COX (1939–)

Born in 1939, Philip Cox graduated from Sydney University in 1962 with first-class honours. His early work experience was in the office of Bruce Rickard. In 1963, Cox, with Ian McKay, was commissioned to design the St Andrews Presbyterian Preparatory College, Leppington, New South Wales, and the CB Alexander Presbyterian Agricultural College of Tocal, on an extensive site at Paterson in the Hunter Valley.

Philip Cox and Associates was formed in 1967 and over the years other partners have joined, with the firm's name changing accordingly. It is now known as Cox Richardson Architects and Planners, with offices throughout Australia and one in Jakarta.

Cox was influenced by the romantic school of Australian landscape painting and his best works are characterised by a subtle and sensitive relationship with the sites.

Philip Cox has received many awards including the Gold Medal from the Royal Australian Institute of Architects in 1984 and an Honorary Fellowship of the American Institute of Architects in the same year. He was made a member of the Order of Australia in 1988. Among his numerous projects are the Yulara Tourist Resort, Uluru, Sydney International Aquatic and Athletic Centres, the Sydney Football Stadium, the National Tennis Centre, the Sydney Harbour Casino, the Sydney Exhibition Centre, the Brisbane Convention and Exhibition Centre and the Cairns Convention Centre.

TOURS

Unlike planned Australian cities such as Melbourne and Adelaide, Sydney has evolved as a private city of clustered interconnected suburbs, which until very recently were concentrated on the Hawkesbury River, the ocean coastline and the harbour foreshore. Ignoring the grid, Sydney reflects the contours and geography of its setting. By car, Sydney is a very easy city to see, but many areas around the habour are also accessible by ferry and inner city areas are well-covered by bus routes.

The eight tour areas which follow, have been chosen because they are representative of contrasting periods and styles of architecture, or they cover an area with a high concentration of buildings found in this book.

Each area includes the location of buildings listed, which are either visible or not visible directly from the public way. However, Sydney's geography with its ridges and valleys, means many buildings which are concealed at their point of immediate access may nevertheless be observed from a distance.

Each tour area reveals a different character to Sydney. The City Centre shows the ages of Sydney: the low-rise hand-made city of three storeys, the medium-rise city of six storeys and then thirteen storeys after lifts were introduced, and the high-rise city to sixty storeys after height restrictions were lifted in 1958. The City South area shows a collision of mixed uses and mixed building styles; the Inner East area captures two periods — Regency and Art Deco; the Eastern Suburbs area shows an eclectic mix of houses of the wealthy; Appian Way in Burwood is an unusual philanthropic development at the time of Federation; Hunters Hill shows the bourgeois influence of French settlers; Castlecrag/Middle Harbour show houses with a new consciousness of breaking with the European past; and Pittwater/Palm Beach, remote until the 1930s, is now the expensive weekend retreat area for many people who have their first house in the city.

1. CITY CENTRE

*Darling
Harbour*

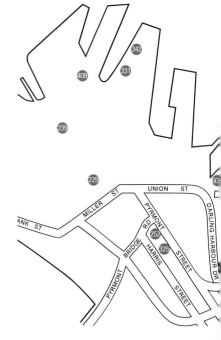

The city centre is a small and confined area, yet it is the largest repository of important architecture in New South Wales. The city has been 'written' over in progressive waves of development; originally three-storey buildings, followed by six- to seven-storey buildings, thirteen-storey buildings from 1912 and 25- to 50-storey buildings after 1960. Historic fragments are scattered within the confines of a magnificent topography. The Rocks area, saved from demolition and development during the 1970s, gives Sydney a historical setting against which the later development of the city can be judged.

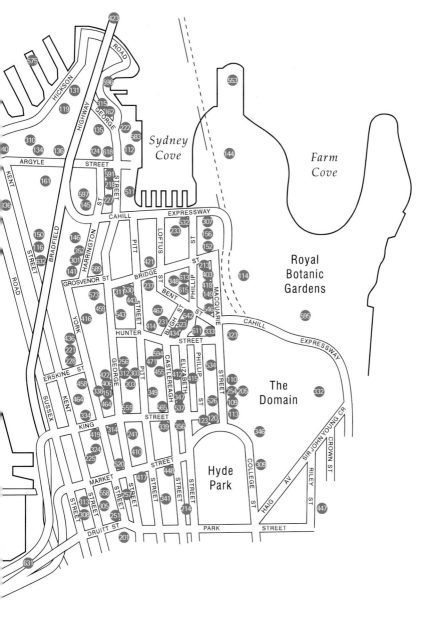

CITY CENTRE CONTINUED

228 **Watch House Terraces**
105a Clarence Street

231 **Former NSW Club**
31 Bligh Street
William Wardell

233 **Customs House**
Alfred, Loftus and Young Streets
James Barnet; Tonkin Zulaikha

237 **Lands Department Building**
Bridge, Loftus and Bent Streets
James Barnet

239 **Pyrmont Community Centre**
Former Pyrmont Public School
85 John Street
William E Kemp

241 **The Strand Arcade**
412–414 George Street
John B Spencer

251 **Former Gresham Hotel**
149 York and Druitt Streets
Ambrose Thornley Jnr

252 **Former John Taylor Warehouse**
Pyrmont Street and Pyrmont Bridge Roads
Arthur Blacket

254 **Sydney Hospital and Eye Hospital**
Macquarie Street
Thomas Rowe; McConnel Smith & Johnson

256 **Société Générale House**
348 George Street
Edward Raht

257 **Queen Victoria Building**
George, Market, York and Druitt Streets
George McRae

301 **St Patrick's Convent**
145 Harrington and Grosvenor Street
Sheerin & Hennessy

303 **Colonial Mutual Life Assurance**
10a–16 Martin Place
John Kirkpatrick

305 **Former Edwards Dunlop Warehouse**
414–418 Kent Street
1897 Robertson & Marks

307 **Former NSW Board of Health Building**
93 Macquarie Street
WL Vernon

308 **CW Foley and Co Warehouse**
230–232 Sussex Street

309 **St Mary's Cathedral**
College and Cathedral Streets
William Wardell

310 **Apartment Building**
73 Windmill Street

311 **Burns Philp & Co Building**
5–11 Bridge Street
McCredie and Anderson

312 **Government Insurance Office**
2 Martin Place and George Street
Edward Raht

313 **Former Dunlop Warehouse**
435–441 Kent Street

314 **Forbes Hotel**
30 York and King Streets
Sheerin & Hennessy

315 **The Earth Exchange**
18 Hickson Road
WL Vernon

323 **The State Library of NSW**
Macquarie Street
WL Vernon

324 **W Horace Friend Warehouse**
197–199 Clarence Street
Robertson & Marks

325 **Pyrmont Fire Station**
Gipps Street and Pyrmont Bridge Road
WL Vernon

331 **Royal Australian Navy Establishment**
Wharfs 17 and 18, Darling Harbour
WL Vernon

332 **Art Gallery of NSW**
Art Gallery Road
Vernon; Farmer; Andersons

333 **Wyoming**
175–181 Macquarie Streets
JB Clamp

334 **RTA House**
120–122 Clarence and King Streets
Spain & Cosh

336 **High Street Housing**
High Street
HD Walsh

338 **National Cash Register House**
14–16 York Street

339 **Culwulla Chambers**
65–71 Castlereagh Street
Spain, Cosh & Minnett

341 **Banking House**
226–230 Pitt Street
John Reid

342 **Former Ordinance Stores**
Darling Harbour
WL Vernon; Jackson Teece Chesterman Willis

343 **Palisade Hotel**
Munn and Bettington Streets
HD Walsh

346 **Registrar General's Department**
Prince Albert Road
WL Vernon

347 **Castlereagh Chambers**
64-68 Castlereagh Street
Wilson Neave & Berry

348 **Education Department Building**
35–39 Bridge Street
George McRae

349 **Commonwealth Banking Corporation**
Martin Place and Pitt Streets
John Kirkpatrick

352 **St Patrick's Hall**
133–137 Harrington Street
Hennessy & Hennessy

356 **The Trust Building**
72 Castlereagh Street
Robertson & Marks

403 **The Astor**
123 Macquarie Street
Esplin & Mould

406 **National Australia Bank**
343 George Street
Kent & Massie

409 **Point Street Flats**
12–20 Point Street
Leslie Wilkinson

410 **'The Block' Dymocks Building**
424–430 George Street
FHB Wilton

412 **Commonwealth Savings Bank**
48–50 Martin Place
Ross & Rowe

414 **Wales House**
Cnr Pitt and O'Connell Streets
Manson & Pickering

415 **Legal Offices** Former Sun Building
60 Elizabeth Street
JA Kethel

2. CITY SOUTH

133. East Sydney TAFE

202. Australian Museum

The southern edge of the city centre is generally low lying land which gradually rises from Darling Harbour to Moore Park and the swamps at Centennial Park. Any initial concept of orderly town planning in the form of a European grid extending the city to the south was simply ignored. Instead, settlers were drawn to private residential pockets in and around the harbour foreshore. The southern areas around Surry Hills and Camperdown were once considered slums, with major clearances occurring around the turn of the century. Warehouses and factories were located near the wharves with large breweries situated on the main roads south — South Dowling Street (Resch's Brewery) and Parramatta Road (Kent Brewery). This is Sydney's largest mixed-use urban area.

243. Capitol Theatre

329. Downing Centre

427. Anzac Memorial

547. Reader's Digest

625. House, Engelen + Moore

318 **Chamberlain Hotel**
420–428 Pitt Street

322 **Fire Station**
St John's Road
WL Vernon

329 **Downing Centre**
Former Mark Foy's Department Store
143–147 Liverpool Street
McRedie & Anderson; Ross & Rowe; NSWGA

337 **Traveller's Rest Hotel**
Former City Markets Building
9 Ultimo Road
George McRae

350 **Strickland Flats**
Cnr Meagher, Balfour and Cleveland Streets
Robert H Broderick

405 **Physics Building**
University of Sydney
Leslie Wilkinson

413 **Sydney Institute of Technology**
Former Marcus Clarke Emporium
827–837 George Street
Spain & Cosh

427 **Anzac War Memorial**
Hyde Park South
C Bruce Dellit

442 **Sydney Dental Hospital**
Cnr Chalmers and Elizabeth Streets
Stephenson, Meldrum & Turner

453 **Mario's Restaurant**
Former Packard Car Showroom
38 Yurong Street
Lipson & Kaad; Gordon & Valich

454 + 538 **Metropolitan Water, Sewerage and Drainage Board Building**
Cnr Pitt and Bathurst Streets
Budden & Mackey; McConnel, Smith & Johnson

462 **Motor Traders Association of NSW**
Former 20th Century Fox Film Corporation Building
43–51 Brisbane Street
EC Pitt & CC Phillips

470 **Beyond Pictures** Former Paramount Pictures Studios
53–55 Brisbane Street
Herbert, Wilson & Pynor

527 **Office Building**
72–84 Mary Street
HP Oser, Fombertaux & Associates

547 **Reader's Digest**
Cooper, Waterloo & Adelaide Streets
John James

585 **Darling Harbour Exhibition Centre**
Darling Harbour
Philip Cox, Richardson, Taylor & Partners

586 **Powerhouse Museum**
500 Harris Street
NSWGA

587 **Office Building**
59 Buckingham Street
Allen, Jack & Cottier

601 **ABC Ultimo Centre**
700 Harris Street
Ancher, Mortlock & Woolley

617 **Crown Street Housing Project**
Albion and Crown Street
Travis McEwen Group

622 **Housing**
63–80 Mary Ann Street
Allen, Jack & Cottier with Design 5

625 **House**
44 George Street
Engelen + Moore

629 **Converted Warehouse**
24 Taylor Street
Kerridge & Wallace

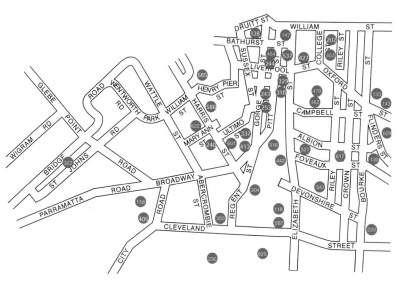

3. INNER EAST

1. Zink & Sons Shop

3. East Sydney TAFE

9. Tusculum

11. Boomerang

13. Rockwall

16. Wyldefel Gardens

19. City Ford

1. **Zink & Sons Shop**
   56 Oxford Street (444)
2. **Darlinghurst Courthouse**
   Taylor Square (143)
   M Lewis; J Barnet
3. **East Sydney TAFE**
   Forbes and Burton Sts (133)
   M Lewis; G Barney; J Barnet
4. **Houses**
   4 and 5 Darley Place (207)
5. **Darlinghurst Public School**
   Womerah and Barcom Ave
   Charles Mayes (219)
6. **Film Studios**
   32 Orwell Street
   RJ Magoffin & Ass. (461)
7. **Kingsclere**
   Greenknowe and Macleay Sts
   Halligan & Wilton (344)
8. **Wychbury**
   5 and 7 Manning Street
   Emil Sodersten (424)
9. **Tusculum**
   3 Manning Street
   Verge + others (126)
10. **Birtley Towers**
    8 Birtley Place
    Emil Sodersten (428)
11. **Boomerang**
    42 Billyard Avenue
    Neville Hampson (408)
12. **Elizabeth Bay House**
    7 Onslow Avenue
    John Verge (127)
13. **Rockwall**
    Macleay Street
    John Verge (139)
14. **Macleay Regis**
    12 Macleay Street
    Pitt & Phillips (460)
15. **Apartments**
    17 Wilde Street
    Aaron Bolot (510)
16. **Wyldefel Gardens**
    8a Wylde Street
    Crowle & Brogan (432)
17. **St Columbkilles Church**
    McElhone Street (224)
18. **Woolloomooloo Deep Sea Wharf**
    Henry D Walsh (357)
19. **City Ford**
    Kennedy and Crown Streets
    Lipson & Kaad (447)
20. **Peejays**
    William and Boomerang Sts
    Stephenson & Turner (446)

Potts Point, named after Joseph Hyde Potts, and Elizabeth Bay, granted to Alexander Macleay in 1829, were the first residential areas to be settled by the well-to-do. Early villas like 'Tusculum' and 'Rockwall' were subject to 'villa conditions' which established a minimum value and the direction to which their main facade must face. This was short lived, and subdivision into smaller lots soon occurred. Connected by one of the first tram services, Kings Cross became an early centre for quality high-rise apartment living and an entertainment district sprinkled with theatres, cinemas, coffee houses and burlesque revues. Over time, this strip has degenerated into an area of pornographic sideshows and prostitution mixed with dignified hotels and good restaurants.

In the 1970s, there were plans to demolish the old Kings Cross buildings and develop the area. This was prevented by 'Green Bans' instituted by a union campaign led by Jack Mundey and the Builders Labourers Federation of NSW in the 1970s. Today, the area is cosmopolitan, trendy and seedy.

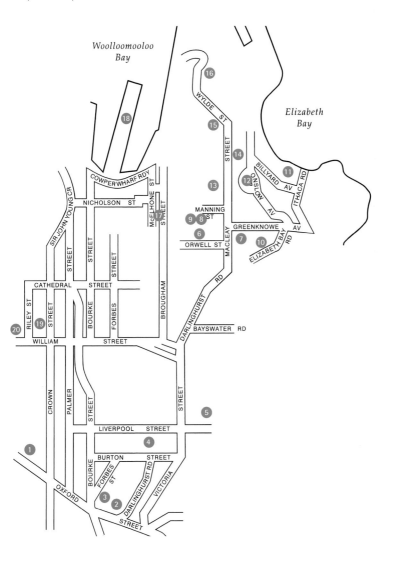

4. EASTERN SUBURBS

The harbourside suburbs to the east of the city centre are shaped by undulating bays and points which extend as far as South Head where the harbour meets the sea. Large gracious estates were established on the 'points' (Darling Point, Point Piper), the slopes behind were settled by the wealthier middle classes, while the shallow bays were natural settings for commerce, jetties, shops and moorings. Two areas dense with residential architecture are Point Piper and Bellevue Hill. While planning controls during the 1960s and 1970s encouraged subdivision and redevelopment of the large estates on Darling Point and Point Piper for apartment towers, some of the spaciousness of earlier days is still retained at Vaucluse, thanks to the Vaucluse House Estate.

1. Houses, Wilkinson

4. House, Wilson, Neave and Berry

6. Caerleon

14. The Chilterns

19. The Hermitage

23. Vaucluse House

24. Wentworth Memorial Church

Port

Jackson

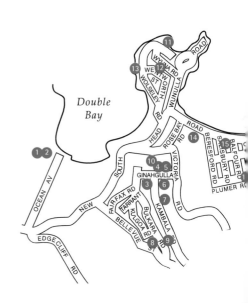

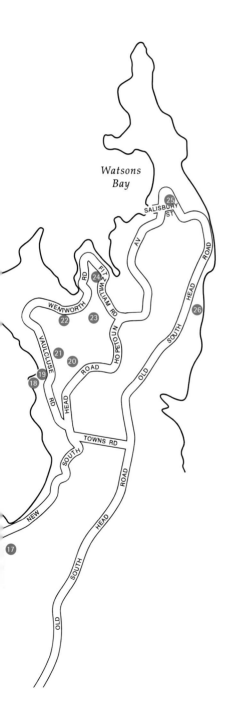

Watsons
Bay

1. *4 Wiston Gardens*
   Leslie Wilkinson (425)
2. *6 Wiston Gardens*
   Leslie Wilkinson (426)
3. *7 Ginahgulla Road*
   Dawson-Brown + Ackert (600)
4. *12 Ginahgulla Road*
   Wilson, Neave and Berry (411)
5. *14 Ginahgulla Road*
   Leslie Wilkinson
6. **Caerleon**
   15 Ginahgulla Road (229)
7. *65 Kambala Road*
   Sydney Ancher (441)
8. *12 Bulkara Road*
   Architectural Projects (623)
9. *9 Bulkara Road*
   Alec Tzannes (619)
10. *24a, 24b, 22b Victoria Road*
    Douglas Snelling (516)
11. *1 Wolseley Crescent*
    Eric Nicholls (439)
12. *22 Wyuna Road* (525)
    Arthur Baldwinson
13. *110 Wolseley Road*
    Richard Christianson (608)
14. **The Chilterns**
    593 New South Head Road
    Douglas Forsyth Evans (513)
15. *609 New South Head Road*
    Ken Willoughby (528)
16. **Shops**
    O'Sullivan and Plumer Roads (420)
17. **The Royal Sydney Golf Club**
    Kent Road (327)
18. *22d Vaucluse Road*
    Douglas Snelling (515)
19. **The Hermitage**
    22 Vaucluse Road (212)
20. *11a Gilliver Avenue*
    Crick & Furse (438)
21. *40 Wentworth Road*
    Guilford Bell (552)
22. **Greenway**
    24 Wentworth Road
    Leslie Wilkinson (404)
23. **Vaucluse House**
    Wentworth and Olola Roads (122)
24. **Wentworth Memorial Church**
    Fitzwilliam Street
    Clarke Gazzard & Partners (539)
25. *294 Old South Head Road*
    Graham Jahn (592)
26. **Macquarie Lighthouse**
    Old South Head Road (215)

5. APPIAN WAY, BURWOOD

House, Appian Way

1. **St Cloud** 1893
2. **Lulworth** 1905
3. **Colonna** 1905
4. **Atella** 1905
5. **Capri** 1908
6. **Erica** 1908
7. **Vallambrosa** 1908
8. **Casa Nuova** 1906
9. **Brescia** 1911
10. **Ravenna** 1911
11. **Toscanna** 1911
12. **Del Osa** 1908
13. **Melvania** 1908
14. **St Ellero** 1910
15. **Brianza** 1908
16. **Brindisi** 1906
17. **Verona** 1907
18. **Amalfi** 1907
19. **Alba Longa** 1907
20. **Olevanus** 1909
21. **Capua** 1905
22. **Ariccia** 1908
23. **Aventine** 1906
24. **Casa Tasso**
25. **Ostia**
26. **Roma** 1906
27. **Talofa** 1906
28. **Dimora** 1906
29. **Torcello** 1907
30. **Ravenscroft** 1907
31. **Cordova** 1910
32. **Langlo** 1911
33. **Mounterey** 1910
34. **Ravenswood** 1905
35. **Iwanora** 1906
36. **Lavinia** 1906
37. **Winton** 1907

Australian Federation in 1901 marked the end of a devastating economic depression that had lasted for almost ten years. The new Federation precinct built along 'The Appian Way' in Burwood represented for its creator, George Hoskins, an ideal suburban environment for the Sydney of the new century.

Created between 1903 and 1911, the planning was unique for its time, though no evidence exists that Hoskins engaged an architect or planner. The estate was distinguished by an abundance of street trees, the use of curved alignments in place of straight, and the incorporation of a recreation area which included a tennis court, croquet lawn, bowling green and pavilion.

Hoskins agreed to share the cost of making the road, plantations and the footpaths with the local council, and also to lend the council the necessary funds for its share. The large allotments and individual designs of houses departed from the usual profit-orientated schemes, suggesting Hoskins intended the estate to be an investment for himself and his family. The substantial houses which he built were leased rather than sold, and a family estate company was formed so that Hoskins could stay involved with the project.

The new suburb of Burwood represented a solid middle-class way of life, designed to attract the most respectable residents. It embodied confidence in the future and set the scene for the possibilities of 'the garden suburb'.

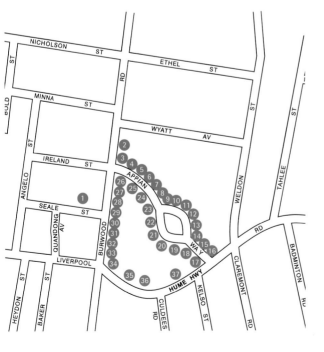

6. HUNTERS HILL

5. Coorabel

7. Loombah

11. All Saints Church of England

18. Eurondella

14. St Claire

13. Yandra

16. Wybalena

1. **Figtree House** 1848
   1 Reiby Road
   Didier Joubert (partly)
2. **St Mark's Church** 1858
   Figtree Road
   Edmund Blacket
3. **Saintonge** 1885
   24 Avenue Road
4. **The Bungalow** 1881
   22 Avenue Road
   Didier Joubert
5. **Coorabel** 1874 and **Annabel Lea** 1874
   28 Joubert Street
   Didier Joubert
6. **Euthella** 1896
   2 Joubert Street
7. **Loombah** 1880
   3 Stanley Road
8. **Lyndhurst** 1880s
   5 Stanley Road
9. **Cambridge** 1870s
   19 Lyndhurst Crescent
   Jeanneret
10. **The Haven** 1861
    1 McBride Avenue
11. **All Saints Church of England** 1885
    Ferry Street
    Horbury Hunt
12. **Passy** 1858
    1 Passy Avenue
    Jules Joubert
13. **Yandra** 1894
    30 Woolwich Road
    CE Jeanneret
14. **St Claire** 1879
    2 Wybalena Road
    CE Jeanneret
15. **Waiwere** 1878
    9 Woolwich Road
    CE Jeanneret
16. **Wybalena** 1874
    3 Jeanneret Avenue
    CE Jeanneret (210)
17. **Norwood** 1893
    27 Woolwich Road
    CE Jeanneret
18. **Eurondella** 1898
    29 Woolwich Road

Hunters Hill is renowned for the contribution of the Joubert brothers to its architecture. They arrived in Sydney from France in the 1830s and, in 1847, Didier Joubert purchased the 120-acre 'Figtree Farm' from Mary Reiby. Mary had come to Australia as a thirteen-year-old orphan convict, charged with horse stealing. She became a prosperous business woman, continuing a successful trading company after the death of her husband, Tom Reiby, and investing in property throughout the Sydney region. Before its purchase by Didier Joubert, Figtree Farm had been leased to Joseph Fowles, who chronicled Sydney in his illustrated publication of 1848.

Jules Joubert bought land adjoining Didier's in 1855 and the brothers began developing the area, transforming its reputation from a hideaway for criminals to a desirable settlement. Between 1861 and 1871, the population of Hunters Hill rose from 479 to 1,425 people. With the purchase of the steam yacht *Ysobel* in 1860, the Jouberts began a ferry service to Sydney. Didier built houses such as 'Coorabel', 'Annabel Lea' and 'St Malo' (the latter demolished to make way for the North Western Freeway). Jules's houses were less conservative and, among them, 'Windermere', 'Innisfree' and 'The Haven' are notable. Stonemasons were imported from Lombardy, who built stone-walled streets as well as houses, including 'Passy' for the French Consul.

Hunters Hill attracted other French settlers and became known for some time as 'The French Village'. Charles Edward Jeanneret, who was an investor in land, building and transport, was responsible for such houses as 'Wybalena', 'Cambridge', 'Lyndcote' and 'St Claire'. He served in local government as an alderman and as a mayor, as did Didier Joubert. Also among the French settlers were the Marist Fathers, who added The Priory, now in the grounds of Gladesville Hospital, and St Joseph's College, to the architecture of the area.

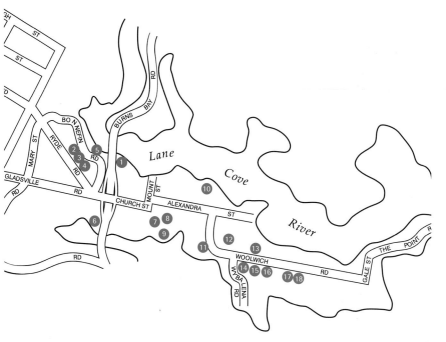

7. CASTLECRAG/MIDDLE HARBOUR

1. House, Frischknecht

2. House, Gruzman

4. House, Burley Griffin

10. House, Nicholls

20. House, Muller

21. House, Buhrich

Walter Burley Griffin and his wife Marion came to Australia in 1912, having won the competition for the design of Canberra. When problems with the project led to Griffin's resignation in 1920, he turned his attention to developing 263 hectares of land at Middle Harbour, purchased with funds raised by 'The Greater Sydney Development Association', founded by Griffin for this purpose.

Griffin's idea was to create an estate in harmony with the environment. Roads would follow the contours of the terrain and pedestrian and vehicular traffic would be separated, communal areas would be linked by walking tracks, allotments would maximise views and homes would be orientated towards internal recreation spaces. Covenants were put in place to protect the GSDA's objectives, including the banning of residential apartment buildings and houses with pitched roofs (a pet hate of the Griffins). There were to be no fences or boundaries, to give the impression that the whole landscape belonged to the individual. Castlecrag had twenty-eight reserves and ornamental parks, and the landscaping used Australian native flora.

Shareholders of the GSDA received free land, provided they built a house on it; five took up the offer and built investment properties in Edinburgh Road and the Parapet. The houses were usually small with flat roofs, decorative windows and stone fireplaces. Materials were predominantly sandstone, quarried on the site, and 'Knitlock', Griffin's invention of interlocking pre-cast structural tiles. Lots were 12.2 metres x 36.6 metres, sized for the average income-earner.

Today, many of the houses have been added to, not always in keeping with Walter Burley Griffin's image of habitable elements in the landscape.

Griffin believed: 'Our sordid environment is the consequence of an egotism that hardly even questions wanton sacrifice to immediate and personal — not social — advantage.'

Castlecrag was to be his testament.

1. *1a North Arm Road*
   Paul Frischknecht (577)
2. *17 North Arm Road*
   Neville Gruzman (519)
3. *31 Rembrandt Drive*
   Neville Gruzman (531)
4. *136 and 140 Edinburgh Road* c. 1921
   Walter Burley Griffin (401)
5. *4 The Parapet 1921*
   Walter Burley Griffin (401)
6. *8 The Parapet 1922*
   Walter Burley Griffin (401)
7. *12 The Parapet*
   Eric Nicholls (450)
8. *14 The Parapet 1922*
   Walter Burley Griffin (401)
9. *158 Edinburgh Road 1926*
   Walter Burley Griffin (401)
10. *3 The Bastion*
    Eric Nicholls (449)
11. *23 The Bastion 1925*
    Walter Burley Griffin (401)
12. *2 The Barbette 1930*
    Walter Burley Griffin (401)
13. *4 The Barbette*
    Walter Burley Griffin (401)
14. *8 The Barbette 1934*
    Walter Burley Griffin (401)
15. *8 Rockley Street*
    Alex Popov (590)
16. *80 The Bulwark*
    Bill & Ruth Lucas (524)
17. *41 The Scarpe*
    Kloots and Morgan (561)
18. *15 The Citadel 1929*
    Walter Burley Griffin (401)
19. *215 Edinburgh Road*
    Eric Nicholls
20. *265 Edinburgh Road*
    Peter Muller (512)
21. *375 Edinburgh Road*
    Hugh Buhrich (551)
22. *Upper Ciff Avenue*
    Hill Thalis (626)

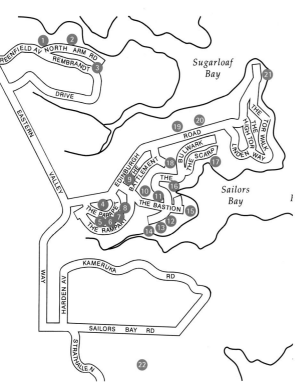

8. PITTWATER/PALM BEACH

4. House, Stutchbury

5. Kumale

12. Houses, Seidler

14. House, Muller

The northern peninsula is defined by the expanse of Pittwater on one side and the Pacific Ocean on the other. It was relatively undeveloped and inaccessible for more than a century. The earliest pockets of settlement related to river trade on the Hawkesbury River, with a few small farms which grew wheat and oats.

Between 1810 and 1850, the governors granted large land parcels between 50 and 700 acres. One of the largest estates was granted to Father J Therry, encompassing all the land between Whale Beach and Newport. Believing that the Hunter Valley coal seam ran along the coast, Therry dug a mine shaft, without success, which descended 220 feet at Bilgola Headland near Avalon Golf Links.

The area's inaccessibility determined its character for decades. Between 1900 and 1930, the area was lauded as the Riviera of Australia, and seaside living came into vogue after the prohibition on seaside bathing was lifted after 1910. Many of the original parcels were subdivided and auctioned, generally failing to sell until the 1920s when native flora and fauna recording and naturalist pursuits became popular. Despite the brief introduction of the tram between Narrabeen and Manly in 1938, the area remained an outlying resort until the 1950s when it started to become densely settled, with Palm Beach, Church Point and Bayview being the most desirable addresses.

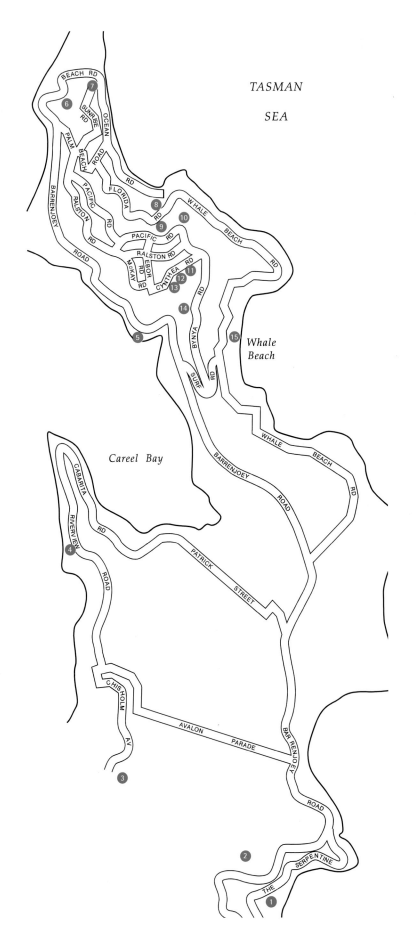

TASMAN

SEA

BEACH RD

SUNRISE RD

OCEAN

PALM

BEACH

ROAD

BARRENJOEY

RD

FLORIDA

PACIFIC

RD

RALSTON

RD

ROAD

WHALE

BEACH

RD

RD

RD

PACIFIC

RD

RALSTON RD

McKAY

EBOR

CYNTHEA

RD

RD

BYNYA

RD

Whale
Beach

SURF

RD

Careel Bay

CABARITA

RIVERVIEW

RD

ROAD

BARRENJOEY

ROAD

PATRICK

STREET

WHALE

BEACH

RD

CHISHOLM

AV.

AVALON   PARADE

BARRENJOEY

ROAD

THE   SERPENTINE

ACKNOWLEDGEMENTS

Our thanks extend to the following individuals and organisations for the provision of materials, information, and editorial assistance: Terence Measham, Kathleen Hackett, Gara Baldwin — Powerhouse Museum, Jennifer Broomhead, Janelle Thoms — State Library of New South Wales; Stephen Davies — National Trust of Australia; Jonathan Chancellor — *The Sydney Morning Herald*; Jan Griffiths — Hunters Hill Historical Society; Caroline Kades — Pittwater Council; Peter Todd — Design 5 Architects; Keith Cottier — Allen Jack & Cottier; David Jackson and Neville Thomas — Jackson Teece Chesterman & Willis; Richard Francis-Jones — MGT Architects; Geoff Searl — Avalon Historical Society; Anthony Rowan — Woollahra Council; Steve Dawkins — Government House, NSW Public Works and Services; Leanne Zilka, Andrew Mitchell — Historic Houses Trust; Warren Clarke — Sydney Home Nursing Service.

Original measured drawings:
'Ingelholme' — Angelo Pirrello (UTS)
'Caerleon' — Glennis Cowell (UTS)
'The Gables' — Susan Vincent (UTS)
'Highlands' — Graham Turner (UTS)
'Eryldene' — Clive Lucas Stapleton & Partners
50 Murdoch Street, Cremorne — Kim Bazeley
Fort Denison — National Parks and Wildlife Service
'Montana' — Sydney Nursing Home Service
Strickland House — Robert Brown
Abbotsford House — Nettleton Tribe Partnership
Mt Wilga — Department of Housing and Construction
'Nioka' — Kraig Carlstrom

Acknowledgement of plan sources:
Robert Moore, Crawford Partners, Jackson Teece Chesterman Willis, Dr John Phillips, Kim Crestani, Dawn Herman, Jennifer Taylor, Harry Seidler, Michelle Cramer, *The Sydney Morning Herald*, Neville Gruzman, Neil Durbach, Bruce Rickard, Stan Symonds, Howard Tanner, Glenn Murcutt, Everard Kloots, Furio Valich, Alexander Tzannes, Ed Duc, Paul Frischnecht, Ken Woolley, Jim Koopman, Philip Cox, Allen Jack & Cottier, Alex Popov, Lionel Glendenning, Bill MacMahon, Denton Corker Marshall, Luigi Roselli, Richard Christianson, Frank Stanisic, Stutchbury & Pape, Margaret Krempff, Jennifer Hill, Sam Marshall, Engelen Moore, Philip Thallis and Peter John Cantrill, Virginia Kerridge.

INDEX